THE HEART IN THE AGE
OF SHAKESPEARE

When Hamlet says he wears Horatio in his "heart of heart," he is claiming that the strongest bonds between people are forged, stored, and understood in the heart. *The Heart in the Age of Shakespeare* sets out to trace the sources and subsequent impact of Hamlet's conviction. The book presents the case that, by studying the interlocking anatomical, religious, and literary discourses of the heart between 1550 and 1650, we can open a new window on the culture that produced such works as *The Faerie Queene*, Catholic and Protestant emblem books, George Herbert's lyrics, and William Harvey's treatise on the circulation of the blood. By crossing several disciplinary boundaries and combining the material with the metaphorical, the book identifies a complex set of cardiological concerns in the dramatic works of Shakespeare and his contemporaries.

WILLIAM W. E. SLIGHTS is Professor Emeritus in the Department of English, University of Saskatchewan. He is the author of *Managing Readers: Printed Marginalia in English Renaissance Books* (2001) and *Ben Jonson and the Art of Secrecy* (1994), and has published widely in books and journals including *Shakespeare Survey* and *Renaissance Quarterly*. In 2007 he was the recipient of the Canadian Society for Renaissance Studies Lifetime Achievement Award.

THE HEART IN THE AGE
OF SHAKESPEARE

WILLIAM W. E. SLIGHTS

CAMBRIDGE
UNIVERSITY PRESS

CAMBRIDGE UNIVERSITY PRESS
Cambridge, New York, Melbourne, Madrid, Cape Town, Singapore, São Paulo, Delhi

Cambridge University Press
The Edinburgh Building, Cambridge CB2 8RU, UK

Published in the United States of America by Cambridge University Press, New York

www.cambridge.org
Information on this title: www.cambridge.org/9780521889438

First published 2008

Printed in the United Kingdom at the University Press, Cambridge

A catalogue record for this publication is available from the British Library

Library of Congress Cataloguing in Publication Data
Slights, William W. E.
The heart in the age of Shakespeare / William W. E. Slights.
p. cm.
Includes bibliographical references and index.
ISBN 978-0-521-88943-8 (hardback)
1. English literature – Early modern, 1500–1700 – History and criticism.
2. Heart in literature. 3. Literature and science – England – History – 16th century.
4. Literature and science – England – History – 17th century.
5. Heart – Symbolic aspects. 6. Shakespeare, William, 1564–1616 – Symbolism.
I. Title.
PR428.H43S55 2008
820.9'3561–dc22   2008027084

ISBN 978-0-521-88943-8 hardback

For Madeleine and Will Ahern,
who are all heart

Immortal Shakespeare! Still thy lips impart
The noblest comment on the human heart.
                    Elizabeth Barrett, *An Essay on Mind* (1826)

How to explain
that which has no state
but the state of grace
erotic music
touching places deep
and worn an evensong resonating
the open strings of the heart
that belong to the state of longing
                    Heather Pyrcz, "The Book of Longing" (2006)

Contents

Illustrations

Chapter 5

Chapter 6

Acknowledgments

Between 1991 and 1993 a dazzling exhibit mounted by the Boston Institute of Contemporary Art and titled "*El Corazón Sangrante* / The Bleeding Heart" toured seven cities in Central and North America. One was Saskatoon, Saskatchewan, Canada, where I saw it – repeatedly. The show was devoted to the image and icon of the bleeding heart, and it included Aztec artifacts, baroque paintings, and contemporary installations with hubcaps and dozens of pipettes of blood dripping down a blank wall. Individually and collectively these heart-based pieces had immense visual and mental impact. Here was an image that for centuries had stirred visceral terror, religious fervor, medical curiosity, and delicate beauty in works ranging from anonymous Catholic icons to the highly sexual images of Frida Kahlo.

But what struck me over and over again was the way these works resonated with literary texts by Shakespeare and his contemporaries that I had been lecturing and writing about for several decades. I found here a pastoral treatment of the bleeding heart that might have served to comfort a character from a John Webster play or a John Donne poem. Here too was a painting of a heart brutally ripped from an innocent victim, the perfect complement to lines by Marlowe and Shakespeare that echoed in my head as I stood in the gallery. To paraphrase Lady Macbeth, who would have thought the old man (Shakespeare, that is) to have so much blood in him? And so many hearts yearning and breaking and dancing and bursting? It would take me years to accumulate, sort, and understand all these hearts.

And then there were the ancillary hearts, the ones whose wit and humanity kept me going through the years of my research. Their creators deserve to be acknowledged. There was the scene in the animated Jim Carey film *The Mask* (1994) when the hero's heart stretched far out of his elastic breast as he first spotted his true love. And the peculiar Benetton advertisement that ran in *The New Yorker* (April 26, 1996) and elsewhere, showing three nearly identical (pigs', I'm assured) hearts labelled "WHITE," "BLACK," and "YELLOW" and followed by a page showing a little blonde girl and a black girl with their arms around each other and another page with the manacled hands of a white and a black prisoner. Somehow the would-be consumer was to get from disemboweled hearts to interracial bonding and racial injustice. More relevant to the ageing heart researcher was Matt Gerberg's 1997 *New Yorker* cartoon in which a balding, paunchy man sits on an examination table while his stethoscope-wielding doctor says, "Good. Now start it up again." Finally, there was my favorite, the cover of a Routledge "Literary and Cultural Studies" catalogue that appeared in my mailbox in 1997 picturing a robed and haloed Elvis Presley revealing his flaming heart, complete with cross and thorns, while he raises his hand in benediction, presumably over those professors who might purchase the publisher's books. These were the late, indeed post, modern instances of the symbol and the reality I had chosen to pursue through the art, medicine, philosophy, and literature of the early modern period, and they did my heart good.

As I have traveled to museums and libraries over the past fifteen years in search of hearts, bleeding and whole, medical and religious, I have been helped by a great many institutions and individuals. For day-to-day help, the libraries of the University of Saskatchewan and Acadia University deserve repeated thanks. The Huntington Library and Art Gallery, the Folger Library, the British Library, the Yale Library of Medical History, the Osler Library at McGill University, and the Wellcome Institute have all provided me with helpful materials in a courteous and timely manner. Between June 21 and September 16, 2007, the Wellcome Collection mounted a sumptuous exhibition, curated by Emily Jo Sergant and James Peto and called simply "The Heart." The exhibition encompassed heart knowledge from ancient Egypt through the discoveries of Galen, Leonardo, and William Harvey to the pop songs, Valentine cards, and open-heart surgeries of our own time. The show reminded me of the pleasant hours I spent tracking down heart images in the Wellcome archives and of the persistent, ever-growing medical and cultural fascination with the heart in the twenty-first century.

I particularly want to thank Rick Bowers, Robert Erickson, and Albert Tricomi, who read entire drafts of the manuscript and made invaluable suggestions about everything from pertinent cartoon characters to omitted chapters. Others who have generously shared their knowledge about medieval and early modern history, emblems, poetry, science, and art include Doris Bietenholz (a fellow Saskatoonian who published her own heart book on Valentine's Day, 1995), Barbara Bowen, Jann Boyd, Steven Buhler, Peter Burnell, Richard Cunningham, Anthony Harding, Richard Hillman, Carole Levin, Yin Liu, Raymond Stephanson, Mark Stein, Lewis Stiles, Kevin

Whetter, and Kurt Wittlin. I was kindly invited to lecture on material from the book by the Renaissance Group at the University of Illinois at Urbana-Champaign, the Body Project conference at the University of Saskatchewan, the Faculty Exchange Lecture Committee at the University of Regina, the Authors at Acadia series at Acadia University, and the English Lecture Series at Dalhousie University. For these invitations I wish to thank particularly Achsah Guibbory and Michael Shapiro, Len Findlay, Jeanne Shami and Ken Mitchell, Ralph Stewart, and Ronald Huebert.

An earlier version of Chapter 4 appeared as "The Narrative Heart of the Renaissance" in *Renaissance and Reformation/Renaissance et Réforme* 26 (2002): 5–23, and Chapter 5 was published as "My Heart upon my Sleeve: Early Modern Interiority, Anatomy and Villainy" in *The Dalhousie Review* 85 (2005): 163–79. I am grateful for permission to reprint this material.

While writing the book, I have been helped in myriad ways by two first-rate scholars at the University of Saskatchewan, Shelley Woloshyn and Pamela Giles. Dr. Giles, with the help of her husband Craig Bowman, has tracked down and evaluated research materials, negotiated with libraries and galleries for permission to publish illustrations, spent hours checking quotations, and generated an index that I hope will serve readers well. The protracted labors of these good friends have certainly made this a better and more useful book. Any errors and infelicities are my own.

For providing me witty and rigorous feedback throughout the entire process of writing *The Heart in the Age of Shakespeare*, I reserve my deepest thanks for my family: Camille and Jessica Slights; Stephen, Madeleine, and Will Ahern. In the final years of its composition, Will and Madeleine have found my heart ready at a moment's notice to sing and dance with them.

I have benefited substantially in writing the book from funds awarded by the President's Research Fund at the University of Saskatchewan and from two generous grants from the Social Sciences and Humanities Research Council of Canada. I am proud to have been adopted by a university and a country that continues to support individual scholars in the pursuit of their intellectual passions and curiosities.

CHAPTER I

A window on the heart

The satirist Lucian of Samosata (*c.* 125–180 CE) imagined how instructive it would be to gaze through a window in a man's breast that would reveal all the secrets of his heart. In Lucian's *Hermotimus* Momus, called upon to judge the human form constructed by Hephaestus, reproves the craftsman because "he had not made windows in his chest which could be opened to let everyone see his desires and thoughts and if he were lying or telling the truth."[1] This literal-minded approach to inadvertent self-revelation is, of course, intended to be humorous, but the idea that the heart is always open to scrutiny – especially to divine scrutiny – is prominent in both ancient and modern thought. Perpetual surveillance of the heart's motives serves as reassurance and as warning in the Bible: "For the worde of God *is* liuelie, & mightie in operation . . . and is a discerner of the thoghtes and the intentes of the heart."[2]

An analogous fantasy of physical and mental transparency is illustrated in a seventeenth-century Dutch emblem book called *Openhertighe Herten* (Open-Hearted Hearts) in the form of a heart with a mullioned window in it.[3] The emblematist offers a graphic representation of the ideal of human transparency in the eye of God. What God sees and mere humans can only labor to piece together from bits of external evidence – a glance, a grimace, an unguarded remark – is a coherent picture of a person's motives. To be able to spy into others' hearts and to read their desires and intentions was a powerfully attractive prospect for churchmen, politicians, and artists in the sixteenth and seventeenth centuries. Just exactly what would be found in the heart was notoriously difficult to predict, but any persons or institutions that

---

[1] Lucian, *Works*, trans. A. M. Harmon, Loeb Classical Library (London: William Heinemann, 1959), 6: 299.
[2] Heb. 4: 12. I quote from *The Geneva Bible: A Facsimile of the 1560 Edition*, intro. Lloyd E. Berry (Madison: University of Wisconsin Press, 1969).
[3] The emblem is reproduced in Mark van Vaeck, "The *Openhertight Herten* in Europe: Remarkable Specimens of Heart Emblematics," *Emblematica* 8 (1994), 278.

could gain a reputation for being discerners of the heart wielded enormous power.

That Charles I and his royal physician, William Harvey, were able to reach through a window in the side of a "*Noble* young Gentleman, *Son* and *Heire* to the honorable the *Vice-Count* of *Mountgomery* in *Ireland*," and touch his heart was much more than a scientific breakthrough. A quality of wonder infiltrates the precise record of their observations in Harvey's *Anatomical exercitations concerning the generation of living creatures* (London: J. Young for O. Pulleyn, 1653).[4] Harvey, who had studied a great many hearts in preparing his immensely influential treatise on the circulation of the blood, *De motu cordis*, a quarter of a century earlier, admits that he was "amazed at the novelty of the thing."[5] The thing had been incorrectly identified by other observers as Hugh Montgomery's lungs, opened to sight and touch through a removable metal plate that protected a hole in his left side caused by a childhood accident and kept perpetually open by an unhealed abscess. The king, fascinated by accounts he had heard, commanded Harvey to examine the young man when he passed through London on his way home from a continental tour. Montgomery cooperated fully:

[H]e discovered all to me, and opened the void part of his *left side*, taking off that small *plate*, which he wore to defend it against any blow or outward injury. Where I presently beheld a vast *hole* in his *breast*, into which I could easily put my three Fore-fingers, and my Thumb; and at the first entrance I perceived a certain *fleshy part* sticking out, which was driven in and out by a reciprocal *motion*, whereupon I gently handled it in my hand. (*Exercitations*, 286)

By coordinating the "*rythme*" of the internal organ with the pulse in Montgomery's wrist, Harvey was able to determine conclusively that what he was handling was "no part of the *Lungs*, but the *Cone* or *Substance* of the *Heart*" (286). This, he further decided, was a spectacle fit for a king, the very king whom he had described as "the heart of the state" in his dedication to *De motu cordis* and who had since been beheaded.

I brought the Young Gentleman himself to our late *King*, that he might see, and handle this strange and singular Accident with his own *Senses;* namely, the *Heart*

[4] Harvey's fascinating account of cardiac manipulation occurs on pp. 285–7 (quotation from p. 285) of the *Exercitations* and has been mined for its biographical revelations in Sir Geoffrey Keynes's *Life of William Harvey* (Oxford: Clarendon Press, 1978), 155–7 and for its political allegory in Jonathan Sawday's "The Transparent Man and the King's Heart," in *The Arts of 17th-Century Science: Representations of the Natural World in European and North American Culture*, ed. Claire Jowitt and Diane Watt (Aldershot: Ashgate, 2002), 12–21.
[5] Harvey, *Anatomical exercitations*, 286. Subsequent references will appear parenthetically.

and its *Ventricles* in their own *pulsation*, in a young, and sprigtly Gentleman, without offense to him: Whereupon the *King* himself consented with me, That the *Heart* is deprived of the *Sense* of *Feeling*. For the Party perceived not that we touched him at all, but meerly by seeing us, or by the *sensation* of the outward *skin*. We likewise took notice of the *motion* of his *Heart*. (*Exercitations*, 287)

Jonathan Sawday construes the phrase "the *Heart* is deprived of the *Sense* of *Feeling*" to mean that Aristotle had been wrong to tout the heart as the seat of sensation and that Descartes was right to call it a purely mechanical pump. The collapse of Charles's (the "late" king's) mystique of monarchy in 1649 becomes allegorically joined in Sawday's account with the harsh demystification of the heart by mid-century scientific probing:

Peering into the human body, we encounter an organ (the heart) disrobed of its former majesty, unfeeling and blindly pumping. The dense web of allegory, resemblance and metaphor which had surrounded the heart in Galenic and Aristotelian physiology has collapsed as completely as the quasi-divinity which had surrounded the King's political *persona* prior to 1649.[6]

But this story of the complete collapse of the metaphorical vitality of the heart is considerably weakened by texts and graphic images that we will consider shortly. What we can safely conclude from Harvey's narrative is that the heart's majesty remained "amaz[ing]" even in the hands of potential Doubting Thomases reaching into a living human body. At the very least, the heart remained the "minister of State" to the Soul and the "Queen Regent of the animal body," as Harvey (quoting Fabricius) says (*Exercitations*, 314). Even when the rule of the monarchy had been temporarily suspended, the regal pageant of the heart continued to be visible through windows that were both metaphoric and literal. As Harvey says later in his book on generation, "we may conclude (with *Aristotle*) That the *Heart*, and not (with the *Physitians*) that the *Brain* is the first *Principle*" (*Exercitations*, 348). Understanding this first principle of life was the responsibility of all monarchs and their subjects.

Elizabeth I's reputed disinclination "to make windows into men's souls" notwithstanding, Shakespeare's age is characterized by fierce competition to read and to control people's hearts. Dominant and emergent institutions – churches, schools, courts – sought to govern the hearts of the nation by radically reconfiguring inherited medieval constructions of social identity. The heart became the locus for the private desires that keep identity in flux, as well as for the sociopolitical affiliations and loyalties that provide a

---

[6] Sawday, "The Transparent Man," 19–20.

degree of stability in human communities. In early modern England, the battle lines were continuously being redrawn between the Old Religion and the New, between prior formulations of the "natural" body and fresh observations of its structure and functions, between established literary forms and new ones. These lines converged in the amatory, political, and devotional heart, where difficult choices were always being made, former alliances abandoned, new forms of practice embraced, and new loves declared. The argument I wish to make is that our habit of scholarly compartmentalization obscures the subtle permeability of intellectual, bodily, and spiritual life in the age of Shakespeare, and, specifically, that we can best understand the early modern heart as the primary point of connection between felt interiority and the systems that helped to make sense of the social and physical universe.

Recovering the full range of the heart's significance for the age of Shakespeare entails learning how its structure and motions were reconceived from ancient natural philosophy by the Renaissance anatomists, how Roman Catholic iconography of the heart was rewritten and redrawn by the Protestant reformers, and how the amatory narratives of the Middle Ages were reinterpreted in the lyric and dramatic poetry of the sixteenth and seventeenth centuries. The many claims made in the early modern period regarding the powers and prerogatives of the heart need to be viewed within a matrix of social and intellectual exchange and as parts of a larger historical process. First, we must know about the inherited systems of thought that defined the physiological and spiritual functions of the heart in early modernity. The main sources of these ideas were (1) the ancient natural philosophers and their redactors, and (2) the Bible and its medieval exegetes. I propose to look at these sometimes contradictory conceptions of the heart and then at the early modern innovations that caused these ideas to change in the period between roughly 1550 and 1650.

The first thing to insist on is that the part cannot be understood apart from the whole system in which it functions, be it physiological, instructional, doctrinal, or poetic. Rather than continuing to study what one collection of essays calls "the body in parts," we need to reintegrate the early modern heart back into the systems that made it intelligible at the time.[7] By far the most influential of these postulated that the body is governed by four humors – blood, phlegm, yellow bile, and black

---

[7] *The Body in Parts: Fantasies of Corporeality in Early Modern Europe*, ed. David Hillman and Carla Mazzio (New York: Routledge, 1997). Many of the essays in this important collection incorporate the wider perspective that I am advocating, but some readers have construed its title too literally.

bile – which function in sympathetic harmony (at least in the healthy body) with the elements of earth, air, fire, and water, which in turn can be symptomatically described as cold, dry, hot, moist, or some combination of these properties. All physiological states and alterations could be conceived within a mandala constructed from these interlocking tetrads. Gender and generation, health and illness, inherited traits and individual inclinations could be accounted for by this firm yet admirably flexible system of thought. The role of the heart in the scheme was crucial. As generator of heat and distributor of refined fluids and *spiritus* to the rest of the body, the heart kept the body alive and well regulated. Its initial beating signaled the start of life, and its cessation marked the moment of death. Though it could not ordinarily be seen or touched and still be able to perform its vital functions, it was the wellspring of life and health. While early modern conceptions of the heart are nearly always inflected with metaphors of spiritual health or corruption, it was the hydraulic, pneumatic, and caloric forces propelling the dynamic humoral system that provided the vocabulary that natural philosophers had long called upon as literal descriptions of the body and its functions.

Well before Christian theologians began their long and careful colloquy on the meaning of scriptural depictions of the heart and its devotional functions, the natural philosophers of antiquity had identified the heart as the vital center of the humoral body. In antiquity, the study of animal bodies, including human ones, was a subset of the amorphous discipline of natural philosophy. An organ such as the heart was not just observed (in "lower" animals) and described, it was made the subject of intense debate. Why did all-creating Nature build the heart with two main chambers (the auricles were often not considered to be integral parts of the heart), thick walls containing few nerves, and an arterial connection to the lungs? Why did the heart attract blood and *spiritus*? How did this organ process and distribute nourishment and air to the entire body? Aristotle's *De generatione animalium* and *De partibus animalium*, a number of Hippocratic texts, and Galen's *De anatomicis administrationibus* and *De usu partium* address these and similarly challenging questions through strenuous deductive and inductive arguments and debates with earlier authorities. A representative passage from Galen's treatise *On the Usefulness of the Parts* (*De usu partium*) describes the ways that Nature has "managed" the design and distribution of the veins and arteries of the heart, giving some of them far thicker walls ("tunics") than others in order to transmit blood in different forms and amounts.

All these facts, then, are weighty proof that Nature did well to make two kinds of vessels, and besides these there are also the considerations that the arteries, which must be constantly in motion, need strong tunics, that a tunic cannot be strong and thin at the same time, and that if, on the other hand, it is made thick, many parts of the body cannot be properly nourished. So Nature has managed all these things excellently both throughout the body of the animal and especially in the heart itself by contriving communication between veins and arteries through those small orifices. This is the reason why the vein [the vena cava] inserted into the heart is larger than the one [*a. pulmonalis*] issuing from it, even though the latter receives blood fused by the heat of the heart. Since a considerable quantity of blood is taken over through the central partition and its perforations into the left ventricle, there is good reason why the vein [*a. pulmonalis*] inserted into the lung is smaller than the one [the vena cava] that introduces the blood into the heart.[8]

The language of logical argument ("weighty proof"; "This is the reason why") transforms sporadically observed phenomena into a coherent, though not always accurate, defense of natural necessity. In this case, Nature cannot quite be shown to manage the movement of blood through a perforated *septum ventriculorum* or central wall since, as the sixteenth-century Flemish anatomist Andreas Vesalius was to argue repeatedly in his lectures and published texts, no such "perforations" exist within the heart. Still, Galen's opinion, or, rather, his persuasive argumentation on this and other matters, remained in the ascendancy until microscopic magnification resolved the issue in the late seventeenth century.

The ancients were drawn to debating not only the structure and function of the heart but also its relation to the soul. The trope of *profundity* emerged early and persistently as a defining quality of philosophical truth. Knowing the depths of natural bodies, not just their outward forms, was the hallmark of genuine value in this area of human endeavor. In the study of "man," no part was considered more profound than the heart, seat of the intangible truths of faith (the *invisibilia*) and the original instigator of corporeal motion. Aristotle, the most widely revered and imitated of the natural philosophers in the early modern period, postulated a soul animated by the heart. In his *On the Soul* and *On the Parts of Animals*, he is concerned to describe precisely what is *not* visible to the eye. He defines *anima*, the force that animates all creatures, in terms of substance, location, and movement but never by visual images. He eventually locates *anima* in the brain, but most of its functions depend upon the heart. *Pneuma*, the refined air that sustains the soul, is produced by the heart and distributed

---

[8] Galen, *On the Usefulness of the Parts of the Body*, trans. Margaret Tallmadge May (Ithaca: Cornell University Press, 1968), 1: 324.

throughout the body. Completely without the evidence of our eyes, we are encouraged to believe that "all motions of sensation, including those produced by what is pleasant and painful, undoubtedly begin in the heart and have their final ending there."[9]

In addition to the rich heritage of classical writing about the heart, Shakespeare's age also drew heavily on biblical heart lore and medieval iconography as a basis for its own mental and material imagery of the heart. In the Old Testament the word "heart" refers to the part of the human responsible for grasping moral and spiritual truths and for willing an appropriate response to those truths. King David enjoins his son Solomon, "knowe thou the God of thy father, and serue him with a perfit hearte, and with a willing minde: for the Lord searcheth all hearts" (1 Chr. 28: 9). Any hesitation to serve will be seen as though through a window. Solomon in turn prays for wisdom so that he may judge God's people fairly: "Giue therefore vnto thy seruant an vndersta[n]ding heart, to iudge thy people" (1 Kings 3: 9). Such active moral processes as understanding and judging were essential to the Bible's account of the heart's role in linking man with God. The heart forged bonds between divinity and humanity; it was the organ of understanding and will on which Scripture relied to communicate its lessons. Communication failed when men's hearts were hardened by sin and deafened to the word of God. Wicked images formed in the sinner's heart are penetrated by God, who, at a crucial moment, feels regret in his own heart that mankind was ever created.

When the Lord sawe that the wickednes of man was great in the earth, and all the imaginacions of the thoghts of his heart *were* onely euil continually, [6] Then it repe[n]ted the Lord, that he had made man in the earth, and he was sorie in his heart. (Gen. 6: 5–6)

The prophet Jeremiah, predictably recognizing the heart's corruption ("The heart is deceitful and wicked aboue all things"), asks "who can knowe it?" The immediate answer is, "I the Lord searche the heart" (Jer. 17: 9–10). David's "perfit hearte" seems to emerge only after an invasive act

---

[9] Aristotle, *Parts of Animals*, trans. A. L. Peck. Loeb Classical Library (London: William Heinemann, 1937), 237. In a letter dated April 28, 1652, William Harvey expresses precisely the opposite view of how the scientist's eyesight comes to be dazzled: "With what labour do we attain the hidden things of truth when we take the averments of our senses as the guide which God has given us for attaining to a knowledge of his works; avoiding that specious path on which the eyesight is dazzled with the brillancy of mere reasoning, and so many are led to wrong conclusions, to probabilities only, and too frequently to sophistical conjectures on things!" *The Works of William Harvey*, as quoted by Stephen Pender in "Signs of Interiority, or Epistemology in the Bodyshop," *Dalhousie Review* 85 (2005): 226 n. 19.

of divine restoration, as God explains in the Book of Ezekiel: "And I wil giue them one heart, and I wil put a newe spirit within their bowels: and I wil take the stonie heart out of their bodies, & wil giue them an heart of flesh" (Ezek. 11: 19). An earlier divine promise states that the Lord will disperse the chosen people among the heathens, where they will be utterly lost, but there is a chance for redemption and continuance if the faithful will "loue the Lord thy God with all thine heart, and with all thy soule" (Deut. 30: 6). But this is a very iffy proposition. There are great sinks of ambiguity in the biblical heart, opportunities for the imagination, judgment, and understanding to be both tainted and redeemed. The early modern clergy and laity eagerly embraced this ambiguity and the ongoing struggle it entailed.

For centuries the Catholic Church used the iconographic and liturgical heart to attract and bind the faithful to it. The Sacred Heart was presented to believers as a powerful metonymy for the Son of God in all His compassion, vulnerability, and suffering. Jesus was the bleeding heart of God made visible. His crown of thorns, symbol of monarchy persisting through pain, was often transferred from the head to the heart of Jesus. The required response to His silent, internal suffering was clear: the truly penitent heart of every Christian had to be offered up willingly to God (and to the Church) if that original act of sacrifice was to retain its full force and meaning. The Church as institution was able to exercise enormous attraction by pressing into service the powerful affectivity that had always been associated with the human heart in Western culture. The model of suffering that gives rise not to hatred but to love and mercy in the human breast performed its remarkable cultural work in Europe without serious opposition for centuries, until two counter-forces caused a profound reassessment of the cultural significance of the heart.

In the course of the sixteenth century, successful challenges to the monopoly on penitent hearts held by the Church of Rome were mounted by two distinct but ideologically related groups, Protestant reformers and professors of anatomy. The leading anatomists – men such as Berengario da Carpi (1460–1530), Realdo Columbo (1515–59), Andreas Vesalius (1514–64), John Caius (1510–73), Ambroise Paré (1509–90), Juan Valverde de Hamusco (1524–64), John Banister (1533–1610), and William Harvey (1578–1657) – uniformly insisted in their published writings on two things: (1) the heart was the furnace that fired all animal and human life, and (2) their studies of the human body, in its parts and its entirety, were intended to demonstrate to the rational mind the majesty of God's creation. Thus, they followed the ancient natural philosophers in keeping the heart at the forefront of their studies, and they paid homage to the teachings of the Church. The most effective renegotiator of the relationship between divine engineering and systematic human observation of the body was Andreas Vesalius. It was his prodigious skills, observational and descriptive as well as surgical, that flung open a window on the human thorax, allowing generations of medical students and the naturally curious to see the heart physically in the anatomy theater and textually in his remarkable volume *De humani corporis fabrica libri septem* (Basel: J. Oporinus, 1543, rev. 1555). Vesalius's *Fabrica*, as his book is generally called, was easily the most influential anatomical textbook for 300 years after its initial publication. In it he looked into the human body through many of the windows previously opened by his teachers, living and dead. His most substantial debt was to Galen, whom he revered and defended, even as he corrected Galen's conceptual errors with his own keen observations of actual human dissections. His handsomely printed volume presented the basic physiological systems, one in each book:

Book I: The Skeleton
Book II: The Muscles
Book III: The Vascular System
Book IV: The Nervous System
Book V: The Gastrointestinal System
Book VI: The Internal Organs
Book VII: The Brain

The structure and function of the heart and lungs are meticulously described and illustrated in Book VI.

Vesalius, at the time a young and somewhat impetuous member of the medical faculty at the University of Padua who had trained in Paris and Louvain, was avid in his pursuit of truths about the body, always preferring observable fact over unfounded opinion and speculation. His section on the heart provides some evidence of his impatience with strict Galenists who prefer the authority of classical texts to the evidence of their own eyes. He is particularly critical of writers who blindly repeat the assertion that there is a supporting bone in the heart. Vesalius writes:

Those who, following Galen, have undertaken to write the description of the human body have declared that there is a bone, in the base of the heart, comparable to that one in the upper part of the larynx called the hyoid from its resemblance to the letter U. Nor was it enough for those men to form a bone in this way in the base of the human heart, but they must add to their discourse that the base of the heart, indeed the whole heart, is strengthened by this bone as is the root of the tongue by that bone placed before the larynx . . . Now let us put aside this sort of imagining of men and let us condemn their stupidity that leads them, full of pride, to prepare the bone of the stag's heart mixed with I-don't-know-what gems and gold for affections of the heart, although the bone of the stag is no different from that of the calf, dog, or swine.[10]

While he is willing to forgive this error in Galen himself, who was forbidden by the mores of his time to dissect human cadavers, Vesalius is determined that the entire medical profession should condemn those who use the imagined heart bone to promote sales of phony medications for heart "affections" or ailments. He also boasts of the "innumerable places where I have already shown the anatomical lapses of Galen."[11] But examples such as these from the *Fabrica* are far outnumbered by positive references to the great classical master of physiology. While carefully blowing the cobwebs off the ancient medical texts, Vesalius adds to the literature an important one of his own.

The *Fabrica* has a healthy infusion of artfulness and even whimsy that helped to alter basic attitudes toward the role of the physician in the theater of the body. The justly famous historiated capital letters, used throughout the first and second editions as well as in the *Epitome* of the *Fabrica*, helped to make it the kind of book that serious collectors preserved and artists consulted. In the capital letters, a series of pudgy, naked *putti* perform the tasks of the anatomist. In the large capital "Q" (there is also a smaller capital "Q" showing a group of *putti* removing a fetus from a dog), a dissector works with his scalpel on a live pig lashed down to a dissecting table while a lector reads from an authoritative anatomical text and five other *putti*, whom Samuel W. Lambert fancifully identifies as "young students" of Vesalius, observe the procedure (Fig. 1).[12] A pair of winged *putti* in the upper corners of the block may suggest a divine operation in progress, but the grinning figure at the lower left opening up what looks like a straight razor or scalpel and the one at the right testing the sharpness of the point on the "Q" with his finger indicate a lower form of comedy. Pulling these playful figures down from the

---

[10] *Fabrica* (1543), 94, quoted in C. D. O'Malley, *Andreas Vesalius of Brussels, 1514–1564* (Berkeley: University of California Press, 1965), 158. To date, only parts of the *Fabrica* have been translated into English. O'Malley translates brief passages in the body of his biography of Vesalius cited above and includes an appendix of longer passages (317–77), including part of Book VI on dissecting the heart and lungs (361–70). An ambitious project aimed at translating the entire work has so far produced one volume, the first of Vesalius's seven books, *On the Fabric of the Human Body, Book I*, trans. William Frank Richardson and John Burd Carman (San Francisco: Norman Publishing, 1998). *The Epitome of Andreas Vesalius* has been translated by L. R. Lind (New York: Macmillan, 1949).

[11] *Fabrica* (1543), 276; quoted in O'Malley, *Andreas Vesalius*, 168.

[12] Samuel W. Lambert, Willy Wiegand, and William M. Ivins, Jr., *Three Vesalian Essays to Accompany the "Icones Anatomicae" of 1934* with a foreword by Archibald Malloch (New York: Macmillan, 1952), 13–15.

Figure 1. Large historiated capital "Q." Andreas Vesalius, *De humani corporis fabrica libri septem* (Basel: Ex officina Joannis Oporini, 1543), 562, reproduced by permission of the Rare Book and Manuscript Library, University of Illinois at Urbana-Champaign, Urbana, IL. Shelfmark F. 611 V63d1543. This humorous woodcut from Vesalius's influential anatomy textbook shows a group of *putti* engaged in the vivisection of a pig, under the direction of a lector.

vaulted ceilings of *palazzi* and the upper corners of vast mythological canvases and turning them loose in a physiology textbook produces a parody that tends to infantilize the sometimes ghoulish activities of the anatomist. Other letters depict grave- and gibbet-robbing, common methods of providing cadavers for the dissecting tables in university lecture theaters such as the one depicted in the famous frontispiece of the *Fabrica*. Like little dimpled, misbehaving cupids, the *putti* make light of the serious business of life and death in the hands of the anatomical technician.

Several narratives intertwine in Vesalius's masterwork: the proud but occasionally defensive story of what anatomists really do; the unfolding of his respectful but sometimes testy relationship with Galen and the Galenists of sixteenth-century Europe; the history of the birth, growth, and decay of the human body; the drama of unveiling the layered secrets of the flesh in the course of dissection. As we will see, bits of these stories were incorporated into early modern literary texts, where they took on a metaphoric coloration and emotional force that the anatomists and other natural philosophers could hardly have imagined.

Like his fellow anatomists, Vesalius insists that the Creator be understood through a systematic study of the natural body. The approach to God through the material body introduced believers to a new way of experiencing and evaluating the deity – to a new cultural language – just as surely as did the more overtly controversial claims of astronomers such as Nicholas Copernicus (1473–1543), Galileo Galilei (1564–1642), and Johannes Kepler (1571–1630). Demonstrating in the anatomy theater the ideally central location of the heart and the ingenious communications system linking it to the rest of the body entailed understanding God as never before, through a system of observational inquiry and logical argumentation that functioned very differently from the meditative disciplines and ritualized celebrations that had shaped the worship of God previously. The challenge to the Old Religion and to former representations of the penitent heart from this new direction was as traumatic in its way as the head-on confrontation mounted by political and theological opponents of the Catholic Church.

The political rebellion against the ecclesiastical power structures of Rome and its persuasive methods of enlisting and retaining believers had its centers in Geneva and Wittenberg but soon spread to England. When required to, the Protestant reformers justified their attacks on the Church of Rome with philosophical rationales remarkably similar to the assumptions underlying the proto-scientific inquiry into the structure and motions of the macrocosmic universe and the microcosmic human body. The argument went roughly like this: if we observe carefully the individual Christian soul in its progress toward God, we see that direct access to scriptural teaching and direct address of one's prayers to God – without the intercession of priests or saints – creates a newly energized convocation of the faithful. The Protestant regime of introspection – analogous in some, but not all, ways to firsthand observation of the human body in the process of dissection – depended heavily upon appropriating the image and discipline of the penitent heart from Catholic religious practice and turning them to its own ends. From the most articulate, university-trained Protestant apologist to the least educated agricultural laborer, there was tacit agreement that the heart was the unique residence of the conscience, the voice of God within each person, and hence the only organ, anatomical or political, that could afford direct union with the Almighty. The reformed heart thus became the most powerful possible means of representing graphically, poetically, and theologically the individual Christian's relationship with God. The primary meaning of the heart in Reformation iconography is uniform across the spectrum of English Protestant churches from the "highest" Laudian to the "lowest" Calvinist, who, though they differed enormously in the degree of inner turmoil they confessed to, invariably located the struggle for self-knowledge and salvation in the heart.

The struggle was often terrifying and the outcome never assured. As I will have occasion to point out frequently in the course of this study, particularly in the chapter on stage villains, circumstances can force unbridgable chasms to open between the heart's secret truths and public declarations of belief. The disjoining circumstances are often political in nature, and the political disruption of spiritual profession was never more violent in England than during the reigns of Edward VI, Mary, and Elizabeth, as accounts of the recalcitrant tongues and tortured hearts of both Catholic and Protestant martyrs make clear. The violent exposure of these disjunctions between heart and tongue underlie the central conflicts of early modern Church politics. Only by resolving publicly not to pry into the souls of her subjects was Elizabeth able to make her Settlement work on the level of outward conformity. The policy of tolerating inward dissent led eventually to major rifts within the Church of England, but in the first instance it encouraged a degree of visible unity and uniformity that permitted the nation to pull itself together while individual Englishmen and women sorted out more profound matters of the heart and the soul on their own.

The ecclesiastical politics of the period, along with developments in the natural sciences, helped to shape the underlying cultural codes that over time simultaneously bolstered and disguised such common practices as worshiping the heart, monitoring its rhythmic pulse, and expanding its symbolic meanings in religious and artistic contexts. These codes, as Michel Foucault observes, define both the historical moment and its subsequent reconstruction by the historian:

The fundamental codes of a culture – those governing its language, its schemas of perception, its exchanges, its techniques, its values, the hierarchy of its practices – establish for every man, from the very first, the empirical orders with which he will be dealing and within which he will be at home.[13]

The second half of the sixteenth century in England brought such sudden changes in acceptable religious practice and such rapid developments in the study of human anatomy that the heart became a place where few could feel comfortably "at home." These changes produced what I think of as stress fractures in the body of thought that Shakespeare and his contemporaries inherited from the medieval and classical past. These subtle breaks appear in

[13] Michel Foucault, *The Order of Things: An Archaeology of the Human Sciences* (New York: Pantheon Books, 1970), xx.

the form of conflicting cultural responses to the human body and spirit. The most profound and widespread of these responses in early modern England involved the reformers' reconfiguration of the penitent Catholic heart, the renewed anatomical study of the heart's motions, and the reshaping of heart symbolism from late medieval and early Renaissance love poetry into the theatrical site of villainy, anguish, and repentance. Locating continuities and breaks in the transmission of a material and poetic subject/object as complex as the heart entails searching for its cultural traces, high and low. I have studied popular emblems, jewelry, proverbs, epics, playing cards, religious icons, legends, and anatomy textbooks in order to learn just how completely the early modern theater embraced and transformed this ideologically fraught body part.

Early modern cultural shifts relating to the body and its parts have been recorded by an impressive group of commentators in the course of the last decade, though not with my specific focus on the heart in the age of Shakespeare. A major point of disagreement and revisionist theorizing concerns the reception of the traditional anatomical and physiological texts that I have been discussing. Recent "body criticism" has proffered conflicting accounts of the process of reception, highlighting the disabling as well as the enabling impact of ancient medical and philosophical works on the perception of embodiment in the sixteenth and seventeenth centuries. One of the most influential and controversial of these accounts is Jonathan Sawday's in *The Body Emblazoned: Dissection and the Human Body in Renaissance Culture*.[14]

For Sawday, Renaissance anatomy was a revolutionary undertaking, departing abruptly from past teachings and tracing a distinctively new path into future mechanistic and vitalistic science. Sawday believes that the conflation of organic and mechanical structures and motions characteristic of anatomical studies in the period rendered largely obsolete the corpus of classical and medieval natural philosophy concerning the body. An intermediate stage in this process, outlined in Sawday's chapter "The Renaissance Body: From Colonization to Invention," involved acute anxiety and deep distress in the minds of those who had been initiated by earlier sixteenth-century anatomists into mysteries of the inward body that exceeded the powers of the mind to formulate rational explanations. Sawday's prime example here, John Donne, repeatedly invoked analogies with New World exploration to chart the intricate terrain of his own interior

---

[14] Jonathan Sawday, *The Body Emblazoned: Dissection and the Human Body in Renaissance Culture* (London: Routledge, 1995). Subsequent references will appear parenthetically.

body, particularly during major illnesses, but found no comfort in the strangeness he encountered there. The inner world, Sawday suggests, would remain a landscape of uncertainty and dread until fresh, more manageable analogies could be found to domesticate it. Sawday puts the case that the spectacle of the early dissecting tables was profoundly upsetting to spectators, and the careful regimentation of its procedures and precise classification of its results insufficient to calm their anxieties. Only a completely revised array of analogies, involving man-made machines, could make the body feel manageable, according to Sawday. In an article published a decade after *The Body Emblazoned*, he argues that this kind of mechanistic analogy was presciently available to Montaigne in the form of French, German, and Italian waterworks that systematically produced the kind of free flow of fluids that the philosopher could only wish for in his own stone-blocked urinary tract.[15] Comparing the functions of the body, especially the action of the heart, to those of a mechanical pump has become emblematic of the Scientific Revolution. Pursuing a similar line of argument, Jonathan Miller insists that "One of the reasons why the anatomy and physiology of the heart took so long to develop was the lack of satisfactory metaphors for what was seen." The key "conjectural model" of the heart's function, he claims (not for the first time) was the fire-pump, concluding that "it seems unlikely that Harvey would have departed so radically from the traditional theory if the technological images of propulsion had not encouraged him to think along such lines."[16] Miller and Sawday are convinced that a seismic shift occurred in body science during the seventeenth century, and they invoke a kind of demystified materialism and mechanism to understand it.

Like Sawday and Miller, David Hillman argues for what he calls in his book *Shakespeare's Entrails* an "emergent psychology of somatic inwardness."[17] Why, he asks, were Shakespeare and others of his time so obsessed with the guts? He frames answers to his question in a surprising variety of terms, drawn from twentieth-century psychology (particularly Freudian and Lacanian) and early modern theology. He emphasizes a crisis of faith that turned thinking people into Doubting Thomases, determined to penetrate others' insides to find evidence of their beliefs or lack of them. While he does not quite convince me that late sixteenth-century theologians

---

[15] Jonathan Sawday, "In Search of the Philosopher's Stone: Montaigne, Interiority and Machines," *The Dalhousie Review* 85 (2005): 195–220.

[16] Jonathan Miller, "The Pump: Harvey and the Circulation of the Blood," in *Blood: Art, Power, Politics and Pathology*, ed. James M. Bradburne (Munich: Prestel, 2002), 100–7, quotations from 101 and 105.

[17] David Hillman, *Shakespeare's Entrails: Belief, Scepticism and the Interior of the Body* (Basingstoke: Palgrave, 2007), 3.

and artists placed *more* emphasis on Christ's "willing enfleshment" (page 37) than, for example, the author of the York Crucifixion play, I am in full agreement that a deeply skeptical mindset lies behind the increasing demands in the period for observable evidence and logical demonstrations in matters of the heart.

The most thoroughly nuanced modern accounts of the history of anatomical theory and surgical practice from Vesalius to Harvey have, however, tended to concentrate on continuity and incremental refinements of proto-body science rather than on the overt hostilities and thrilling reversals implicit in the revolutionary model of historical change. The work of Andrew Cunningham and Nancy G. Siraisi is preeminent in this debate.[18] Cunningham has little patience with the notion of a "Scientific Revolution" rooted in the anatomical experimentation of the sixteenth century and still less with the view that anatomists were regarded as outlaws poking into physically unsavory and socially forbidden realms. Instead he portrays early modern anatomists as conscientious textual scholars and serious medical teachers bringing the learning of the past into line with their own practice and the medical needs of their own world. Siraisi, too, finds the Renaissance anatomists respectful of their ancient predecessors and careful not to treat the subjects of their dissections with disrespect. While Siraisi and Cunningham present useful assessments of the anatomical project, they say little about how such experiential study of the human body could affect the way people thought about the divine artistry exhibited in the process of dissection. Relying on learned men to reveal and confirm the structural and functional perfection of the Creator's work was ideologically very different from accepting it as an article of faith.[19] Revealing the *arcana Dei* might, indeed, be confused with rivaling it. Even without a direct challenge to religious orthodoxy by the doctors of anatomy, their systematic scrutiny of the human interior set up demanding new standards for ocular and reproducible results in the study of the early modern self.

The figure who placed the heart at the center of the debate over methodologies in the systematic study of human physiology was William Harvey. Harvey's *De motu cordis* (1628) made the heart not just the object of another story of vital heat, spirits, and passions, but rather the subject

---

[18] See especially Andrew Cunningham, *The Anatomical Renaissance: The Resurrection of the Anatomical Projects of the Ancients* (Aldershot: Scolar Press, 1997) and Nancy G. Siraisi, *Medieval and Early Renaissance Medicine: An Introduction to Knowledge and Practice* (Chicago: University of Chicago Press, 1990).

[19] Following the lead of Stanley Cavell, David Hillman finds the rejection or disowning of received knowledge a central tenet of early modern thought. I want to argue that what was occurring was a critical re-examination of the knowledges of the past rather than their outright rejection.

of an extended argument aimed at persuading readers that this organ was the sole efficient cause of blood being propelled in its constant recirculation through the arteries and veins. Harvey presented a strategic blend of previously accepted and freshly devised experiments that rendered his conclusions extraordinarily compelling. It had been long accepted, for instance, that there were trapdoors in the blood vessels. Arguing that these "valves," as Harvey called them, kept the blood moving away from the heart in the arteries and toward it in the veins, he was able to demonstrate the circulation of the blood in living dogs, wounded people, and fresh cadavers by using carefully placed ligatures along the course traveled by the blood. The only illustration in his book depicts an arm tourniquet of the sort used regularly by barber-surgeons in letting blood, but Harvey includes it not to demonstrate the cure for a superflux of humors but rather to track the direction of blood movement by temporarily arresting it. While medical texts required many illustrations of anatomical structures and surgical procedures, Harvey's purpose and pedagogical method was quite different. He set out to create an intelligible model of how the heart could push a very large quantity of blood through the body, much more blood, he observed, than the liver could possibly produce from nutrient intake. The familiar and the innovative experiments combined to produce a persuasive case, one that drew strength from past physiologies and laid down new directions for both physical and, somewhat surprisingly, social science.

Not everyone was on side, however. Colleagues of Harvey's in the Royal Society published refutations. Such influential European university professors as Jean Riolan wrote heated letters and learned treatises denouncing Harvey's supposed rejection of Aristotelian natural philosophy and the teachings of Galen. Harvey admitted that he couldn't answer all the questions that his investigations raised, such as how blood got transferred from arteries to veins at the body's extremities. It wasn't until 1660 that Marcello Malpighi actually saw blood moving through capillaries from the arterial system to the venous in a frog's lungs. And Harvey had not even tried to address the philosophical issues of design and teleology in his account of the heart's function, except briefly to discuss final causes in his last chapter.

Still, Harvey's way of working and his conclusions gained influential adherents. In the *Discours de la méthode* (1637) Descartes admired Harvey's experimental methods of deriving reproducible results under controlled conditions. Hobbes speaks glowingly in the Epistle to his *De corpore politico* (1650) of Harvey's groundbreaking work on the heart and blood and says in the introduction to the *Leviathan* (1651) that the heart-spring drives the entire body.[20] James Harrington's *Commonwealth of Oceana* (1656) uses the model of the Harveian heart for a two-chambered legislature and the movement of the blood as a way to organize the circulation of political offices and powers. Bypassing the mechanistic models of Galileo and other early physical scientists, Harrington outlined a social science based on the premises of the most recent physiologists. His political theory found practical application in John Adams's work on the new American constitution.[21] In this way, the early modern discourse of the heart came to resonate far beyond its origins in theology and anatomy.

As Eric Jager demonstrates in his elegant study, *The Book of the Heart*, the heart was strongly identified with the act of recording the experience of selfhood in book form throughout the Middle Ages, though not in the proto-scientific form we have just been considering. The heart was frequently represented as a codex (as opposed to biblical tables or the scrolls of the Torah) in which magical aspects of the self (rather than the Bible's communications of God) were recorded for public consumption. While similar uses of the book-heart metaphor persisted into the early modern period, Jager focuses his research mainly on the medieval period:

> Although I trace the self-text metaphor from antiquity to modernity, I devote most of my attention, as my title suggests, to the medieval millennium during which this metaphor, as a book of the heart created in the image of the manuscript codex, reached the height of its ideological power and poetic expression. The period from roughly 400 C.E. to 1500, or from the ascendancy of the codex in the late Roman Empire to the advent of the printed book during the late Middle Ages, saw not only the full flowering of the book of the heart as a literary trope, but also its transformation into a pictorial image and even a tangible artifact.[22]

After reading Augustine's autobiography as a story metaphorically written upon the heart, Jager discusses fifteenth-century manuscript codices literally produced in the shape of hearts, arguing persuasively that the cultural confluence of privacy in the acts of writing and reading, along with meditations on the secrets of the heart, produced an enduring metaphor of the self. He touches on the extension of this phenomenon into the age of print, but his primary focus is on medieval manuscripts and their narratives of the heart. His study makes clear that cultural continuity is at least as

---

[20] See Sir William Molesworth, *The English Works of Thomas Hobbes*, 11 vols. (London, 1839–45; reprinted Aalen, 1962).

[21] I am indebted here to I. Bernard Cohen's informative essay, "Harrington and Harvey: A Theory of the State Based on the New Physiology," *Journal of the History of Ideas* 55 (1994): 187–210.

[22] Eric Jager, *The Book of the Heart* (Chicago: University of Chicago Press, 2000), xiv.

important as cultural change in matters of the heart. The heart was the key, Jager observes in his chapter "The Scriptorium of the Heart," not only to perpetuating the life of the body but also to understanding the life of the soul and the passions. God's image and His Word were inscribed in the heart/conscience of the faithful. Love and hate resided in the heart, and people were most fully themselves within their hearts. Accounts of the inner being became increasingly dense and detailed as the lives of early modern statesmen, merchants, and even stage-players were added to those of the medieval saints. Acts of individual introspection, owing a great deal to earlier forms of Catholic meditation, provided the core of early modern life-writing in diaries and lyric poetry. The heart was fully integrated into these explorations of inwardness.

Establishing the place of the heart in the early modern conception of human interiority requires not only getting past our own preoccupation with medicalizing the organ in its moments of crisis but also allowing for the fusion rather than the strenuous separation of mental and physical states of self-awareness. The excellent work of Michael Schoenfeldt has helped to open up our corporeal thinking well beyond the works of the four English poets (Edmund Spenser, William Shakespeare, George Herbert, and John Milton) that he studies in *Bodies and Selves in Early Modern England*. Schoenfeldt wisely advocates the study of interiority in the period through the historically appropriate lens of Galenic humoral psychophysiology:

Whereas our post-Cartesian ontology imagines psychological inwardness and physiological materialism as necessarily separate realms of existence, and thus renders corporeal language for emotion highly metaphorical, the Galenic regime of the humoral self that supplies these [early modern English] writers with much of their vocabulary of inwardness demanded the invasion of social and psychological realms by biological and environmental processes.[23]

He goes on to say that "in early modern England, the consuming subject was pressured by Galenic physiology, classical ethics, and Protestant theology to conceive all acts of ingestion and excretion as very literal acts of self-fashioning" (11). All these systems of thinking shaped the way the inner, feeling self found its habitation within the material body and the social structures beyond it. The rules governing concealment and revelation of inner truths were changing rapidly in the period and with them the approved but often transgressed boundaries between inner and outer, the

---

[23] Michael C. Schoenfeldt, *Bodies and Selves in Early Modern England: Physiology and Inwardness in Spenser, Shakespeare, Herbert, and Milton* (Cambridge: Cambridge University Press, 1999), 8. Subsequent references will appear parenthetically.

private self and the society of others, invisibility and transparency. Negotiating and respecting these boundaries was an important part of the discipline of natural philosophy from classical times to the Enlightenment. Self-writers, both biographers and autobiographers, always ran the risk of revealing too many of the secrets of the heart, opening the window of the confessional too wide.

For all the encouragement to look into one's heart and write, giving literal as well as metaphorical shape to felt experience, there have always been stringent taboos associated with this powerful organ.[24] While cultures that valued heroic strength and courage perpetuated the idea that these qualities could be enhanced by devouring the heart of one's conquered opponents,[25] in societies that viewed the heart as charged with love, sacred and profane, there were strong prohibitions against eating the heart. The violation of this taboo affords storytellers the opportunity to tap into feelings of profound horror and mysterious sacramentalism. Dante, for example, exploits the power of this transgression at the moment in the *Vita Nuova* when he dreams of seeing Beatrice being forced to eat his own flaming heart.[26] In *A Perverse History of the Human Heart* Milad Doueihi

---

[24] On the physical and metaphorical shaping of the heart see Pierre Vinken, *The Shape of the Heart* (Amsterdam: Elsevier, 1999).

[25] Appropriation of another's heart as a token of bravery generally stops short of ingestion. Shakespeare, for example, follows a prominent strand of the medieval legend of Richard Cœur de Lion when he has the King of France refer to "Richard, that robb'd the lion of his heart" (*The Life and Death of King John* 2.1.3). Unless otherwise noted, quotations of Shakespeare are from *The Riverside Shakespeare*, ed. G. Blakemore Evans *et al.* (Boston: Houghton Mifflin, 1997). According to some versions of the Cœur de Lion legend, however, the imprisoned Richard not only rips out the heart of the lion sent to kill him, he devours it before his captor, King Modred:

> King Richard . . . squeezed the blood,
> And in the salt he dipped the heart,
> As everyone stood back, apart.
> Dripping and raw, this heart he ate.
> Modred stunned and desolate,
> Muttered, "In truth I understand,
> This is no mortal, but Devil's hand,
> That has my stalwart lion slain,
> And ripped his heart by might and main,
> And of it here now eats his fill.
> He is rightly called for this fierce skill,
> A king christened of great renown,
> 'Strong Richard Cœur de Lion!'"

Richard the Lion-Hearted and Other Medieval English Romances, trans. Bradford B. Broughton (New York: Dutton, 1966), 178, lines 1105–16. Richard's action combines the heroic with the demonic.

[26] See the discussion of this passage in Chapter 5.

offers a heavily theorized account of the anthropological significance of the eaten-heart trope and its narratives, extending from the thirteenth-century *Lai d'Ignaure* to the seventeenth-century treatment of the Eucharist by Jean-Pierre Camus in such works as *Les Spectacles d'Horreur*. *The Knight of Curtesy and the Lady of Faguell*, a late thirteenth-century English version of the romance story that Doueihi doesn't discuss, shows a number of variations worth investigating as we consider the transition from medieval to early modern narratives of the heart.

In *The Knight of Curtesy* the relationship between the lady and the titular hero is utterly chaste. The knight's quest carries him as far as the Holy Land, carrying with him the blonde braid that the lady cut off and presented him as her parting favor. When the knight is fatally wounded by Saracens, he directs his servant to return the braid, along with his heart, to Faguell:

> Out of mi body . . . cut mi herte
> And wrappe it in this yelowe here;
> And when thou doest from hence departe,
> Unto my lady thou do it bere. (lines 381–4)[27]

The lady's husband intercepts the messenger and commands his cook to prepare the heart to be served to his wife. When he brutally informs her that she has eaten the heart of her beloved, she stoically refuses all other food and starves to death.

> That herte shal certayne with me dye;
> I haue rec[e]iued thereon the sacrament;
> All erthly fode here I denye;
> For wo and paine my life is spente (lines 461–4)

What is remarkable in this particular romance is the complete sympathy with the lady, who gives first her hair and then her life to honor the knight's courteous heart. Her husband ironically becomes complicit in the consummation of the heart-bond between the knight and his lady. He is, though, unable to fathom the secrets of the heart, which point toward later conceptions of human bonds that set aside the horror of the eaten-heart stories in order to focus on the humanist value of friendship.

Doueihi presents the view that by the time of Francis Bacon's essay "Of Friendship" heart-cannibalism has been translated into the language of

---

[27] *The Knight of Curtesy and the Fair Lady of Faguell*, ed. Elizabeth McCausland (Northampton, MA: Smith College, 1922).

friends who are able to bridge the gap between self and Other. Doueihi writes:

Cor ne edito: Pythagoras' absolute prohibition is now simply a parable of and for the heart, that is, a linguistic and discursive object in quest of interpretation whose truth lies at the center of new, emerging representations of the body and its organs, of the heart and its figures, of self and identity. Pythagoras' prohibition now names a parabolic form of cannibalism, a figurative transmutation of the body of the other into one's self and of one's self into another body under the guise of friendship. "Eat not the heart," for the heart is what can no longer be eaten because it is inhabited by words that mirror the self in its quest for a friend. In other words, Bacon's heart, in the manner of Dante's Lord of Love, exhibits itself, shows its most inner parts, to the one who mirrors himself in the same fashion by opening up his own heart. The heart, the organ of life and speech, the organ of rebirth and regeneration, the organ of the sacred and the magical, has finally been fully humanized. It has been given to man as the tool and instrument of friendship, as the means of mastering the self and the flesh in and through the words that inhabit the heart.[28]

The occurrence of the *cœur mangé* in discourses ranging from love poetry to the expository essay suggests that the metaphor of devouring the heart of the beloved was felt to be an accurate, not just a fanciful, description of intense interpersonal feelings at the outer limits of social tolerance.

By the start of the early modern period, the heart is far more than a bodily organ that generates heat and distributes *spiritus* to other parts of the body. It is also a storehouse and transmitter of language that allows people to communicate intimately with those they truly love. This sensitive and articulate heart to which God speaks and from which the good Christian speaks to others has its origins, as we have seen, in the Bible. As the English Puritan Thomas Watson explains in *Heaven Taken by Storm*, God is the sole author of the Bible and the heart the primary organ for receiving, understanding, and storing His Word: "The word is of divine original, and reveals the *deep things of God* to us. That there is a numen or deity is ingraven in mans heart."[29] Watson's term "numen" (Gr. πνεῦμα, *pneuma* or breath) is meant to invoke the Bible's account of God's physiological presence as His spirit is breathed into the heart.

Robert A. Erickson's brilliant study of the biblical heart in the work of John Milton, Aphra Behn, and Samuel Richardson, *The Language of the*

---

[28] Milad Doueihi, *A Perverse History of the Human Heart* (Cambridge, MA: Harvard University Press, 1997), 73–4.

[29] Thomas Watson, *Heaven Taken by Storm; or, The Holy Violence a Christian is to Put Forth in the Pursuit after Glory* (London: by R. W. for T. Parkhurst, 1669), 24.

Heart, 1600–1750, has shed enormous light on the literary impact of heart lore during what we might call the *long* early modern period. The languaged heart, he argues, is also a powerfully gendered heart. He traces "a movement from a strongly masculinist heroic version of the heart in Harvey (one that incorporates a projective sense of the heart's power) to a no less powerful but more feminist heroic narrative in Richardson (one that incorporates a more receptive sense of the heart's power)."[30] The divine heart, in its generative and its communicative aspects, is also aggressively male. In his section on "The Semiotic God," Erickson says:

Besides being represented as a seminal God of astonishing fertility and creativity (the ultimate fertility god of all such deities in the ancient Near East), the God of the Old Testament is a powerful God of signs or "tokens." I take the term semiotic in its most literal sense of "sign-making," with the emphasis on creating, inflicting, memorializing. I wish first to explore God's marking activity on the human body (especially the male body), and on the earth or land ("the land is mine" [Lev. 25: 23]), and why that activity is important to the biblical narrative of the heart. We shall see that the emphasis on written discourse in Exodus (in conjunction with the emphasis on oral discourse in Genesis) is primarily significant for our master narrative because of the eventual metonymic identification of stone tablets and the human heart in Jeremiah and, most importantly for Christians in early modern England, the discourse of the heart in the Gospels and that of the Spirit's writing in the heart in the Epistles of St. Paul. The account which I give here of God's writing, and writing as a male act of power, culminates in the trope of the written heart.[31]

God's power is transmitted into the Christian heart in the form of understanding, as Paul tells the Corinthians: "For God that commanded the light to shine out of darknes, *is he* which hathe shined in our hearts, to giue the light of the knowledge of the glorie of God in the face of Iesus Christ" (2 Cor. 4: 6). Before the thinking heart can be so enlightened, however, the true believer must first soften, break, or surgically alter the hardness of his heart. The striking image for this latter procedure is circumcision: "Circumcise therefore the foreskin of your heart, and harden your neks no more" (Deut. 10: 16). As John Donne explains in his sermon preached at St. Dunstan's on New Year's Day, 1624/5, this verse is concerned with purifying the profoundest recesses of the inner self, the heart, where the word of God is imprinted on man's most tender flesh. But that private, interior place becomes as well the penis in this odd injunction, suggesting that the

---

[30] Robert A. Erickson, *The Language of the Heart, 1600–1750* (Philadelphia: University of Pennsylvania Press, 1997), xi.
[31] Erickson, *The Language of the Heart*, 35.

Figure 2. Emblem 13, "Cordis circvmcisio" [The Circumcized Heart]. Benedict van Haeften, *Schola Cordis*, (1629), trans. Christopher Harvey (London: for H. Blunden, 1647), 52, reproduced by permission of the Rare Books Division, The New York Public Library, Astor, Lenox and Tilden Foundations. The angel presents the figure on the left with a knife to cut away the fashionable gauds from the heart.

discourse of sacred interiority is simultaneously the discourse of sexual privacy and male initiation.[32] All that is effeminate, gaudy, or corrupt must be cut away from the heart. An almost comical version of the surgical scene is depicted in an emblem from the seventeenth-century collection called *Schola Cordis* (Fig. 2).[33] An angel provides a knife to excise the vain trumpery (a violin, a jester's head, and other signs of frivolity) from the encumbered heart. The accompanying epigram and ode liken the procedure to the

---

[32] Erickson, commenting on allusions to the circumcised heart in Jer. 4: 4 and 4: 9, says, "the male heart must be circumcised, opened, revitalized, made receptive to a new truth" (*The Language of the Heart*, 51). He lists several other biblical references to this injunction (233 n. 27) and notes the frequent conflation of sexual and textual hearts, concluding that the heart is as much a site of reproductive power as are the penis and the womb. Generative power is attributed by the ancients to the male's greater heat.

[33] Benedict van Haeften, *Schola Cordis* (1629), trans. Christopher Harvey (London: for H. Blunden, 1647), 52.

suffering of Christ on the cross, though the discomfort of having to de-accessorize hardly seems commensurate.

The circumcized heart is a purified heart, a pen poised to reinscribe God's originary act of creation and a table prepared to receive His Word. The inner record of one's dialogue with God, written in the heart, became increasingly important in the Reformation. As Jager remarks, "The inherited notion of the heart as a book containing God's word, a devotional memory, or a moral record of the individual's life was well suited to the Protestant culture of individual Bible study and self-examination."[34] Difficulties arose for the fathers of the Reformed Church as they attempted to devise ways to represent the devout man's inner encounter with himself and his God. The dramatic and often highly ornamental icons that decorated Catholic churches were anathema to many Protestants. The flaming, lacerated, and bleeding heart of Jesus bespoke a gaudy tradition of papist assaults on the senses, and puritanical iconoclasm enjoyed its own violent day destroying such images in the continental centers of reform and in England.[35] Altarpieces and crucifixes were stripped from many churches in a sixteenth-century revival of earlier passionate outbursts of iconoclasm, and the Sacred Heart, like other powerful Christian symbols, all but disappeared from the institutional and domestic display places of religious art in Protestant countries.[36] The prohibition, however, was replaced by a somewhat different conception of religious iconography and the heart's place, particularly in Lutheran thought. As the art historian Joseph Koerner explains, the practice of such artists as Lucas Cranach the Elder was guided by Luther's rethinking of the problem of religious icons:

Likening the inner portrait of Christ to a reflection, Luther makes the inner image a spontaneous, natural event. Iconoclasm thus becomes absurd, for even without being manually fabricated, crucifixes will be formed anyway. Whereas in

---

[34] Jager, *The Book of the Heart*, 139.

[35] Quoting the Puritan divine William Perkins's *Warning Against the Idolatry of the Last Times* (1601), Huston Diehl arrives at the generalization that "English Calvinists warn[ed] especially of the danger of 'erect[ing] unto themselves Idols within their own hearts, and commit[ting] a most secret and spirituall idolatrie, which the world cannot discerne.'" *Staging Reform, Reforming the Stage: Protestantism and Popular Theater in Early Modern England* (Ithaca: Cornell University Press, 1997), 164–5.

[36] Eamon Duffy makes the important observation, however, that immediately following Elizabeth's accession, there was "no great iconoclastic enthusiasm" among a religiously conservative populace whose devotional habits had been formed in the "traditional" Catholic faith and who had found themselves having to reverse the direction of their reformations rather frequently in the preceding years. See *The Stripping of the Altars: Traditional Religion in England, c. 1400–c. 1580* (New Haven: Yale University Press, 1992), quotation from p. 574. The more strenuous stripping occurred later in Elizabeth's reign, when a more zealous group of reformers succeeded to the ecclesiastical hierarchy.

1522 he had called them adiaphora and wished them gone, here he suggests that images are even salvifically necessary, for faith takes place *as* that image-filled machinery of the heart.[37]

The elder Cranach's altarpiece in Luther's Wittenberg church places a crucifix prominently between the portrait of the great minister preaching and his congregation, while Lucas Cranach the Younger's *Colditz Altarpiece* (1584) is in the shape of a heart, depicting the Annunciation and the Fall on the outside, and the Birth, Crucifixion, and Resurrection on the inside. Clearly, images of the heart would remain central to the Protestant reconstruction of the spiritual self.

Christ's Passion is just one example, though the supreme one, of the embodiment of the passions in general, which made their home in the heart, as the Catholic priest and controversialist Thomas Wright explained in 1604:

[T]he affections and passions . . . must have some corporall organ and instrument, and what more convenient than the heart? for, as the brayne fitteth best, for the softnesse and moysture, to receyve the formes and prints of obiects for vnderstanding; even so the heart endued with most fiery spirites, fitteth best for affecting.[38]

While Wright's distinction between "vnderstanding" and "affecting" is far from settled in the early seventeenth century, it serves to establish the importance of the emotions in the proto-scientific as well as the poetic discourse of the period. A number of recent commentators hold the view that the growing concern with brain-based rationality gradually displaced the heart as the defining organ of human identity in the latter half of the seventeenth century.[39] My own studies point to a somewhat different conclusion, one that sees the heart continue to have immense significance as a determining force in creating and storing all aspects of human understanding. The passage quoted above from Wright's *Passions of the*

[37] Joseph Leo Koerner, *The Reformation of the Image* (London: Reaktion Books, 2004), 161. The theological shift that moves the chief icon of Christ's passion from the category of "indifferent things" (adiaphora) into the far smaller group of things essential to salvation insured the continued centrality of the heart, both Christ's and the sinner's, in the everyday experience of Protestants.

[38] Thomas Wright, *The Passions of the Minde in Generall* (London: V. Simmes [and A. Islip] for W. Burre [and T. Thorpe], 1604), 33.

[39] In Jager's perhaps too neat formulation, "the empiricist psychology of the seventeenth and eighteenth centuries . . . exchanged the book of the heart for the book of the brain" (*The Book of the Heart*, xxi). Scott Manning Stevens finds that "The heart, though its signification is not easily defined, has proven an enduring symbol of both the spiritual and physical worlds," while "The brain, on the other hand, seems tied to its own physicality and function, oddly separate from the more evocative term 'mind.'" See Stevens's "Sacred Heart and Secular Brain" in *The Body in Parts: Fantasies of Corporeality in Early Modern Europe*, ed. David Hillman and Carla Mazzio (New York: Routledge, 1997), 262–82, quotation from p. 278.

Minde relies on Galenic elementalism ("softnesse" and "fiery spirites") to characterize the body's organs, and, like Galen, Wright comes back to the way we feel our bodies reacting to external and internal stimuli to determine the properties and functions of the organs: "who loveth extreamely, and feeleth not that passion to dissolve his hearte? who reioyceth and proveth not his heart dilated . . . ?"[40] As Gail Kern Paster has shown, the directly felt humoral body provides the basis for the emotional dynamics of one of the greatest periods in English drama. Shakespeare conceived of the passions of such widely different characters as Cleopatra and Falstaff in terms of a predominantly Galenic psychophysiology, and in this system "the organ most in charge of the emotions was the heart."[41]

The heart is the most effective and efficient intermediary in the life of the humoral body because it is the only internal organ that processes both nourishment and thought. Paster's study of the early modern conception of the passions repeatedly makes the point that inner affective experience was understood as an aspect of the physics of temperature and hydraulic flow within the body. The interior flow of humors, heat, and "spirit," according to such essayists as Wright, Bacon, and Burton, as well as the popular dramatists of the day – Jonson, Shakespeare, Middleton – interacted continually with the external environment. One's experience of a calm or a troubled interior self depended on spirits being absorbed from the heavens and the ambient air as well as from everything one ingested. Just as there was no fixed division between the processes of mind and body, so too there was none between the inner world of the passions and the surrounding natural world. The entire, interconnected system of physical and spiritual health was regulated by vital heat, and the heart, as we have seen, was thought to supply that heat. The degree of heat in a body governed its gender, its complexion, its health, and its passions.

We always view the heart through the window of our own theoretical assumptions. Our particular angle of inquiry determines what we see through that window. Scholars who have undertaken the systematic study of the heart in the last century have generally worked as anthropologists, art historians, theologians, students of anatomy and other medical sciences,

---

[40] Wright, *The Passions of the Minde*, 33. The same sense of exuberant dilation is evident in a "hymn" entitled "The Hart Consecrated," which appears in a collection of meditations by the Jesuit Stephanus Luzvic: "IESV, behold the hart dilates / It-selfe to thee, and consecrates / It's [*sic*] triple power, and al within." See the English translation of Luzvic's volume, *The Devout Hart or royal throne of the pacifical Salomon* (Rouen: J. Cousturier, 1634), 15. The poem bears a passing resemblance to George Herbert's "*IESU*," published the year before.

[41] Gail Kern Paster, *Humoring the Body: Emotions and the Shakespearean Stage* (Chicago: University of Chicago Press, 2004), 12.

or literary historians. My own practice in what follows is to use as many of these disciplines and types of evidence as possible in order to generate a series of what Albert H. Tricomi calls "functional historical narratives" of the heart.[42] Looking more closely at the approaches listed above, it becomes clear that scholars have been both enabled and restricted by their disciplinary training in their attempts to formulate these narratives.

The anthropologist generally tends to study material evidence of the ways that knowledge of the natural and spiritual world is organized within and across cultures. Anthropologists have discovered images of the heart in Egyptian funerary art from the period before 1400 BCE. They interpret the heart shape in that culture as an aspect of the practice of removing the viscera in the mummification process and then needing to replace what has been removed with a specially preserved heart or a facsimile of it so that the deceased could present this vital part of the self in the other world to be "weighed in scales against the feather of truth, emblem of the goddess Maat."[43] It was thought to be essential for the heart to speak on behalf of the dead soul in the realm beyond death.[44] Fusions of cultural practice and belief systems are as important to the anthropologist studying the heart-shaped Valentine cards of Victorian England as to the Egyptologist. The late nineteenth-century translation and sublimation of desire for one's "sweetheart" into the form of a heart-shaped greeting card places the mysteries of love into a culturally acceptable format. Associations of the heart with the soul and with sexual love were assimilated into early modern culture in some of these same ways, as we know through the survival of works of art, great and small, from the period.

The art historian studies these works in an effort to locate patterns of continuity and change in artistic representation of the natural and imagined world. A woodcut of a disdainful woman tormenting her lover's heart in a dozen different ways (Fig. 21) can be directly related to a series of medieval romance narratives, but it can also be seen to emerge from the philosophical discourse of the passions and from representations of the Passion of Christ, depicting, for example, Jesus proffering his flaming or bloody heart to a faithful Christian. The Devotion of the Sacred Heart has been an important part of the iconography of the Church of Rome from

---

[42] Albert H. Tricomi, *Reading Tudor-Stuart Texts through Cultural Historicism* (Gainesville: University of Florida Press, 1996), 14.

[43] Louisa Young, "The Human Heart: An Overview," in *The Heart*, ed. James Peto (New Haven: Yale University Press; London: Wellcome Collection, 2007), 10.

[44] See Doris Bietenholz, *How Come This ♡ Means Love? A Study of the Origin of the ♡ Symbol of Love* (Saskatoon, Canada: D. Bietenholz, 1995), 3.

the eleventh century to the present. Such images, radically transformed in Protestant nations at the time of the Reformation, establish the crucial place of the heart in the theology of the early modern period.

A student of the history of religion concerned with placing the heart within a theological and devotional context works largely in the realm of metaphor. As we have noted, the heart is the book or table where divine commandments are written, covenants and struggles with God recorded, and acts of faith memorialized. For Christians, the Bible is the richest source of heart theology. Hundreds of references in both Old and New Testament attest to the wickedness of the human heart and the beneficence of the divine one. St. Paul expressly prefers the metaphorical book of the heart to any other record of the Word of God. Writing directly to God, he acknowledges:

2. Ye are our epistle, written in our hearts, which is vnderstand [sic] and red of all men, 3. In that ye are manifest, to be the epistle of Christ, ministred by vs, and written, not with yncke, but with the Spirit of the liuing God, not in tables of stone, but in fleshlie tables of the heart. (2 Cor. 3: 2–3)

But that divine text, internally recorded, shares the same space with the treacheries of fallen man, and only God commands a window on the heart, according to the forty-fourth Psalm:

20. If we haue forgotte[n] ye Name of our God, & holden vp our ha[n]ds to a strange god, 21. Shal not God searche this out? for he knoweth the secrets of the heart.

Despite the heart's propensity to harbor evil intentions, it is singled out repeatedly in the Bible as the instrument of moral discernment, the only means we have for acting conscientiously: "Giue therefore vnto thy seruant an vndersta[n]ding heart, to iudge thy people, that I may discerne betwene good & bad: for who is able to iudge this thy mighty people?" (1 Kings 3: 9). In post-Reformation England, the direct inheritors of the biblical tradition of moral judgment were the casuists who analyzed individual cases of conscience. These rigorous, systematic thinkers found in the heart the power to resolve moral dilemmas within a context of immutable divine law and constantly shifting social realities. In their practice, they shared much with students of the physical heart, the anatomists. Their writings brought systematic analysis and rigorous record-keeping to activities that otherwise might have been dismissed as fantasy, the easy error that could suppose a bush a bear, a vein an artery, a sin a virtue.

The last group of modern commentators I want to consider are the literary historicists, whose archival research and respect for the distinctiveness of the past have taken their findings well beyond fantasy. In the course of the present chapter we have encountered the work of recent scholars who have connected the functions of the early modern body and – in the cases of Eric Jager, Milad Douiehi, and Robert A. Erickson – specifically the heart, to early narratives of literacy, villainy, and heroism. Each of these writers develops the idea that inscribing language in or on the heart captures the philosophical valorization of verbal discourse and interiority in a single, distinctively literary trope. The critical activity of reading what is inscribed in the heart of a fictional character is a hypertextual exercise for these commentators. That is, they have learned to read the signs of the humoral body and the state of the conscience in the words of fictional characters, often looking through a window obscured by the characters' own uncertainty, duplicity, erroneous self-analysis, and turbulent passions. The present study carries these interpretive strategies into one of the richest periods of drama in England, the age of Shakespeare.

Consider for a moment the case of King Lear, who twice refers explicitly to a debilitating medical condition called *passio hysterica* or "the suffocation of the mother" in which vapors were said to rise from the womb, causing strangulation in the throat and giddiness in the head.[45] Shakespeare, however, stops the appalling, un-manning attack at the heart:

> Oh how this mother swells up toward my heart!
> *Hysterica passio*, down, thou climbing sorrow,
> Thy element's below . . .
> Oh me, my heart! my rising heart! But down!
>
> (*King Lear* 2.4.56–8, 121)

The heart, center of the passions and pathway to Lear's many vulnerabilities, has a will of its own, against which the subject-king rages helplessly. Later in the action, he names a very different kind of heart in his middle daughter and commands that the dissecting knife be put to use to reveal her hard-heartedness to the world: "Then let them anatomize Regan; see what breeds about her heart. Is there any cause in nature that make these hard hearts?" (3.6.76–8). Lear has finally become the natural philosopher, concerned with mothering, fathering, and breeding. He is at the same time the theologian, seeking divine punishment for hardness of heart, a biblical sign of turning away from the Father (Exod. 10: 1; John 12: 40; Rom. 2: 5). What "breeds" around Regan's heart is greed and ingratitude, and around Lear's is, first, pride, then, terror at his loss of self. The story of King Lear's

---

[45] See the note on 2.2.246–7 in *King Lear*, Arden Third Series, ed. R. A. Foakes (London: Thomas Nelson and Sons, 1997), 241–2.

suffering is the story of the heart in agony, and the literary historicist could do worse than approach the play via the cultural history of this remarkable organ.

Historicist approaches to literary texts work at the material as well as the ideological level. Knowledge of the anatomical Renaissance and of the iconography of the Protestant Reformation form a solid groundwork for what Clifford Geertz might consider a "thick" reading not only of Lear's outburst against Regan, but also Busirane's diabolical inscriptions on Amoret's heart in *The Fairie Queene* (Book III) and Giovanni's ecstatic display of his sister's heart on the point of his dagger at the end of John Ford's *'Tis Pity She's a Whore*. The violation of legal and cultural proscriptions concerning the heart in these actions partly explains their dramatic power on the early modern stage. The history of the period's literary texts includes their performance as acted or read cultural experiences, and denying the many differences between that period's culture and our own in a quest for universal human values will lead only to misconstruing these works. In a persuasive explanation of cultural historicism as a theoretical methodology, Albert Tricomi makes an impassioned plea for a radical broadening of the ideological emphases that dominated literary criticism in the late twentieth century. He adamantly refuses to accept the commonly held view "that the postmodern condition signifies an end to history."

Rather, it signifies another beginning from which other beginnings become possible . . . [A] viable cultural historicism must, through the inclusion of canonical and noncanonical literary and theatrical texts, iconographic representations, and recursive cultural practices, continue to develop procedures for reading texts symbolically, processually, and diachronically from multiple perspectives. In literary studies, in particular, modernist criticism must find ways of breaking out of its cerebral, inveterately suspicious manner of reading, as if all texts spoke a repressive language from the center. That is why I have stressed the importance of treating the affectivity of the textual past. Our affective responses, constructed and historicized as they are, are part of the meaning that the past holds for us. By continuing to revise and reform current critical practices in ways such as this, we work toward ensuring that studies in cultural historicism remain adaptable and pertinent.[46]

In what follows, I have taken Tricomi's words to heart and have attempted to include the broad range of primary materials that he recommends and to incorporate the kinds of open, historically informed reading practices that he champions. My inclination, however, is to

---

[46] Tricomi, *Reading Tudor-Stuart Texts*, 156.

explore the aesthetic and philosophical values of the texts I work with rather than the overtly political ideologies that struggled to assert their control by manipulating the symbolism of the heart. I have had to work hard to construct the early modern imaginary of the heart in the terms of that age and not just our own. I have also tried to remain mindful of A. D. Nuttall's caveat that "although knowledge of the historical genesis can on occasion illuminate a given work, the greater part of the artistic achievement of our best playwright [and, I would add, many lesser ones] is *internally* generated."[47]

Each of the following chapters looks into a different kind of heart: the graphic heart, the passionate heart, the narrative heart, the villainous heart, and the Shakespearean heart. This scheme cuts across others that I might have used, so that anatomical, theological, and amatory hearts appear in each chapter. The insights of Galen, Calvin, and Shakespeare are likely to contend with as well as to complement one another in each chapter, my object being to study the intellectual and cultural diversity of this enigmatic organ.

Chapter 2 presents a series of readings of graphic heart images from the late Middle Ages to the Enlightenment, mainly concentrating on the hundred-year period from the mid-sixteenth to the mid-seventeenth century that I have called "the age of Shakespeare." I am concerned here with not only the codification and transmission of heart-knowledge through anatomical illustration but also with the impact of religious art in the late Renaissance. One of the most difficult problems addressed by the graphic artists of the period was how to transmute the essentially violent and bloody process of evisceration into anatomically informative, religiously inspiring, and aesthetically pleasing forms. Heart images of all these kinds rest on one or another conception of a natural creator at work (what Galen calls the *Opifex* of all things) and a strongly teleological notion of what the heart is intended ultimately to accomplish for humans and other animals. In order to provide a sense of how broad a gestural meaning could be in a simple engraving, I begin with a highly schematic late fifteenth-century image of the heart embracing the entire world as the source of life and love. From there I move to a sixteenth-century manuscript codex image of an Aztec heart sacrifice, and then to several engravings and paintings representing the Sacred Heart of Jesus. This intensely iconic movement within the Church of Rome was significantly altered in a rich continental Protestant emblem literature that continued

---

[47] A. D. Nuttall, *Shakespeare the Thinker* (New Haven: Yale University Press, 2007), 23.

to project a symbolic significance for the heart that was widely embraced in England throughout the seventeenth century. In this tradition the heart became an exemplary organ as preserver of the true image of Christ and the residence of the Christian conscience. The transition in conceptions of the heart was marked by acrimonious debates and gruesome tortures that included cutting out the hearts of martyrs, Catholic and Protestant. To the hotly contested religious image of the wavering penitent heart, the martyrological literature of the period added the resolved, steadfast heart.

Intricately related to the religious transformations of the heart icon was the development of anatomical illustration as an artistic genre. Artists such as Leonardo da Vinci and anatomists such as Berengario da Carpi recognized very early the interconnectedness of their disciplines.[48] A fairly detailed knowledge of the underlying structures of the human body was essential to convincing figure drawing, while the application of the artist's techniques for handling line, shading, and perspective could contribute immeasurably to the presentation of human physiology in medical textbooks. The goals of anatomist and artist were not entirely consonant, however, and authors such as Vesalius in his *Fabrica* had to keep a tight rein on the early anatomical illustrators. The series of muscle-men and bone-men in the *Fabrica* strike poses reminiscent of antique statuary but also reveal with remarkable precision the proportions and structure of particular muscle and bone groups.[49] Subtle woodcuts of the contents of the thorax place the heart in relation to the lungs and diaphragm, while diagrams of the vascular system do everything but represent the circulation of the blood.

Central though heart images were to university instruction in medicine, illustrations of fictional lovers' hearts likely had a wider viewing audience. Representations of the heart in the throes of desire from medieval to early modern erotic narratives demonstrate the pervasiveness of heart lore in the culture at large. Books, lockets, badges, playing cards, and other material representations of the heart suggest that amatory narratives retained a powerful visual component for a culture that was busy replacing the heroic epic with the domestic love story.

---

[48] Dr. Francis Wells, consultant cardiothoracic surgeon at Papworth Hospital, Cambridge, sensitively explores Leonardo's achievements in anatomy, drawing, engineering, and lateral thinking in his essay "The Renaissance Heart: The Drawings of Leonardo da Vinci" in *The Heart*, ed. James Peto, 70–94.

[49] See Glen Harcourt, "Andreas Vesalius and the Anatomy of Antique Sculpture," *Representations* 17 (1987): 28–61. Harcourt finds strong resemblances between the anatomical illustrations and such works as the Belevedere Torso, the Canon of Polykleitos, and the Capitoline Antinous.

Chapter 3, on "The Organ of Affection and Motion, Truth and Conflict," tracks the prominence of the heart from Galenic humor theory into a broad realm of metaphors in which the heart is vital fountain, supreme ruler, and storehouse of both nurturing impulses and vengeful memories. After characterizing the distinctive contributions of head, hand, and heart to physical and spiritual exercise, I turn to Phineas Fletcher's remarkable geographical/anatomical poem *The Purple Island* (1633) with its carefully annotated description of the heart city, Kerdia, "Where life, and lifes companion, heat, abideth; / And their attendants, passions untam'd."[50] Like Harvey's *De motu cordis*, published five years earlier, *The Purple Island* is filled with metaphors of anatomical and national governance and its failures. The heart can rule the body only so long as the heat of its passions is moderated by careful diet, the strictly regulated intake of nutrients and output of excrements. Controlling the motive and emotive functions of the heart is a prominent theme as well in John Davies of Hereford's *Microcosmos: The Discovery of the Little World, with the government thereof*, published a quarter century before Fletcher's body poem. In Davies's epigrammatic phrase, "The *Hartes affects*, produce the *Heades effects*" in a hierarchy that harks back to Aristotle.[51] While the poems by Davies and Fletcher lack the narrative and imaginative complexity of the works by Spenser and Shakespeare that figure prominently in Chapter 5, they work subtly with body language to reveal the politics of moderation and systematic explanation against which the heroic exceptionalism of greater literary works defines itself. One work of Shakespeare's, Sonnet 62 ("Sin of self-love possesseth all mine eye"), serves as a miniaturized literary conclusion to the discussion in Chapter 3 of the affective nature of the conscience, which John Calvin's *Institutes* and *Commentaries* characteristically locate in the heart.

Chapter 4 brings together a group of early modern narratives built around the dangerous passions of the heart. English poets inherited from their continental predecessors not only well-developed traditions of sacred heart lore and graphically rich anatomical texts, but also an established poetics of the heart that paradoxically combines comfort and terror in this single, complex organ. While Dante's *Rime petrose* (the Stony-Hearted Lady poems) dramatize the extravagant suffering of rejected lovers, the central event in the *Vita Nuova* is the poet's transformation, caused by a

---

[50] Phineas Fletcher, *The Purple Island*, in *The Poetical Works*, ed. Frederick S. Boas (Cambridge: Cambridge University Press, 1909), 1: 50.

[51] John Davies of Hereford, *The Microcosmos: The Discovery of the Little World, with the government thereof* (Oxford: J. Barnes, 1603), 78.

dream-vision of the naked Beatrice being fed his own flaming heart. Equally stunning passages in Book III of Edmund Spenser's *Fairie Queene* capture this rapturous combination of erotic energy and poetic commitment as Britomart rescues the extracted heart of Amoret from the enchanter Busirane. The biblical metaphors of heart-inscription, satanic enslavement, and, eventually, salvation involving sacrifice are the bedrock on which Spenser constructs much of his religious-amatory allegory.

A process of de-metaphorization characterizes the material and symbolic hearts incorporated into early modern drama from Shakespeare's *Titus Andronicus* to John Fletcher's *The Mad Lover* and John Ford's *'Tis Pity She's a Whore*. Traditional affective metaphors are literalized in each of these plays by the processes of amputation and dissection. A heart is ceremonially presented to a young woman in a golden cup; another is brandished wildly on the point of a dagger. And still, the heart preserves a magical aura that keeps it from being simply a bloody piece of meat or an affectively neutral specimen from the anatomist's laboratory. Heart symbolism was transposed from a religious arena to an aggressively secular and sexual one without losing any of its power as a political instrument. The civic controls placed on the activity of public dissection and the advent of specifically mechanistic metaphors for the actions of the heart could never quite displace the frisson that accompanies the public extraction of a human heart. Horror always attends upon the futile attempt to make visible the secrets of the heart. The self that resides in the heart finds magnificent expression in the early modern language of the heart, but it is inevitably, spectacularly destroyed by the surgeon's knife. That occluded self, consumed by lust, jealousy, or despair, and very occasionally comforted in the inner sanctum of the heart, is repeatedly discovered to view by the poets and dramatists of the period.

The discovery of interiority, like that of the New World, was, in fact, an excited rediscovery of what had been well known to past cultures, but the excitement made it all feel new to the religious, medical, and literary writers of the time. The special case of early modern literary villainy is the focus of Chapter 5, "'My Heart Upon My Sleeve': Early Modern Interiority, Anatomy, and Villainy." A long line of villains including Aaron, Richard III, Edmund, Jachimo, Flaminio, and Bosola move across the early modern English stage, offering tantalizing glimpses of their black hearts. None is so enigmatic as Iago, who shares his scheming and a bewildering array of plausible motives with the audience in soliloquy, while famously refusing to wear his heart upon his sleeve. Discovering the secrets of his interiority has seemed to some commentators as straightforward as Edward May's surgical removal of a huge, coiled serpent from the heart of John Pennant in 1639, but the arch-villain's flat assertion, "I am not what I am," remains as inscrutable as God's own tautological mystery: "I AM THAT I AM" (Exod. 3: 14).

The work of the literary and cultural critic falls somewhere between the positivism of the surgeon and the gnomic rhetoric of the Bible – hence the attraction of Shakespearean texts that stand at the intersection of the anatomical Renaissance and the Protestant Reformation as a place to explore the complexities of the early modern heart. While the heart was the locus of health and faith for the anatomist and the preacher, for dramatists it generated and spread envy, hatred, and shame.

Chapter 6, my final one, addresses the question of whether we can identify something called the Shakespearean heart. As a starting point for this inquiry, I have assembled a cluster of images from the plays that associate the shame of betrayal with attacks on the heart by venomous snakes. Dramatic circumstances in each case reveal that, ironically, the betrayal has not actually occurred, or at least not in the way the angry and frightened speaker imagines, but the fantasy that a lover/friend has turned mortal serpent is devastating. The result is a peculiar estrangement of the heart's passions from the organs of agency, particularly the hand and the tongue. Audiences of Shakespeare's tragedies may observe this kind of estrangement in the behavior of the tragic heroes as, for example, Hamlet struggles to bring his actions into line with the truths he is convinced of in his heart. Familial divisions in *King Lear* originate in the proud heart and end in the isolated, penitent heart, defined in a specifically Protestant manner. Shakespeare's Sonnets, too, develop a concept of the heart estranged from the rest of the body, in particular an inner self shamefully betrayed by the eye, the hand, and the sexual organs. Readers are repeatedly invited to do the impossible: to "read the mind's construction in the face," or the gesture, only to find that they are gazing into a glass darkly, not through the clear window that Momus thought could reveal all inner truths.

The motions of the heart had not, then, in current parlance been "reduced to a science" in the age of Shakespeare, though they were being measured and assessed in ever-changing ways. Fresh knowledge demanded fresh assertions of faith in the invisible and unfathomable. In Dean John Donne's epigrammatic phrase, "Faith is not on this side Knowledge, but beyond it."[52] In a sermon preached at St. Paul's in 1624 Donne tempers the demands for accurate, observable measurements put forward by Galileo and his followers:

[52] John Donne, *Sermons*, ed. George R. Potter and Evelyn M. Simpson (Berkeley: University of California Press, 1957), 3: 359.

[F]or things created, we have instruments to measure them; we know the compasse of a Meridian, and the depth of a Diameter of the Earth, and we know this, even of the uppermost spheare in the heavens: But when we come to the Throne of God himselfe, the Orbe of the Saints, and Angels that see his face, and the vertues, and powers that flow from thence, we have no balance to weigh them, no instruments to measure them, no hearts to conceive them.[53]

What Donne refers to as the "naked thinking heart" in his poem "The Blosome" is not up to the task of conceiving either children or the vast scope of God. The carefully measured science of Galileo was not, then, universally embraced as the measure of all things. Still, Donne invokes the well-developed science of cartography in his poem "The good-morrow" as a precise illustration of the affection of "true plaine hearts" as seen reflected in the lovers' eyes:

> My face in thine eye, thine in mine appeares,
> And true plaine hearts doe in the faces rest,
> Where can we finde two better hemispheares
> Without sharpe North, without declining West? (lines 15–18)[54]

The two hemispheres were those represented in sixteenth-century cordiform maps based on the Stabius–Werner projections. These flat maps of the world show the parallels as arcs of circles centered on the North pole; the central meridian is a vertical line, and the other meridians curve to form a heart shape.[55] It is easy to imagine Donne, poetic herald of the New Science, finding in a map such as Johannes Honter's (1546, Fig. 3) an exacting science of measurement that also presents an image of lovers' hearts as revealed through the windows of their eyes.[56] Thus the affections are provided a local habitation, a name, and a memorable shape.

The sexualized, theologized, and medicalized heart maintained its distinguished place throughout early modern life and discourse. Truths that had to be retained in the core of the self were said to be "learned by heart"; those who sank into profound despair were "sick at heart"; the most significant problems and emotions were "matters of the heart." And they still

[53] Donne, *Sermons* (Berkeley: University of California Press, 1953), 6: 174.

[54] *The Poems of John Donne*, ed. Herbert J. C. Grierson (Oxford: Oxford University Press, 1912), 1: 7.

[55] See Robert L. Sharp, "Donne's 'Good-morrow' and Cordiform Maps," *Modern Language Notes* 69 (1954): 493–5. Maps of the kind I have just described by Johannes Stabius (*c.* 1500), Johannes Werner (1514), and Peter Apianus (1520) circulated widely in Europe. For other examples of these maps see George Kish, "The Cosmographic Heart: Cordiform Maps of the 16th Century," *Imago Mundi* 19 (1965): 13–21.

[56] Thomas Wright, explaining the physical means of recognizing true love, tells of a man who looked at his wife and "thorow the window of her eie, he beheld the chastitie of her heart." *The Passions of the Minde*, 54.

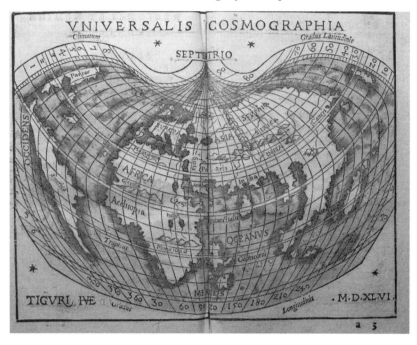

Figure 3. "Vniversalis cosmographia," a cordiform map. Johannes Honter, *Rvdimentorvm cosmographicorum* (Tigvri, apvd Froschouerum, [1549]), reproduced by permission of the Rare Book and Manuscript Library, University of Illinois at Urbana-Champaign, Urbana, IL. Shelfmark IUA06872. In this cartographic projection, to which Donne alludes in "The good-morrow," the longitudinal lines form the shape of a heart.

are, though the metaphors have become deadened with the passage of time. One of the goals of what follows is to experience again the living pulse of the early modern heart and the vitality of the heart's language in the art, philosophy, literature, and everyday life of the period. Another is to develop strategies for looking into the window of the heart that reveal more than the compromising secrets that Lucian's Momus wished to spy out.

CHAPTER 2

Reading the graphic heart

Before considering the range of ways that artists and illustrators devised for picturing the heart from the late Middle Ages to the Enlightenment, we need to address the question of why so much energy and ingenuity were expended imagining and drawing the activities of an organ so definitively hidden from view as the living heart. The activities associated with the heart in the representative images I have selected for analysis (Figs. 4 to 21) include housecleaning, nursing, painting, and viniculture. This list suggests that the artists were engaged in a project of domesticating the mysteries of the sacred, the amatory, and the anatomical heart, but such a conclusion oversimplifies the effect of depicting the *invisibilia*, the attributes of faith, with artistic techniques that are highly symbolic and at times exceedingly cryptic. The point of all this two-dimensional representation is not that the inner body is flat and lacks depths of meaning but rather that purely verbal descriptions of human interiority could be made far more immediate and memorable through graphic illustration.

The interplay of text and image received an enormous boost with the advent of the printed book. Though they were far less decorative than the scribal images incorporated in manuscripts, the monochrome woodcuts and copperplate engravings in sixteenth-century books placed the reader in the conceptual space of the page.[1] Blocks of text were relieved by representations of activities that humanized theological concepts and anatomical speculations. Ideas could be schematically tabulated and emotional states given a recognizable shape. Image and text printed together effectively extended the culture's conception of the material body through space and time. People did not have to travel to remote anatomy theaters to experience the immediacy of the inner body, and this same pictorial immediacy has been preserved as part of our intellectual and artistic heritage.

---

[1] Michael Camille, "Reading the Printed Image," in *Printing the Written Word: The Social History of Books, circa 1450–1520*, ed. Sandra Hindman (Ithaca: Cornell University Press, 1991), 284.

Confirmation and transmission of inner body knowledge were indebted not only to newly translated and edited classical texts in the Renaissance but also to the evolving methods of image making. The reading public was eager for graphic representations of the interior body and its relation to the external world, and printers were quick to deliver. Pictures of the heart, with its distinctive and ancient shape, proliferated in religious, medical, and historical texts.[2] These illustrations were done in a wide range of styles and for a variety of purposes. The work of an artist/engraver whose experience was limited to textbook theories of the heart's structure and functions tended to be highly simplified and schematic. On the other hand, a meticulously engraved copper plate of body parts based on close observation looked very different and was informed by its own set of theoretical assumptions. An image whose purpose was religious instruction was driven by a very specific conception of society's needs and the body's teleology, while an anatomical "fugitive sheet" tells a different, but often interconnected, story about the significance of body knowledge.[3] Each story needs to be heard and collated with the others, since no single way of representing the human body – no single "scientific" or religious model – dominated the early modern world. This world was, in many ways, more open to contending views of corporeality than is our own.

A peculiar set of problems always attends the visual representation of the body's internal organs. Moral and aesthetic concerns intersect with technical matters such as perspective, proportion, and surface textures. These concerns were more easily dealt with in some contexts than in others. Late medieval and early Renaissance artists creating images of the heart did not need to be convinced of the virtues of producing images to show illiterate audiences the seat of godly understanding in the human breast. Their images were largely informed by a set of metaphors drawn from Holy Scripture, saints' lives, classical myth, and the like. They avoided naturalistic representation of the bodily organ and instead imaginatively represented its spiritual attributes and actions. The situation was more

---

[2] See Pierre Vinken, *The Shape of the Heart* (Amsterdam: Elsevier Science, 1999) and Doris Bietenholz, *How Come This ♡ Means Love? A Study of the Origin of the ♡ Symbol of Love* (Saskatoon, Canada: D. Bietenholz, 1995) on the changing shape of the heart from ancient Egyptian times to the present.

[3] A fugitive sheet was a kind of anatomical broadside sheet, never intended to be bound together with a text. Some of them, such as a group of three in the Yale Medical Library dated between 1578 and 1625, include glued-on flaps that can be lifted to reveal deeper layers of dissection. For a comprehensive survey of extant examples of this form see Andrea Carlino, *Paper Bodies: A Catalogue of Anatomical Fugitive Sheets, 1538–1687*, trans. Noga Arikhas (London: Wellcome Institute for the History of Medicine, 1999).

complicated for anatomical illustrators, who were left to make the case for invading the divinely constructed space of the human body in order to expose its secrets to plain view. A group of highly trained and experienced medical men attached to the medical and anatomical faculties of such universities as those of Padua, Bologna, Paris, and Leiden made the case for externalizing in detailed drawings and engravings what was ordinarily withheld from view: the blood-vessels, muscles, bones, and organs of the body. These men explained and defended their descriptive and instructional methods and goals at length in letters and prefaces to printed compendia of anatomical knowledge.

One of the greatest of these authors, Andreas Vesalius, repeatedly refers to the *"Opifex rerum"* or designer of all things, acknowledged as the original maker whose actions are merely being shadowed at a great remove by the illustrators of his magisterial anatomical text book, the *Fabrica*. To cite just one example, he explicitly attributes to the industry of the Creator the brilliant solution to the problem of joining bones firmly yet flexibly with ligaments:

> For unless the joints of the bones and cartilages were held together with ligaments nothing would prevent the bones or the cartilages from being dislocated in the course of some movement or other . . . Lest that happen, God the highest opifex of things surrounded all the joints of the bones and cartilages with ligaments, strong indeed but also capable of considerable stretching. Greatly to be wondered at is the industry of the Creator.[4]

Human anatomists and artists could never have devised this ingenious design, but it was up to them to present it clearly and in all its glorious detail to serious, advanced students of anatomy. A generation earlier Leonardo da Vinci had asserted the absolute necessity of including illustrations in any competent study of the whole man: "Dispel from your mind the thought that an understanding of the human body in every aspect of its structure can be given in words; for the more thoroughly you describe, the more you will confuse: it is therefore necessary to draw as

---

[4] Vesalius, *Fabrica* (1543), 2.1, 215, as translated by Nancy G. Siraisi in "Vesalius and the Reading of Galen's Teleology," *Renaissance Quarterly* 50 (1997): 1–37, quotation from p. 15. Siraisi concludes that "The way in which Vesalius used the theme of the work of Nature and the Opifex yielded a disciplined version of providential rhetoric about the human body, supported chiefly by observed anatomical detail" (30). Vesalius was working within a distinguished classical tradition that included Aristotle's "immanent, active, but impersonal principle" of Nature, Cicero's understanding of natural perfection as evidence for divine providence, Galen's Platonic notion of "a divine Craftsman" or Demiurgos, and Lactantius's Christianized account of the beneficent Creator of the natural universe (Siraisi, "Vesalius and the Reading of Galen's Teleology," 3–4).

well as to describe."[5] Putting this exhortation into practice himself, Leonardo produced elegant and detailed drawings of the body and its parts which, though not published until the late eighteenth century, circulated in manuscript form through the medical as well as the artistic communities. Just as no self-respecting artist could hope to limn the body without knowledge of its underlying skeletal and muscular structure, neither could professors of anatomy demonstrate their subject without the aid of artistic renderings of the body as a whole and in parts. This marriage between the skills of medical and artistic practitioners developed with surprising rapidity in the sixteenth century in the fertile common ground of humanistic conceptions of God's most engrossing creation.[6]

Another remarkable marriage that was arranged, consummated, and severely tested during this period was the union between Christian and proto-scientific conceptions of the body. It is easy to view these two ideologies as mutually antagonistic, but it can also be misleading to do so. A shared paradox of violence and nurture helped to maintain the often strained relation between these two discourses in matters of the heart. The powerful link between physical pain and spiritual peace had always been present in Christian understandings of the heart: tribulation brings the inner peace that passeth understanding. These same extremes were similarly balanced in the natural philosophy that defined the motions of the heart for proto-scientists in the sixteenth century. The healthy heart attracted *spiritus* and generated vital heat, but the slightest disturbance could destroy this rhythm of life. The basic Christian mindset that associated the heart with agony *and* faith was reinforced – not attacked, as people often think – by early modern anatomical science and medical practice. The heart images that we are about to inspect display both the tensions and the strong bonds that developed during the Reformation through the interplay of anatomy and religion.

A good place to begin a study of early modern graphic representations of the heart is with an artistically naïve but conceptually dense image from a late fifteenth-century dialogue between Knowledge and Aristotle in a volume entitled *Le pèlerinage de vie humaine* (*The Pilgrimage of Life*, Fig. 4). The image accompanying one of Aristotle's responses is of the whole world, symbolized by a "T-in-O" map, contained within a stylized

---

[5] *The Notebooks*, fol. A14[r], as quoted by Robert Herrlinger in *History of Medical Illustration from Antiquity to A.D. 1600* (London: Pitman Medical and Scientific Publishing, 1970), 70.

[6] See Ludmilla Jordanova, "Happy Marriage and Dangerous Liaisons: Artists and Anatomy," in *The Quick and the Dead: Artists and Anatomy*, ed. Deanna Petherbridge and Ludmilla Jordanova (Berkeley: University of California Press, 1997), 100–13.

Figure 4. "The Heart Holding the World." Guillaume de Deguileville, *Le pèlerinage de vie humaine* (en castellano) [El pelegrino de la vida], trans. Vincente de Mazuelo (Toulouse: Henry Mayer, 1490), D2ᵛ, reproduced by permission of the Biblioteca Nacional, Madrid. Shelfmark Inc/1362. In this iconic woodcut, the inverted T-in-O map of the world is wholly contained within the expansive heart of humanity.

heart. Medieval cartographers used the intersecting lines of the T (inverted in this instance) to demarcate three continents (Asia, Europe, and Africa), which are surrounded by the O representing the world's oceans. The orientation of this particular world map has been rotated 180 degrees: generally the full half of the circle, representing Asia in the east, is at the top of the map with the smaller continents of Europe and Africa at the bottom. The continents are divided by the Red Sea and the Mediterranean. This diagram of the world became so familiar from the eleventh century onward as to be recognizable without any written labels. The point where the lines of the T intersect always represents the location of Jerusalem. As the heart is the center of the human body and the mainspring of physical and spiritual life, so is the Temple in Jerusalem the point of initiation and subsequent intersection of the Christian, Jewish, and Muslim faiths.[7] Taken together, this particular schematic woodcut represents the power of the heart, both divine and human, to encompass and contain the entire physical world. The illustrator is not concerned with the details of the natural world but rather with the emotional embrace of the heart. The image celebrates in highly compressed, symbolic language the quality of God's all-embracing love.[8] And for the humanist writer and illustrator the potential for loving embrace extends as well into the hearts of all people. The knowledge represented in the dialogue combines Christian and pagan insights. As "Aristotiles" concludes after explaining that there will always be some space left over in the triangular heart when the circular world is inscribed within it, "Conclujo q[ue] todo el mundo no hartaria el coraçon del hombre. E ves lo manifiesto en esta figura" (All the world would not be enough to fill the heart of man. And you see it manifested in this figure.).[9] Of course, if the heart's roughly triangular shape were drawn inside the world's circle, there would also be some world-space left over, and the opposite conclusion would be "proved." The point, however, is that within the language of the heart, even Euclidian geometry can be pressed into service to "demonstrate" certain deeply felt truths. By conflating the traditional figures of T-in-O map and heart, the woodcut designer has mapped the physical world onto the spiritual.

---

[7] See Stephen Greenblatt, *Marvelous Possessions: The Wonder of the New World* (Chicago: University of Chicago Press, 1991), 41–3 and 83.

[8] The biblical source of the idea that God placed the gift of the whole world in man's heart is Eccles. 3: 11: "He hathe made euerie thing beautiful in his time: also he hathe set the worlde in their heart."

[9] Guillaume de Deguileville, *Le pèlerinage de vie humaine* (Toulouse, 1490), sig. D II^v. The image is discussed in Michael Camille, "Reading the Printed Image," 285. Preaching in London at the end of the sixteenth century, Thomas Playfere drew upon this same ancient idea: "[T]his infinite number of worldes, which should haue beene created, could not haue filled the verie least *heart*, of any one man, without the creatour himselfe. This Orontius an excellent Mathematitian sheweth, who describing the whole world in the forme of an *heart*, leaueth many voide spaces in his heart which he cannot fil vp with the world." See Playfere's *Hearts Delight. A Sermon preached at Pauls Crosse in London in Easter terme. 1593* (Cambridge: J. Legat, 1603), 49.

Figure 5. Aztec heart sacrifice. *Codex Magliabechiano*, 70ʳ. Sixteenth century, reproduced by permission of the Biblioteca Nazionale Centrale di Firenze (Florence). Shelfmark Magl. CL. XIII.3 (B. R. 232). The heart of the sacrificial victim flies out of his chest as the priest cuts him open.

"The Heart Holding the World" is a visually static representation of a conceptual property of the heart, namely its comprehensiveness. The dynamics of the image exist solely on the conceptual level. The totality of God's creation is compressed cartographically into the terrestrial T contained within the oceanic O, which is then surrounded by the stylized heart. The image is not at all dynamic or dramatic, but it succinctly captures the triangulated relationship of God, man, and the physical universe.

In sharp contrast is the tumult surrounding the Aztec ritual of heart sacrifice included in the sixteenth-century *Codex Magliabechiano* (Fig. 5).[10] The terrifying act of dissecting a living human victim in order to extract the vital spirit of his heart – here improbably shown flying out of the unfortunate man's breast – is dramatically represented in this notebook

[10] The drawings in this volume and their cultural significance are discussed at length in *The Book of the Life of the Ancient Mexicans: containing an account of their rites and superstitions: an anonymous Hispano-Mexican manuscript preserved at the Biblioteca Nazionale Centrale, Florence, Italy*, reproduced in facsimile, with introduction, translation, and commentary by Zelia Nuttall and Elizabeth Hill Boone (Berkeley: University of California Press, 1983), in two parts.

sketch by a European artist, right down to the victim's screams. The gigantic bird deity mounted on the temple near the altar seems to rear back in amazement as the highly stylized heart is propelled into the air by the action of the priest's stone knife. A second victim, his torso slashed open and bleeding, is being dragged down the temple steps from the altar. The priest, his assistants, and a half-dozen spectators, all clothed in exotic robes and headgear, register their responses to this astounding sacrificial moment with facial expressions ranging from scowls to smiles to open-mouthed amazement. The soaring heart is far more rounded at its bottom end than the heart symbol ordinarily is, and the three-lobed ornamentation at the top alludes only sketchily to the auricles or "ears" of the heart, or perhaps to the severed major veins and arteries depicted in most contemporary anatomical drawings.

The reason the sketch was included in a collection of drawings of domestic activities of the Aztec people was certainly not anatomical but, rather, anthropological.[11] Supposed eyewitness records of the exotic ways of the New World were highly prized in Europe. By implication, the artist is recording the cultural difference between "barbaric" indigenes (there are also sketches of imagined cannibal banquets in this codex) and the Christian conquistadors. Performing human sacrifice in order to obtain pure heart's blood to nourish the sun, to adorn the temple walls, or to sprinkle on the fields to increase their fertility is represented as totally alien to the artist's sensibility. But an unsettling irony often overtakes such symbolically charged images: other associations with heart iconology and blood sacrifice ("This is my blood, which is shed for you . . . Drink it in remembrance of me") rise unbidden in the viewer's consciousness. What one religion celebrates literally and dramatically, the other celebrates symbolically and metonymically. However hard the scandalized European adventurers tried in their verbal accounts to dissociate themselves from the "natives," the ritual violence here graphically associated with the heart continues to suggest parallels with Christian images such as the ones we will look at shortly. As David Freedberg provocatively argues in *The Power of Images*, suppression of the visceral nature of responses to representations of the body can inadvertently serve as a guide to how those images actually affected viewers.[12] Elevated aesthetics,

---

[11] For a detailed anthropological and medical account of a related set of heart rituals, see Francis Robicsek and Donald M. Hales, "Maya Heart Sacrifice: Cultural Perspective and Surgical Technique," in *Ritual Human Sacrifice in Mesoamerica*, ed. Elizabeth H. Boone (Washington, DC: Dumbarton Oaks, 1984), 90.

[12] David Freedberg, *The Power of Images: Studies in the History and Theory of Response* (Chicago: University of Chicago Press, 1989). See especially Chapter 14, "Idolatry and Iconoclasm."

enervating rationalization, and religious convention have regularly been invoked to contain the potentially transgressive power of images such as the bleeding heart. The attempted suppression and displacement seldom work.

The high drama of human sacrifice is often sublimated in Christian iconography, but the violent treatment and the adoration of the heart remain powerful recurring themes. The Devotion of the Sacred Heart of Jesus was established as early as the twelfth century. Bernard of Clairvaux's prayers addressed to *Cor Jesu dulcissimum* (the most sweet heart of Jesus) stress both the triumph of His love and the corporeal depths of His suffering. Christ's heart is an integral part of the passion narrative, though it remains invisible in many graphic renderings of the scene. Its location is indicated, however, by the point of insertion of the Roman soldier's lance. Vladimir Gurewich observes that while many early medieval representations locate the wound on Christ's right side, it gradually migrates to the left with the growing devotional enthusiasm for the Sacred Heart in Europe following the fifteenth century.[13] Works by Dürer, Rembrandt, and Blake include this later, anatomically heart-directed thrust. The resulting wound provides the devout Christian direct access to the Sacred Heart.

In a powerfully iconic woodcut from 1492, "The Five Wounds of Christ" (Fig. 6), parts of Christ's body have been rearranged in order to thematize the repeated piercing of His flesh at the time of the Crucifixion. The overall arrangement resembles a medallion or perhaps a grotesque blossom that transforms the events of the Passion into a memorial icon. While we tend to associate the term "icon" (Gr. εἰκών, L. *icōn*) with images of sacred personages that themselves become objects of veneration, especially in the Eastern Orthodox Church, it had quite different meanings in early modern England. In *The Arte of Rhetoricke*, George Puttenham uses the term to mean something like "simile," referring to an "*Icon*, or resemblance by imagerie."[14] In the case of the "Five Wounds of Christ" the relevant rhetorical figure would be synecdoche, the body parts standing for the whole of Christ's sacrifice.[15] His hands and feet are grouped around His pierced and bleeding heart. The nails that pinned Him to the cross have been removed, but they remain prominently displayed, suggesting that this

---

[13] Vladimir Gurewich, "Observations on the Iconography of the Wound in Christ's Side, with Special Reference to Its Position," *Journal of the Warburg and Courtauld Institutes* 20 (1957): 358–62.

[14] George Puttenham, *The Arte of English Poesie* (London: R. Field, 1589), 205. Puttenham explains that the rhetorical term "icon" is used when "alluding to the painters terme, who yeldeth to th'eye a visible representation of the thing he describes and painteth in his table" (204).

[15] A drawing in a fifteenth-century Carthusian miscellany (London BL Add. 37049, fol. 20ʳ) shows the Five Wounds all within Christ's pierced heart. See Carolyn Walker Bynum, "Violent Imagery in Late Medieval Piety," *GHI Bulletin* 30 (2001), Plate 10 on p. 19.

Figure 6. The Five Wounds of Christ. *Epistolae et Evangelia (Plenarium): Boek der prophecien leccien epistolen unde ewangelien* (Lübeck: Mohnkopf [The Poppy Printer], 1492), reproduced by permission of the Pierpont Morgan Library, New York, NY. Shelfmark ChL518. Christ's body has disappeared from this icon of his wounds, leaving only the injured parts visible. The central lance wound was believed to open directly to His heart, the source of sacramental blood and living water.

is an icon of torture. Only the crown of thorns is missing. The Roman soldier's spearhead still penetrates the heart, which has been provided a rough three-dimensionality by the addition of curved shading lines. Droplets of blood fall from the pierced heart and are also arranged in a circle around the wounded body parts. The sacramental heart's blood symbolically embraces the scene of bodily mutilation much as the ocean encompasses the land in the T-in-O map and the heart encloses the entire natural world in that image. The remaining frame in the present icon, decorated with vines and a pair of birds holding a blank banner, may seem to modern sensibilities to be at odds with the painful body-piercing depicted in the central medallion, but a late fifteenth-century viewer would not likely have found the juxtaposition of divine suffering and bucolic peace at all incongruous.

The piercing of Christ's heart on the cross continues to be a prime subject for inspirational art and a reminder of the sharp, cruel pain that each sinful act delivers to the still-suffering Christ. This distinctly male form of punishment and heroic endurance is paralleled in the history of religious art by a complementary and equally poignant image of suffering combined with nurturing in the female heart. In an early fourteenth-century relief sculpture of *Charitas*, Giovanni di Balduccio of Pisa captures the spirit of Christian giving through the act of breast feeding (Fig. 7). The figure of Charitas holds a self-identifying scroll unfurled in her right hand and casts her eyes toward heaven as she feeds two babies with streams of milk from her left breast.[16] But there is a gaping hole where the breast should be that suggests not a lactating mother so much as a sacrificial victim whose heart has been pierced, resulting in streams of her lifeblood flowing into the mouths of the children of God. The entire flow of the piece moves from the unseen heavenly presence being regarded beyond the upper left corner of the niche to the two babies at the lower right. The river of divine love appears to break through the stone at the figure's left breast and drops into the infants' mouths. The heart of Charitas, or divine love, appears to be the immediate source of nourishment, but there is also a higher, ultimate source hovering over the image. The life-giving substance flows *through* her invisible heart, thus recalling Christ's blood being shed for the redemption of all sinners.

There is little sense of pain in the Charitas image. Her act of self-less giving generates, instead, a feeling of beatific intermediacy. The emotional situation changes significantly when bleeding and burning hearts appear in full view in a pair of paintings of female saints, Catherine of Siena and Marguerite-Marie Alacoque, exchanging their hearts with

---

[16] The sculpture is from the Church of Orsanmichele in Florence and is now in the collection of the National Gallery of Art in Washington, DC. It was brought to my attention by Steven Buhler. The piece is reminiscent of Giotto's thirteenth-century *Caritas*, which depicts a female figure holding an overflowing bowl of fruit in her right hand while with the left she holds up her own pinecone-shaped heart as an offering to God, who receives it in both hands. Giotto's sculpture is reproduced in Bietenholz, *How Come This ♡ Means Love*, 55.

Figure 7. *Charitas* [Charity]. Giovanni di Balduccio, *c.* 1330, marble, 45.1 × 35.3 cm. Church of Orsanmichele, Florence, reproduced by permission of the National Art Gallery, Washington, DC, Samuel H. Kress Collection. Acc. no. 1960.5.4. In this sculptural relief the breast of the allegorical figure of Charity is opened to send heart-blood / milk into the mouth of the two hungry infants.

Christ.[17] These works fuse pain with pleasure in a moment of religious ecstasy that is both intensely pious and highly sexual. The amorously inflamed heart of the lover from innumerable medieval romances finds a shocking new context for display in the hands of devout nuns offering themselves to Christ and receiving Him into themselves. The story of embracing Christ's heart-wound is told of Lutgarde d'Aywière, who,

[17] Emily Jo Sargent discusses both these female saints, using other images, in "The Sacred Heart: Christian Symbolism," in *The Heart*, ed. James Peto (New Haven: Yale University Press; London: Wellcome Collection, 2007), pp. 102–14.

around the year 1206, confided in her confessor that a divine voice had summoned her to church where, "[f]rom the Cross, an arm broke away, embraced her, pressed her against His right side, and [she] placed her mouth on His wound. She drank in sweetness so powerful that she was from that time stronger and more alert to the service of God."[18] In her meditation on the Crucifixion, Marguerite of Oingt says that she took Christ down from the cross and "put him between the arms of my heart," and Catherine of Siena, in an ecstatic vision, placed Christ's detached foreskin on her finger as a wedding ring so as to marry herself to His suffering.[19]

This kind of detailed verbal and iconic description of a spiritual/sexual experience later proved to be deeply troubling to the Protestant reformers of early modern England and, as we will see, provided a powerful motive for waves of iconoclasm in the seventeenth century. The oral gratification highlighted in Lutgarde's description far exceeds in its sensory specificity the many contemporary descriptions of the joys of receiving the body and blood of Christ in the Mass. The fact that these experiences happened so frequently to female devotees of the Sacred Heart lends a particularly sexual coloring to the ritual "Interchange of Hearts" in which the suppliant artfully but also viscerally experienced Christ. Giovanni di Paolo's *St. Catherine Exchanging Her Heart with Christ* (Fig. 8) depicts the saint holding her still-dripping heart, her inmost being, out to Christ in her right hand while her left covers her breast where she has removed her heart. Christ hovers above the rooftops but is not shown holding his own heart as part of the "Exchange."[20] The painting was probably made in connection with the furious debates presided over by Pope Pius II in 1464 about whether the blood shed during the Crucifixion was sacred.[21] As graphic in its way as Giovanni's painting is an account of Marguerite-Marie Alacoque (1647–91), a Visitandine nun and member of the Order of the Béguines in France who, in the early 1670s, claimed to find refuge in the side of Christ.[22] One eighteenth-century depiction of Marguerite-Marie shows her on one knee before a crucifix, holding up her flaming heart while arrows emitted from the eyes of Christ

---

[18] Quoted in Olivier Debroise, "Heart Attacks: On a Culture of Missed Encounters and Misunderstandings," in *El Corazón Sangrante/The Bleeding Heart*, catalogue of an exhibit mounted by the Institute of Contemporary Art, Boston (Seattle: University of Washington Press, 1991), 15.

[19] For Marguerite's and Catherine's stories, see Caroline Walker Bynum, *Fragmentation and Redemption: Essays on Gender and the Human Body in Medieval Religion* (New York: Zone Books, 1991), pp. 168 and 86.

[20] Carole Levin kindly directed me to this painting.

[21] Keith Christiansen, Laurence B. Kanter, and Carl Brandon Strehlke, eds., *Painting in Renaissance Siena, 1420–1500* (New York: Metropolitan Museum of Art, distributed by H. N. Abrams, 1988), 230.

[22] For a full account of Sister Marguerite-Marie's pivotal role in establishing the Devotion of the Sacré Cœur in seventeenth-century France, see Raymond Anthony Jonas, *France and the Cult of the Sacred Heart: An Epic Tale for Modern Times* (Berkeley: University of California Press, 2000).

Figure 8. *St. Catherine Exchanging Her Heart with Christ.* Giovanni di Paolo, fifteenth century, tempera and gold on wood, 29.8 × 24.1 cm, reproduced by permission of the Metropolitan Museum of Art, New York, NY. The painting represents Catherine's part in her vision of the heart exchange. Other representations of the scene depict Christ pressing the saint's mouth to the wound in His side.

pierce it.[23] The small Lamb of God looks back at her quizzically, registering the amazement that any onlooker at such a miracle must feel. That quality

[23] This beautifully executed little work is reproduced in color in N. Boyadjian, *Le Cœur, son histoire, son symbolisme, son iconographie et ses maladies* (Antwerp: Esco Books, 1980), 99.

of wonder at the detachability of the heart is only infrequently included in such pictures. The chief participant in the miracle seems coolly focused but otherwise unaffected by her cardiectomy.

An eighteenth-century French engraving of Ste. Marguerite-Marie receiving the heart of Christ (Fig. 9) casts the event in a highly dramatic fashion. God sits on high surrounded by the heavenly host, while below a notably muscular Christ appears to be throwing His flaming heart, encompassed by the crown of thorns, to the kneeling nun. The divine figures radiate light as Marguerite-Marie presses her right hand to her own heart in a posture of penance. Still another version of the saint's story, this one in prose, links her experience of encountering the Sacred Heart through Christ's side-wound with her unusual methods of treating sick patients by devouring their sweat, pus, vomit, and even their diarrhea.[24] Such visionary literalization – if that conundrum can catch the conflicting elements of this experience – may appear to us simply bizarre and unsavory, but Marguerite-Marie was revered as a deeply spiritual and uniquely gifted healer in her own time and was eventually welcomed into the company of the saints.

Equally astonishing stories are told of Sister Chiara of Montefalco, whose dead body remained miraculously uncorrupted for five days in August of 1308 before she was eviscerated for burial. Her heart was removed and found to contain an intact crucifix. In the days that followed, the nuns again cut into Chiara's heart and found there "the crown of thorns, the whip and column, the rod and sponge, and tiny nails."[25] The techniques for opening up the human body appear to have been readily available to the nuns, and none of the witnesses registered surprise at the procedure or at finding the holy objects in her heart. Though stories of the saintly woman proliferated and viewing her heart reportedly healed some of the townspeople of Montefalco, all attempts to have Chiara beatified failed. Accounts of the treasures in her heart were not unique in the fourteenth

---

[24] *El Corazón Sangrante*, pp. 15–16. Louis Beirnaert, S.J., relates this behavior to a detailed autobiographical account of an oozing sore the size of the palm of her hand on her mother's cheek, an "érésipèle purulent," which she was able to cure with her prayers when the local doctor's ministrations failed. The analogous flowing wound in the side of Christ became for her "un abîme sans fond . . . le recoin secret . . . où la mère dispensait la nourriture et la boisson" in Beirnaert's Freudian reading. These references to maternal nurturing and miraculous faith-healing at the Feast of the Circumcision suggest a complicated and somewhat uneasy blend of spiritual and physical cleansing in discourses of the heart. This is the same uneasiness we encountered in the passage from Deuteronomy concerning circumcision of the heart. See Louis Beirnaert, S. J., "Note sur les attaches psychologiques du symbolisme du cœur chez Sainte Marguerite-Marie" in *Le Cœur*, Les études Carmélitaines (Bruges: Desclée de Brouwer, 1950), 228–33.

[25] See the account in Katharine Park, "The Criminal and the Saintly Body: Autopsy and Dissection in Renaissance Italy," *Renaissance Quarterly* 47 (1994): 1–33, quotation from p. 2.

Figure 9. The Sacred Heart being presented to Marguerite-Marie Alacoque. Frontispiece from *Instruction, pratiques, et prières pour la dévotion au Sacré-Cœur de Jésus: L'Office, vespres et messe de cette dévotion* (Paris, 1752), reproduced by permission of the Obrecht Collection of Gethsemani Abbey, Kentucky; volume housed at the Institute of Cistercian Studies, Western Michigan University. Shelfmark Waldo Rare Books BX2157.I67x. The resurrected Christ appears to throw his flaming, thorn-encircled heart to the kneeling nun.

century: Margarita of Città di Castello, who died a dozen years after Chiara, was similarly embalmed, and her heart "was found to contain three stones engraved with images of the Holy Family."[26] These narratives are all about what Caroline Walker Bynum calls "enfleshing" God and the intense faith of true believers.[27] The earnest and approving tone of these accounts of physical re-embodiments of the Passion in the hearts of the faithful strongly suggests that the material body was not regarded as a source of revulsion in the late Middle Ages. Dissecting these hearts, however astounding the results seem to us, was presented as an avenue to important kinds of knowledge.

Far more domestic and playful than these medieval tales of physically touching and being touched by the persons of the Trinity is a seventeenth-century French emblematic image of the Christian heart being swept clean of sinful desires by the childlike figure of Jesus (Fig. 10).[28] Jesus stands on a puffy cloud and uses a straw broom to sweep a variety of fiendish little characters representing sins out of a heart whose front wall has been removed for the cleaning operation. The diminutive devils with their serpentine lower extremities look desperate, especially the one holding his head at the bottom center. By contrast, a pair of angels with hands clasped stand on clouds at either side of the cleansed heart, looking on in "*admiration*" and "*étonnement.*" Jesus performs a familiarly domestic task, tidying up the heart of the "*Ame fidèle.*" Even the hearts of faithful Christians become polluted with the "*ordures*" of demonic possession. The action being depicted, then, is a joyful exorcism with a particular organ specified as "le centre de tous les désirs."[29] The imagined act of purgation must have functioned for seventeenth-century French culture much as other purgatives and emetics did in the alimentary tract, bringing relief to the congested body. The cleansing itself causes some distress, but the result is imagined as bringing inner peace. While it was in the heart that early modern Christians experienced what we now call "peace of mind," the heart was also the dustbin of trespasses and required vigorous cleaning by divine intervention.

The delicate balance of peace and pollution, pious confidence and disturbing uncertainty is likewise captured in the emblem "Speqve metvqve pavet" ([The heart] is tormented between hope and fear) from George

---

[26] Park, "The Criminal and the Saintly Body," 3.

[27] Bynum, *Fragmentation and Redemption*, 223.

[28] The prose text accompanying the emblem is headed "*IESVS BAILIANT LE cœur d'une Ame fidèle, afin de le nettoyer de ses ordures.*" It is from a collection by G[abriel] d[e] M[ello] called *Les divines opérations de Jésus dans le cœur d'une Ame fidèle* (Paris, 1673), 14. I owe this reference to Barbara C. Bowen.

[29] De Mello, *Les divines opérations*, 15.

O beatam cordis ædem! Animose puer verre,
Te cui cælum dedit sedem Monstra tuo vultu terre,
Purgat suis manibus. Tere tuis pedibus.
Anton.Wierx fecit et excud.

Figure 10. "Iésvs bailiant le Cœur d'une Ame fidèle." Anton Wierix. From G[abriel] d[e] M[ello], *Les divines opérations de Jésus dans le cœur d'une Ame fidèle* (Paris: J. Van-Merle, 1673), 14, reproduced by permission of the Rare Book and Manuscript Library, University of Illinois at Urbana-Champaign, Urbana, IL. Emblems 241 M48D. The young Christ sweeps grotesque monsters representing sins from the heart of a faithful follower.

Wither's 1635 *Collection of Emblemes* (Fig. 11). The strong caesura in the second line of the motto reflects this balance poetically:

> Where strong Desires are entertain'd,
> The Heart 'twixt Hope, and Feare, is pain'd.

The graphic correlatives of this emotional opposition are the symbolic anchor of hope on the left side of the smoking heart in the emblem's *pictura* and at the right the bow, armed, drawn, and aimed toward the heart. Our strongest desires, that is, are poised between hope and fear.

Where strong Desires are entertain'd,
The Heart 'twixt Hope, and Feare, is pain'd.

Figure 11. "Speqve metvqve pavet" [The (heart) is tormented between hope and fear]. George Wither, *A Collection of Emblemes* (London: A. M[atthews], 1635), Emblem 39, reproduced by permission of the Henry E. Huntington Library, San Marino, California. The desperate man's heart is caught precariously between hope (symbolized by the anchor) and fear (the drawn bow).

Wither explores the psychology of this balancing act in surprising ways. Even hope, he argues, can cause torment and despair, while fear can protect us from emotional carelessness:

> A *Groundlesse-Hope*, makes entrance for *Despaire*,
> And with Deceiving showes the Heart betrayes:
> A *Causelesse Feare*, doth *Reasons* force impaire,

And, terrifies the Soule, in doubtfull wayes.
Yet, quite neglect them not; For, *Hope* repells
That *Griefe* sometimes, which would our Hearts oppresse.
And, *Feare* is otherwile the *Sentinell*
Which rouzeth us from dang'rous Carelesnesse.
Thus, *Both* are good: but, *Both* are Plagues to such,
Who either *Fondly feare*, or *Hope too much*.[30]

Hope and fear, desire and doubt, are the poles between which "A Troubled
Minde" fluctuates. Such complex states of mind, we are told, were "in former
times exprest" in the figure of the heart surrounded by symbols of its
emotional states. In the phrase "former times" Wither acknowledges that
there is something archaic about his way of picturing mind as heart.

The archaic heart has a way of reinventing itself in hundreds of new
contexts, and the emblematic tradition in England and on the Continent
supplied mechanisms and formats for perpetuating and renewing this
ancient symbol. Although the emblem form is by its nature universalizing
and, hence, anti-historical, emblem books and the literature they helped
to shape reflect the received wisdom of the culture that produced them.
Emblems tend to epitomize familiar experiences and accepted values
of their culture in a largely non-analytical shorthand. Wither's "Speqve
metvqve pavet" captures in the simple, three-part *pictura* and an alternately
rhymed epigram the blend of hope and fear that often characterizes
emotionally fraught expectations. The heart, not the brain, was for Wither
the appropriate place to locate a self "payned inwardly with secret *Fires*."
The emblem economically conflates the sacred and the profane. Employing
figures from traditional *imprese*, Wither is able to show the interaction of
emotional states with their appropriate moral valences. The anchor
symbolizes the stabilizing effect of strong Christian faith, while the bow
and arrow derive from military *imprese* and Cupid narratives, and the fiery
heart from both secular and spiritual amatory discourse. The sum of what
George Puttenham calls "ciuill life" is compressed in the emblem and is
directed, in Puttenham's terms, toward managing the reader's "will by
hope or by dread." This particular heart emblem illustrates Puttenham's
dictum that the "intent" of this instructional art form is

to insinuat some secret, wittie, morall and braue purpose presented to the beholder,
either to recreate his eye, or please his phantasie, or examine his iudgement, or
occupie his braine or manage his will either by hope or by dread, euery of which

---

[30] George Wither, *A Collection of Emblemes* (London: A. M[atthews], 1635), 39.

respectes be of no litle moment to the interest and ornament of the ciuill life: and therefore giue them no litle commendation.[31]

Hearts "insinuat" themselves into every aspect of civic, domestic, and devotional life, appearing in love poems, stained glass windows, portraits, devotional books, architectural ornaments, tapestries, and medical illustrations. Entire volumes of emblems from the seventeenth century are dedicated to representing the heart in its many guises: Anton Wierix, *Cor Iesu amanti sacracum* (*c.* 1600), Jan van de Velde, *Openhertighe Herten* (Brussels, *c.* 1618–21), Benedict van Haeften, *Schola Cordis* (1629, translated into English by Christopher Harvey in 1647), Francesco Pona, *Cardio morphoseos sive ex corde desumpta emblemata sacra* (Verona, 1645). There were substantial sections devoted to the heart in other emblem collections as well. In her *Index of Icons in English Emblem Books, 1500–1700*, Huston Diehl lists 116 emblems dealing with the heart.[32] Some of this popularity is due to the efforts of Reformation and Counter-Reformation writers and artists to claim the scripturally charged image of the heart as their own and to the culture's more general fascination with representing inner emotional states in graphic and narrative form.

There is nothing idiosyncratic about George Wither's decision to present a heart so hot that it is smoking. As we have seen, Galenic physiology and humors theory specify that the heart is the body's furnace. The Lutheran emblem-maker Daniel Cramer includes both a heart and a heart-shaped furnace in the *pictura* for his emblem "Probor" ("I am tested"; Fig. 12). God's hands emerge from the clouds to slide the heart into the furnace, which emits smoke and flames through a chimney that replaces the aorta in anatomical drawings of the heart. This is the Refiner's fire that not only cleanses and purifies but tests the religious commitment of the faithful. The dramatic but unadorned image conveys the idea of the trial by fire with remarkable economy. While it anticipates the pain that must be suffered by the imperfect heart, it also holds the promise of perfection once the heart has passed through this ritual purgation. The quintessential human self will be cleansed of its impurities in this process, leaving only a pure, spiritual essence. These are orthodox scriptural sentiments and procedures expressed in a strictly puritanical context, and for his symbolic account of them, the emblem-maker has medical, theological, and secular-amatory discourses as precedent. The

[31] George Puttenham, *The Arte of English* Poesie (London: R. Field, 1589), 84 + iii[r].
[32] Huston Diehl, *An Index of Icons in English Emblem Books, 1500–1700* (Norman: University of Oklahoma Press, 1986), 116–21.

Figure 12. "Probor" [I am tested]. Daniel Cramer, *Emblemata sacra* (Frankfurt, 1624), Decas III, 109, reproduced by permission of the Rare Book and Manuscript Library, University of Illinois at Urbana-Champaign, Urbana, IL. Shelfmark Emblems 096.1 C848e1624. The seventeenth-century Lutheran emblem-maker depicts the hands of God refining the heart of the faithful in a heart-shaped furnace.

heart was a well-tried vessel by the mid-seventeenth century, a container of essences and trigger for intense audience responses. While in other contexts the heart is animated by its own imagined motions – it soars and sinks, skips and droops, races and seizes up – in this case it is an inert container lifted by cloudy, celestial hands into a fiery furnace. Enormous aesthetic changes had occurred in the half century since the publication in Paris of an elaborate allegory of painting as an *imitatio dei* contained within the heart of a virtuous woman (Fig. 13).

In contrast to the starkness of the Cramer furnace emblem, Hendrik Goltzius's "Exemplar virtvtvm" (1578) is positively cluttered by the inclusion

Figure 13. "Exemplar virtvtvm" [Christ as an exemplar of virtue]. Hendrik Goltzius, 1578, engraving, 23.7 × 18.3 cm, reproduced by permission of the Rijksmuseum, Amsterdam. In this allegory of the imitation of Christ, the copyist studies the child-shepherd being revealed to her by Jesus in a heart-shaped box. Christ points to the Lamb of God recumbent beside the woman's box of paints. The images surrounding the scene represent the cardinal virtues.

of sixteen mini-emblems illustrating the cardinal virtues, which form an elaborate frame around the engraving's central image. That image, however, reveals the same element of self-reflexivity that we saw in Fig. 12, where God is thrusting a heart into a heart-shaped retort. The Goltzius engraving shows an attentive young female painter copying onto the heart-shaped canvas on her easel the image of the child-shepherd contained in the open heart being held up to her by the Good Shepherd, who points at a lamb lying beside the artist's portable paint box. The allegory is about the good artist and the good Christian as imitators, both of them reiterating the revelations of Christ. The innocence of the child within the adult heart is reinforced by Christ's hand pointing to the recumbent lamb. The meta-artistic act of painting depends on the careful study and faithful reproduction of the divine subject in the imitator's own personal space, her heart. That this highly contrived self-reflexive act is "natural" is suggested by the bucolic setting of the picture, with the town in the far distance, the clouds surrounding Christ's halo, and the overhanging tree at the right side of the image. The artist's traveling box in the right foreground indicates that she has carried the tools of her art into the countryside to capture Nature through divine imitation. The fiction is that she is painting an inner reality *en plein air*. Confirmation of the truth of the allegorical narrative of looking into one's heart appears in the form of the "Exemplar virtvtvm" extracted from the devout heart and placed at the edge of the *pictura*.

A culture that repeats its images of interiority with this kind of insistence will return almost obsessively to traditional icons such as the heart. The long history of faithful Christians inspecting their hearts is recalled in this act of allegorical instruction and social commemoration. Allegorical emblematics, whether theological or political, then, become the language of inner conviction and remain so throughout the period we are studying.

One of the most stunning uses of these emblematics in the entire period is the Rainbow Portrait of Queen Elizabeth I, painted around 1600 and now part of the collection at Hatfield House (Fig. 14). It appears to have been designed with help from the Queen's counselor, Robert Cecil, and a rising young lawyer, Sir John Davies, author of *Hymnes of Astraea* (1599).[33] The rainbow that Elizabeth holds in her right hand, just under the motto "NON SINE SOLE IRIS" (No rainbow without the sun), is an

---

[33] For background material on this painting see Roy Strong, *Gloriana: The Portraits of Queen Elizabeth I* (New York: Thames and Hudson, 1987), 157–61, and Frances A. Yates, "Queen Elizabeth as Astraea," *Journal of the Warburg and Courtauld Institutes* 10 (1947): 27–82. See also Yates's pertinent comments in the appendices to *Astraea: The Imperial Theme in the Sixteenth Century* (London: Routledge & Kegan Paul, 1975), 216–18.

Figure 14. The Rainbow Portrait of Queen Elizabeth I, detail, *c.* 1600, canvas, 127 × 99.1 cm, reproduced by permission of The Marquess of Salisbury, Hatfield House. The queen's cloak is painted with eyes and ears, signifying the watchfulness of her counsellor. On her sleeve, worked in rubies and pearls, is the serpent of Wisdom, who controls the passions of the heart, represented by the heart-shaped jewel suspended from the serpent's mouth.

emblem of divine peace and power drawn from Genesis 9: 13. Connected to this covenantal symbolism and more relevant for our purposes are several detached body parts depicted on the Queen's garments. On her golden cloak are painted eyes and ears, betokening, as Roy Strong says, the intelligence transmitted by her watchful servants (such as Cecil) and judged by her own prudent spirit, represented here by the jewel-encrusted serpent on her left sleeve. Suspended over the serpent's head is a celestial sphere, suggesting the universal scope of the monarch's wisdom. Dangling from its mouth is a ruby heart reminiscent of the heart pendant worn by Valeriano's figure of "Counsel," which harks back once again to Cecil. The wise serpent controls the passionate promptings of the heart, as Davies says in an acrostic addressed to Elizabeth:

> B ut since she hath a hart, we know
> E uer some passions thence do flow,
> T hough euer rul'd with Honor;
> H er Iudgement raignes, they waite below,
> A nd fixe their eyes vpon her.[34]

The straightforward announcement that Elisa-Betha has a heart over which her judgment reigns serves as a reminder of the aging Queen's continuing vitality.[35] This iconic portrait is all about the mythic ideas associated with her sacerdotal body, and the gemlike visual image of that body is her heart.

A hauntingly visceral example of the allegorical habit of mind I have been discussing is the seventeenth-century Mexican artist Juan Correa's painting *Alegoría del Sacramento* (*c.* 1690, Fig. 15), in which the grapevines that produce the sacramental wine for the Eucharist emerge from a nasty wound in the breast of the crucified Christ. Large heart-shaped bunches of purple grapes hang from the vines supported by the cross. Christ is allegorized as the vintner, crushing the grapes/Sacred Heart with his hands to make the wine that will commemorate his own suffering and death. The banner unfurled above the cross displays Christ's words: *Pater ignosce illis* (Father, forgive them). An anxious-looking Pope waits beneath the cross, holding a basin into which the wine/blood flows, then overflows into a large round trough beside which seven recumbent sheep wait to drink. A blue sphere, representing the earth, floats in the trough and supports the kneeling, blood-spattered figure of Christ. The vividly colored painting is nothing if not memorable.

The grisly image of the vine snaking out of Christ's breast in Correa's painting may not have upset a late seventeenth-century Catholic viewer accustomed to explicit representations of the agony of the crucifixion, but puritanical Protestants in England, Germany, and the Low Countries were deeply suspicious of such violent and terrifying images. Solidity and reassurance of salvation were the hallmarks of Protestant emblem books

---

[34] "Hymne XX. Of the Passions of her Heart," in Sir John Davies's *Hymnes of Astraea in acrosticke verse* (London: [R. Field] for J. S[tandish], 1599), 20.
[35] Whoever painted the Rainbow Portrait, whether Marcus Gheeraerts, Isaac Oliver, or another of their contemporaries, has followed the convention of preserving the youth and sensuality of the Queen's person. The passionate heart is associated with youthfulness.

Figure 15. *Alegoría del Sacramento*. Juan Correa, *c.* 1690, oil on canvas, 164 × 106 cm, reproduced by permission of the Denver Art Museum, Denver, CO, Collection of Jan and Frederick Mayer.The painting depicts the crucified Christ squeezing sacramental wine from grapes produced by a vine growing from His chest into a bowl held by the Pope and intended eventually for the faithful flock below.

of the period, not dramatically precarious poses, agonized countenances, and bloodshed. Images such as Wither's anchor and bow-and-arrow tend to distance the viewer from the realities of the body and to move meditation directly to the level of abstraction. It would appear that the emblematic heart sheers off from the anatomical heart at this moment in cultural history, shifting the naturalistic representation of the heart and the body in general to the realm of medical illustration. But the dichotomies are never so clear-cut when we are dealing with an organ/icon so emotionally charged as the heart.

Producing images of the heart always requires evisceration of some kind. Just as the medical anatomist must retract tissue and bone to reveal the internal organs, so too has the creative artist to anatomize his or her subject in order to accomplish the job of raising human consciousness about those parts of experience generally relegated to the inner person. Revealing interiority involves the sometimes brutal act of cutting away the surrounding body. The combined horror and fascination of the moment of incision simply will not be denied. What is discovered inside is, as often as not, fetid and corrupt, as we will see in detail in Chapter 5. Once moral corruption takes up residence in the heart, it requires purgation through dire acts of scrutiny and refinement such as that emblematized in Cramer's "Probor" and the passage from Deuteronomy that we looked at in Chapter 1. Corruption and purification are the polarities within which moral analysis occurs in these images of the heart. Acts of inscription (analogous to God's writing on Moses' tablets) and erasure make and remove traces of the *eidos* within the image, thereby establishing the written word as the preeminent mode of recording private and public commitments in early modern culture. The words, though, gain much of their power from pictorial supplements. The act of digging into the human breast dramatizes the dynamic of concealment and revelation, thus redrawing for the culture the boundaries between what is imagined to be inalienably private and what is necessarily public. Artistic reproductions of the heart image reinscribe complex ideologies that otherwise might remain invisible in English culture, and they also show significant variation during the sixteenth and seventeenth centuries.

A strong affiliation was established in the early modern period between art and anatomy. Artists found it imperative to study and to produce drawings of the bone and muscle structures that define the shape of the body, both in motion and at rest. In turn, what the artists learned from their studies of dissected bodies and anatomical texts could be used to illustrate anatomy books. The collaboration proved to be profitable for everyone. Leonardo da Vinci was fascinated not only with representing the outward form of humans and animals but also their internal organs.[36]

---

[36] See Deanna Petherbridge's section "Leonardo da Vinci and the Grammar of Anatomical Drawing" in *The Quick and the Dead*, 43–8, and Robert Herrlinger's detailed analysis of Leonardo's illustrative techniques in his *History of Medical Illustration from Antiquity to A.D 1600*, trans. Graham Fulton-Smith (London: Pitman Medical and Scientific Publishing, 1970), 67–79.

His descriptive drawing of two aspects of an ox heart, with notes made in his minute hand, solves the problem of representing both surface and volume so ingeniously that it might almost be used to instruct modern-day veterinary students (Fig. 16). Leonardo clearly cared about the mechanics of the heart and its connecting vessels and valves, but he also wanted to trace the heart's motion back to its source. He offers the following advice to any student who consults his notebooks:

Do not fail to follow up the reversive nerves [vagi] as far as the heart; and see whether these [nerves] give movement to the heart or whether the heart moves by itself. And if such movement comes from the reversive nerves which have their origin in the brain, then you will make it clear how the soul has its seat in the ventricles of the brain and the vital spirits have their origin in the left ventricle of the heart. And if this movement of the heart arises from the heart itself then you will say that the seat of the soul is in the heart and likewise that of the vital spirits.[37]

This was a problem that Leonardo never solved, one that had to await micro-technologies and biochemical studies capable of tracking the interaction of actin and myosin under the influence of calcium ions produced by waves of electricity that sweep over the heart in durations of 100 milliseconds.[38] To be sure, neither Leonardo's physics nor modern biochemistry addresses the problem of the heart's relation to the soul. But what Leonardo was really tracking was not just an observable anatomical phenomenon but a textual debate inherited from Aristotle, the Hippocratic texts, and Galen, one that persisted well into the eighteenth century. This conflict between anatomical function and teleological purpose was the root

[37] Leonardo da Vinci, *Notebooks*, fol. 105^r, note V. I quote the translation of the mirror-written Italian from the *Corpus of the Anatomical Studies in the Collection of Her Majesty the Queen at Windsor Castle*, ed. Kenneth D. Keele and Carlo Pedretti (New York: Johnson Rpt. Co. and Harcourt Brace Janovich, 1978), 1: 334. On fols. 50^r and 107^r Leonardo explains the theory of the cardiac furnace (he even supposed that without certain pericardial safeguards the heart might catch fire), a notion that was grist for the poet's mill and that wasn't definitively rejected until William Harvey addressed the issue 150 years later.

[38] A simplified explanation is offered by Lionel H. Opie, Professor of Cardiac Medicine at the University of Cape Town, in his inaugural lecture *The Heart and Its Functions* (Cape Town: University of Cape Town, 1981), 4. For more recent solutions to the mystery – some of them, such as the possibility that heart rhythms are best described by chaos theory, still rather mystifying – see Ary L. Goldberger and David R. Rigney, "Nonlinear Dynamics at the Bedside," in *Theory of the Heart: Biomechanics, Biophysics, and Nonlinear Dynamics of Cardiac Function*, ed. Leon Glass *et al.* (New York: Springer-Verlag, 1991), 583–605. Leonardo actually inserted into his early diagrams of the heart a papillary muscle that he considered the prime mover of the organ. See K. D. Keele, *Leonardo da Vinci on Movement of the Heart and Blood* (London: Harvey and Blythe, 1952), Fig. 20, which follows p. 70 and is discussed by Keele on p. 72.

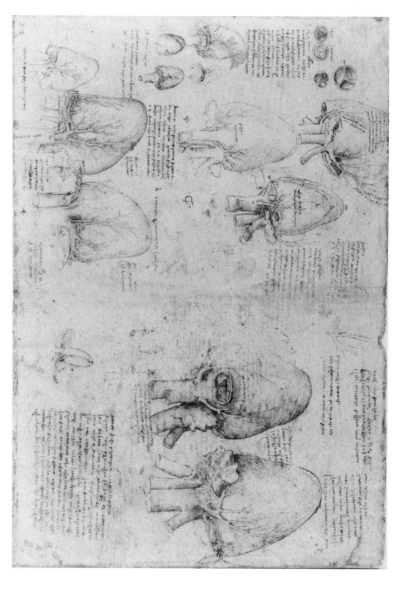

Figure 16. "The Heart and its Blood Vessels." Leonardo da Vinci, *Anatomical Notebooks* (c. 1495–1505), 1974[v], reproduced by permission of The Royal Collection © 2007, Her Majesty Queen Elizabeth II. Leonardo's technique of anatomical illustration is unmatched in the period. His notes surrounding these ox hearts are made in his small, neat mirror-writing.

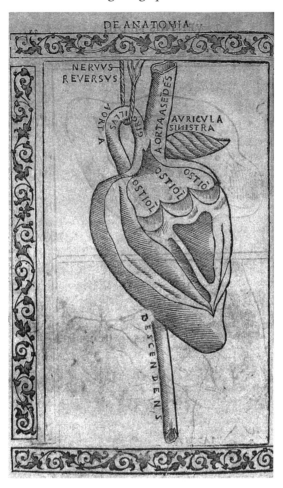

Figure 17. "The Heart and its Vessels." Berengario da Carpi, *Isagogae breves* (Bologna, 1523), 32^r, reproduced by permission of the Wellcome Library, London. Library reference no. EPB783. Anatomical detail and the naming of parts have been kept to a minimum in this schematic illustration for Berengario's medical textbook.

from which grew and branched the competing claims of poets and artists, as well as physicians, for the uses and significance of the heart.

Leonardo's heart sketch does not fully solve the instructional problem of labeling the parts of the organ. Writing directly on an illustration of the heart worked only for the simplest diagrams, such as the one from Jacopo Berengario da Carpi's *Isagogae breves* (Bologna, 1523, Fig. 17). Berengario labels only a half-dozen features, without including, for example, such notable parts as the ventricles and their dividing wall, the septum. Subsequent anatomical illustrators introduced better technologies for connecting names to parts, experimenting with banderols unfurled to the sides of the image, indication lines connecting part to name, and keying systems that referred viewers to numbered or lettered names in the text.[39] Some rough shading helps to distinguish sections of Berengario's heart, but the entire effort seems primitive compared to the work done by Stephen Calcar under the meticulous supervision of Andreas Vesalius for his *Fabrica*.

The *Fabrica* was a beautifully printed and lavishly illustrated book that covered the main physiological systems and set the standard for anatomy texts for the next several hundred years. Like other serious students of the human body who followed him, Vesalius realized the importance of adding a strong visual component to his text because his method of description and instruction relied not just on written texts from the past but also on observations of actual human bodies in various stages of dissection. It is a nice question whether the early modern emphasis on observation in the field of natural studies caused the rapid development of realism in depictions of the anatomized body or, conversely, whether the work of the artists stimulated interest in looking directly at what had previously only been described verbally. In either case, it is clear that the verbal and the pictorial came to complement and to reinforce one another in the most comprehensive anatomies, and no one was as careful as Vesalius about guiding the chief designer of his woodcuts in the production of detailed and comprehensible illustrations. To these admirable qualities Calcar added grace and elegance, knowing that the market for the *Fabrica* would include not only medical students but collectors of showpiece printing. This volume, and the *Epitome* based on it, had to capture the attention and patronage of the most wealthy and refined men in Europe, including the Emperor Charles V, to whom the work was dedicated.

Vesalius and Calcar worked together to devise an astonishing number of ways to present the body, in various stages of dissection, to the eye and the understanding of its various audiences. Minute hatching and shading provide a sense of depth and contour; series of illustrations capture the results of the dissector's work as it unfolds in time; drawings of entire isolated systems (such as the veins, arteries, and nerves) permit a degree of continuity and transparency not available even to an observer present at the dissection; background landscapes and expressively posed, notionally living bodies generate temporal and moral narratives as the skin, muscles,

---

[39] On the development of these labeling schemes see Herrlinger, *History of Medical Illustration*, 59–60.

vessels, and bones seem progressively to disintegrate under the dissector's knife, thus mimicking the natural processes of decay and death. In the process of devising techniques to convey all this information, author and illustrator had to make a huge number of tricky decisions regarding the images for the book. Should they depict typical or individual bodies?[40] (Vesalius chose to avoid diseased or "deformed" [atypical] bodies, while acknowledging in his text that there was considerable diversity in the human form, even among so-called "typical" bodies.)[41] Should illustrations show only what could be seen at a specific stage of dissection from one particular viewpoint, or should they abstract and synthesize entire systems such as the nervous system that could never be viewed together during an anatomy lecture? (Vesalius includes the heart in a diagram of the vascular system, and he also offers larger views of the heart. On the whole, he understood that illustrations worked well to visualize such individual parts as joints and organs, but not always so well as words to describe certain larger systems.) Is it permissible to omit materials that are extraneous to the subject of the illustration, say the spleen or the spinal column, even though they would be prominently visible in that part of the cadaver during a dissection? (Some of each: Vesalius eliminates the ribcage but includes the lungs as a visual and systemic context in his larger views of the heart.) How should illustrations be connected to the text? (In most cases, including his heart images, a series of letters serves to key the parts of the illustration to the names of the parts in the text.) Vesalius and Calcar made so many of the right decisions about these and other matters that the *Fabrica* achieved a comprehensive look at the body that brought together the best of the artist's imagination and the proto-scientist's observations.

In the sixth of the seven books of the *Fabrica*, Vesalius brings us to the heart and lungs. The importance of visual context as a guide to intellectual

---

[40] In his article " 'The Mark of Truth': Looking and Learning in Some Anatomical Illustrations from the Renaissance and Eighteenth Century," Martin Kemp formulates seven probing historical questions that amount to "nothing short of a plea for a revised agenda for the history of anatomical illustration" (89). Not all his questions are directly relevant to the place of heart images in early modern anatomies, but his historically thick descriptions of the illustrating activity – including matters of patronage, artistic technique, intended and unintended audiences – suit my own method of studying the heart admirably. Kemp's article appears in *Medicine and the Five Senses*, ed. W. F. Bynum and R. Porter (Cambridge: Cambridge University Press, 1993), 85–121.

[41] Nancy G. Siraisi, "Vesalius and Human Diversity in *De humani coporis fabrica*," *Journal of the Warburg and Courtauld Institutes* 57 (1994): 60–88. Siraisi uses Vesalius's extensive revisions in the 1555 edition to show that, while he strove to present universal truths based on rational demonstrations – the hallmark of *scientia* as opposed to *artes* in the Aristotelian scheme – he deplored and denounced the way that some earlier writers ignored differences among human bodies and between human and animal anatomy (Galen's frequent error).

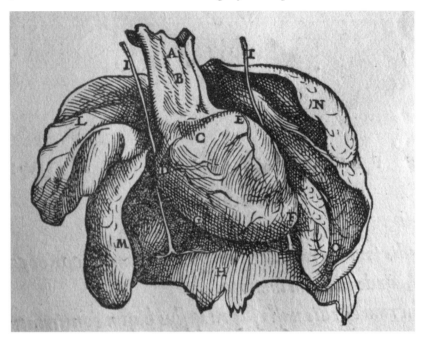

Figure 18. Heart with pericardium, lungs, and part of diaphragm. Andreas Vesalius, *De humani corporis fabrica libri septem* (Basel: Ex officina Joannis Oporini, 1543), 561, reproduced by permission of the Rare Book and Manuscript Library, University of Illinois at Urbana-Champaign, Urbana, IL. Shelfmark F. 611 V63d1543.

understanding is evident in two of his heart illustrations: one with the heart encased in the pericardium and surrounded by the lungs and part of the diaphragm (Fig. 18); the second showing a differently shaped heart, this time with the pericardium cut away (Fig. 19). While more than a dozen parts are keyed by letters to their names in the text, there has been a good deal of necessary abstraction so as to move the parts forward in space and make them systematically, though not photographically, visible. Vesalius was greatly distressed when Thomas Geminus published his *Compendiosa totius anatomie delineatio* (London: J. Herford, 1545) using his own copperplate copies of the most notable of Vesalius's woodcuts and text from the *Epitome*. Given his more flexible medium, Geminus was able to improve somewhat on the precision of the Vesalian originals and greatly on any illustrations previously published in England. Vesalius was further annoyed (though he might have felt flattered as well) by Nicholas Udall's English translation of the *Compendiosa* (London: N. Hyll for T. Geminus, 1553). Vesalius published

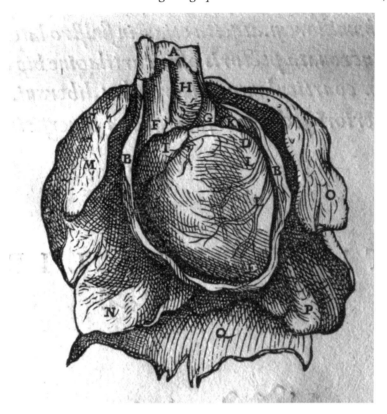

Figure 19. Heart with pericardium cut away. Andreas Vesalius, *De humani corporis fabrica libri septem* (Basel: Ex officina Joannis Oporini, 1543), 562, reproduced by permission of the Rare Book and Manuscript Library, University of Illinois at Urbana-Champaign, Urbana, IL. Shelfmark F. 611 V63d1543.

his own second edition of the *Fabrica* in 1555, as its influence continued to spread. This book, based on firsthand observation of human dissections by the twenty-eight-year-old lecturer in anatomy at the University of Padua must have shocked the entrenched medical faculties who persisted in taking and teaching their Galen literally, without challenging the contradictions between the classical text and the evidence of their eyes in the dissecting theaters of Europe. Vesalius stridently mocks an established tradition of medical instruction when he writes in the preface to the *Fabrica* that:

some conduct the dissection of the human body and others present the account of its parts, the latter like jackdaws aloft in their high chair, with egregious arrogance croaking things they have never investigated but merely committed to memory from the book of others, or reading what has already been described. The former are so ignorant of languages that they are unable to explain their dissections to the spectators and muddle what ought to be displayed according to the instructions of the physician who, since he has never applied his hand to the dissection of the body, haughtily governs the ship from a manual. Thus everything is wrongly taught in the schools, and days are wasted in ridiculous questions so that in such confusion less is presented to the spectators than a butcher in his stall could teach a physician.[42]

Calling his older university colleagues jackdaws and particularly unskilled butchers was hardly diplomatic, but Vesalius was sure he was right about the need for manual as well as textual contact with the anatomized body, and he had allies who shared his conviction. This was an aspect of the culture in which the practical and the intellectual were being vigorously integrated.

While Vesalius's illustrations show some familiarity with the unpublished sketches in da Vinci's notebooks, he would have found little use for the artist's early schematic sketch of the heart, based, as it was, solely on his reading of medical texts (Fig. 20). The sketch looks a good deal like the head of a large-eyed insect with antennae and round ears (the auricles, from L. *auris*). The drawing is obviously not an instructional tool but rather a reverse ekphrasis, moving from verbal description to roughly imagined visual shape, an *aide mémoire* for a naturalist note-taker.

Though the work of anatomical illustrators became increasingly refined and reliable throughout the sixteenth and early seventeenth centuries, crucial information about how the heart performed in the body remained unknown or, at best, theorized by only a few natural philosophers. Oddly, when William Harvey published *De motu cordis* in 1628, providing answers to the most perplexing questions, he included no illustrations of the heart or the vascular system. Yet this is perhaps not so odd, since Harvey's interest was in the motion or function of the heart and its related systems, not primarily in their structure. Words, therefore, and particularly verbs denoting action, were Harvey's tools of choice in laying out his careful arguments for the dynamism of the heart, which, he explained, spasmodically forced blood through a fully connected system of arteries and veins. He writes excitedly about this process and the sequence of experiments that led him to conclude that blood is being circulated within the body, not consumed and replaced, as the followers of Galen insisted. For this purpose, language (Latin, in the first instance) was more precise and convincing than graphic illustrations.

---

[42] Vesalius, *Fabrica*, as quoted in K. B. Roberts and J. D. W. Tomlinson, *The Fabric of the Body: European Traditions of Anatomical Illustration* (Oxford: Clarendon Press, 1992), 133.

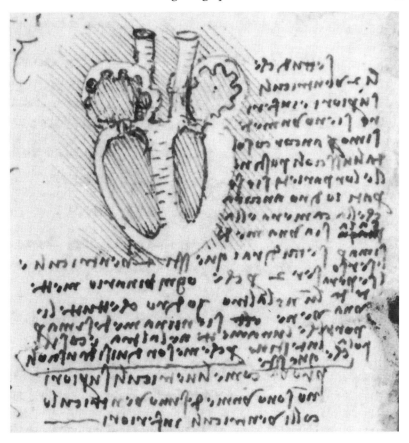

Figure 20. Sketch of the heart. Leonardo da Vinci, *Anatomical Notebooks* (c. 1495–1505), 19062ʳ, reproduced by permission of The Royal Collection © 2007, Her Majesty Queen Elizabeth II. This rough drawing among Leonardo's notes on the heart derives from earlier medical texts rather than being copied from life.

Not that the visual image lacked flexibility and impact. In the world of the secular amatory narratives, the ubiquitous metaphor of the heart suffering the pains of rejection frequently found expression in the visual arts. A German woodcut from the later fifteenth century depicts the mischievous Frau Venus (Fig. 21), practicing her full range of torments as she violates the heart of her kneeling lover by piercing, sawing, pressing, burning, racking, and other violent forms of attack.[43] Her condescending smile and sexy

[43] Executed by Meister Casper von Regensburg in 1485.

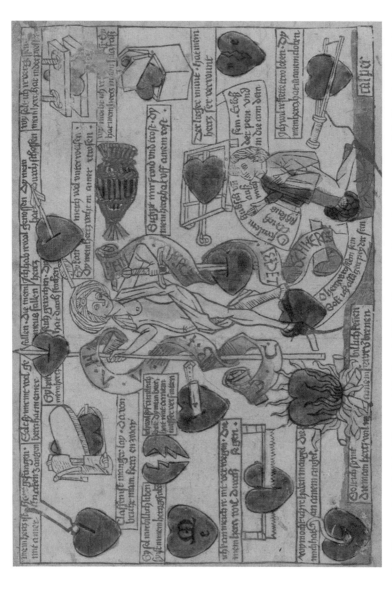

Figure 21. *Frau Venus und der Verliebte* [Venus and Her Lover]. Meister Casper von Regensburg, Regensburg, Germany. Kupferstichkabinett, Staatliche Museen zu Berlin, Berlin, reproduced by permission of Bildarchiv Preussicher Kulturbesitz / Art Resource, New York, NY. The mischievous Frau Venus smiles condescendingly at the kneeling lover whose heart is being attacked in a dozen different ways: by piercing, sawing, pressing, burning, racking, and so forth. This striking copy has the hearts colored red and the serpentine banner highlighted in green.

pose, standing on a heart, link her protean skills for causing heart pain to her sexual arrogance. Labels attached to each heart under attack mimic those in early anatomical drawings, adding to the sense that this is a systematic, exhaustive survey of the pains of love. There is, of course, something vaguely absurd about bringing out all the heavy artillery and torture devices to attack such a vulnerable object as the poor young man's heart. The overkill is itself part of the pleasure of the courtly love situation being visually reiterated.

Women are not the only tormentors in the culturally persistent game of the amorous heart attack. Victims such as Shakespeare's Hermione (*The Winter's Tale*) and Ford's Calantha (*The Broken Heart*) provide eloquent testimonials, through speech and silence, to the emotional wounds inflicted by men. Authors, too, are frequently taken to task for dissecting the secrets of the female heart and are accused of being as callous in their anatomies as their most brutal characters.[44] Probing too deeply into the secrets of the heart brings nothing but pain, the pain suffered by Frau Venus's admirer, the Christian sinner, and the criminal whose body was subject to the indignities of the anatomist. If there was pleasure in the function and study of the healthy human heart, there was also pain in the unceasing process of probing that heart.

---

[44] A late example of this authorial brutality is A. Lemot's lithograph "Flaubert Dissecting Emma Bovary," which originally appeared in *La Parodie* for the week of December 5–12, 1869. The image neatly conflates the anatomy theater with the theater of love's cruelty, which we will explore further in Chapter 5. In addition to his surgical tools (scalpel, bone-saw, shears, and apron), Flaubert is provided with a magnifying glass to inspect his unfortunate heroine's romantic secrets more closely and a pot of ink to write them all down. Emma's bleeding heart on the point of his scalpel demonstrates graphically the cruelty often attributed to surgeons, anatomists, and authors.

CHAPTER 3

The organ of affection and motion, truth and conflict

In earlier chapters I have been concerned with establishing the wealth of anatomical and iconic heart lore available to writers in early modern England. The examples I have used tend toward the conclusion that anatomists, theologians, and poets were not huddled in separate camps, isolated by suspicion of one another's methodologies and goals but were engaged, one way or another, in constructing a generally acceptable body of knowledge about the heart. As I will argue in the present chapter, this body of revealed and constructed knowledge was not stable or unproblematic in Shakespeare's age, but neither was it dominated by anxious contention with earlier conceptions of the heart's physiological and symbolic functions. There were important changes in the way that people thought about the passions and pumping actions of the heart, but they were changes rooted in respect for inherited learning and faith. The terms in which these changes were most often expressed were "affection" (a powerful inclination capable of causing sudden shifts in the body's internal condition) and "motion" (a motive force in the mind or some part of the body, especially the heart, which could come to dominate a person's actions). These changes, often sudden and distressing, raised troubling questions about whether the heart was the originator and repository of lasting "truth" or simply the setting for perpetual "conflict" in matters of feeling and faith. The texts through which I want to trace these changes in early modern experiences and theories of the heart include several plays, a pair of lengthy poetic meditations on the human body, Calvin's *Institutes* and *Commentaries*, and Shakespeare's rigorously introspective Sonnet 62. First, however, we need to consider the concepts of change and continuity as defining features of the period frequently referred to as the Renaissance, of which Shakespeare's age is a small but important part.

The task of understanding the role of the heart in this period has been complicated by our ongoing infatuation with the spirit of change, a concept that has come to define the Renaissance and has diverted attention away from continuities with earlier times that were, I believe, alive in the minds of even the most revolutionary thinkers. For these thinkers, cultural change was unimaginable without cultural continuity. The honorific term "innovative" is of very recent origin, most innovation being viewed in earlier times (often unfairly) as confounding and dangerous. Any theory of sudden, revolutionary change in the ways that society responded to the artistic symbolism, anatomical study, and religious devotion to the heart is difficult to defend on the basis of contemporary records.

Historians of early modern England have understandably been attracted to the Protestant Reformation as a crucial instance of change in the period, but the nature and extent of this change needs to be re-evaluated in the context of heart studies. While the iconoclastic movement in the early Reformation that led to stripping churches of devotional images, among them images of Christ's heart, used to be cited as a precise moment of devotional change in England, Eamon Duffy has argued more recently for a far slower shift in attitudes concerning the iconic trappings of the Old Religion.[1] Further, Joseph Leo Koerner points out that for Martin Luther, the image of the bleeding heart of Jesus was captured within the heart of each and every devout Protestant.[2] In effect, Luther repudiates the iconoclasts in his defense of an internalized, imaged-based faith:

Of this I am certain, that God desires to have his works heard and read, especially the passion of our Lord. But it is impossible for me to hear and bear it in mind without forming mental images of it in my heart. For whether I will or not, when I hear of Christ, an image of a man hanging on a cross takes form in my heart, just as the reflection of my face naturally appears in the water when I look into it. If it is not a sin but good to have the image of Christ in my heart, why should it be a sin to have it in my eyes? This is especially true since the heart is more important than the eyes, and should be less stained by sin because it is the true abode and dwelling place of God.[3]

Such a conception of the power of believers to inscribe the image of their Savior within the heart guarantees a continuity of visual culture from earlier periods and provides a potent counter-argument to the notion of radical change as a model for Renaissance thought. A more inclusive and

---

[1] Eamon Duffy, *The Stripping of the Altars: Traditional Religion in England, c. 1400–c. 1580* (New Haven: Yale University Press, 1992).

[2] Joseph Leo Koerner, *The Reformation of the Image* (London: Reaktion Books, 2004), esp. 212–21.

[3] Martin Luther, "Against the Heavenly Prophets in the Matter of Images and Sacraments (1525), Part I," trans. Bernhard Erling, in *Luther's Works*, American edition, ed. Conrad Bergendorff (Philadelphia: Muhlenberg Press, 1958), 40: 99–100.

compatible model for reconstructing the early modern fascination with the identity-making functions of the heart is one of reverence for a select body of ancient thought, of more or less disciplined observation of natural phenomena, and of carefully revised textual and graphic records of the poetics and physiology of the heart.

It is nonetheless true that fresh and sometimes disturbing responses were registered throughout fifteenth- and sixteenth-century Europe to the re-publication in Latin of medical texts that had survived, primarily in Arabic language versions. That these responses emanated from or propelled the sudden birth of the Burckhardtian Renaissance Individual is, however, doubtful. The residual appeal of Burckhardt's account of a radically altered Renaissance habit of mind, one that eclipsed the stodgy medieval conception of the self mired in such supposedly oppressive institutions as guilds, feudal bonds, and papal dicta, continues to skew our view of the place of the human body in early modern culture.[4] The current popularity of theories of periodization which place a premium on those aspects of earlier cultures that anticipate our modern (or post-modern) one further contributes to a distorted view of how human embodiment shaped early modern thought.

Shifting our view from the broad sweep of historical change to those local changes believed to govern particular living bodies in the age of Shakespeare, we come back to the resonant term "motion." The body part most conspicuously in continuous motion was, of course, the heart. William Harvey used the Latin form of the word "motion" to capture his special emphasis on the dynamics of propulsion emanating from the heart in his title *Exercitatio anatomica de motu cordis et sanguinis in animalium.* His focus on the "motions" of the heart is very much in the tradition of ancient studies of living bodies. Physiological change was described in classical Greek by the term κίυησŋ, kinesis or motion, and included everything from generation to corruption. The early modern English term "motion" was the favored term in physiological and anatomical works, and in other contexts it acquired the allied senses of political instigation (as in proposing a motion), supernatural promptings (as in Samson's "rousing motions" in Milton's *Samson Agonistes*,)[5] and automatic movement (as in a puppet motion). In the later seventeenth century the term "emotion" gained prominence in discussions of the stirrings or agitated movements

---

[4] See Jacob Burckhardt, *The Civilization of the Renaissance in Italy*, trans. S. G. C. Middlemore (London: Phaidon, 1945).

[5] Line 1382. *John Milton: Complete Poems and Major Prose*, ed. Merritt Y. Hughes (New York: Odyssey Press, 1957).

triggered in the body by the passions or "affections" (L. *affectus*), which were often set over against the settled reason. "Affection" denoted an inclination toward or striving after (OED sb 1.2), suggesting discontent with who one is or one's present situation and a longing to *move* to some better mental or physical place. The affections stir one to action, and this stirring often originates in the heart and is noted in the pulse. As Francis Bacon explains in his *Sylva sylvarum, or a naturall history in ten centuries* (1626), "[T]he affects and Passions of the *Heart*, and *Spirits*, are notably disclosed by the *Pulse*."[6] While the primary sense of the terms "motion" and "affection" in medical discourse is concerned with material alteration within the body, the same terms acquire the meaning of spiritual arousal in religious and poetic contexts (OED sb II.2). The crucial link between physical and spiritual motions in the systematic thought of the day was provided by the term "*spiritus*," identifying a substance, both material and immaterial, that flowed freely in the healthy human body.

Although the motions and affections of the heart were often represented by graphic artists as removed from the body, as we saw in Chapter 2, in the discourses of natural philosophy and medicine, they were decidedly not free-floating entities. Their significance was linked to familiar systems of internal organs and their connective sinews, veins, arteries, nerves, and invisible channels for transferring bodily fluids to various corporeal command-centers such as the brain and the liver. The interconnectedness of systems was all-important in physicians' efforts to track health failures to the particular parts that had malfunctioned from the accumulation of superfluous and damaging humors. Galen's *On the Usefulness of the Parts of the Body* made clear to university-trained physicians that use or function animated the interconnected structures within the body.[7] Emphasizing the natural and rational causes and cures for disease, Galen largely followed Aristotle's philosophical rationale for understanding the body's vital motions and emotions, many of them triggered in the heart. Mary Lindemann has conveniently summarized Galen's conception of the heart as it was transmitted by Arabian physicians and textual scholars:

The heart ... was the principal member of the organs of the chest and the arteries, known as *spiritual members* because they distributed a mixture of blood and spiritus (air) throughout the body ... The arterial system, carrying spiritus and blood, did not connect at all with the venous system, except when blood

---

[6] Francis Bacon, *Sylva sylvarum* (London: J. F. for W. Lee, 1651), 25.

[7] Galen, *On the Usefulness of the Parts of the Body*, trans. Margaret T. May (Ithaca: Cornell University Press, 1968).

seeped through small, invisible (in fact, nonexistent) pores in the septum of the heart to allow the blood to mix with spiritus. Blood was not pumped through the body by the heart, but rather ebbed and flowed and was attracted to different organs by their need for nourishment.[8]

However "flawed" this account appears in the wake of subsequent texts by such influential teachers as Andreas Vesalius and William Harvey, Galen's theory of humors and the multiple functions of the heart within that theory are characterized by what Michael Schoenfeldt aptly describes as "seductive coherence" and "experiential suppleness."[9] While the heart has a position of centrality and life-giving instrumentality in this way of thinking about the body and its health, it was clear to the earliest students of anatomy that the brain and spinal column, when functioning properly, also served to direct man's thinking and locomotion, while the liver was believed to "concoct" blood, phlegm, black and yellow bile, thereby nourishing and regulating the body.[10] Broad and carefully refined knowledge of the body's parts was, then, required to guide one through the human body and through the body of physiological writing based on classical authors.

What the ancients had written required and received interpretation. Natural philosophy was not a static body of knowledge, and its language demanded not only translation but elucidation. This branch of knowledge was as much philological and rhetorical as it was "scientific." In 1595 one English redactor arranged *The problems of Aristotle with other philosophers and phisitions ... touching the estate of mans bodie* into a series of what might now be called FAQs or frequently asked questions. The series of twenty-two questions about the heart begins:

Question. *Why are the heart and the lungs called, liuely parts of the body, in Latine* Spiritalia membra?

   Answer. From this word *Spiritus*, which signifieth breath, life, or soule, and because the vitall spirits are ingendred in the heart: but that is no good answer, for so the liuer and the braine might bee so called, which is false: because the liuer is a part which giueth nouriture, and the braine sence and life. And yet the consequence is cleere, because the vitall spirits are ingendered in the liuer, and the sensible or animall spirits in the braine. And therefore the answere is, because that in the heart and in the lungs breath and ayre is receiued, by which we liue.[11]

---

[8] Mary Lindemann, *Medicine and Society in Early Modern Europe* (Cambridge: Cambridge University Press, 1999), 69–70.
[9] Michael C. Schoenfeldt, *Bodies and Selves in Early Modern England: Physiology and Inwardness in Spenser, Shakespeare, Herbert, and Milton* (Cambridge: Cambridge University Press, 1999), 3.
[10] Lindemann, *Medicine and Society*, 69.
[11] *The Problemes of Aristotle* (Edinburgh: R. Waldgrave, 1595), sig. D6ᵛ.

Some explanations, the paraphraser postulates, are less good than others, and the brain and liver from Aristotle's scheme are forced, under heavy pressure from Galenic thinking, to take a back seat to the heart. The liver's "vitall spirits" and the brain's "sensible or animall" ones lack the pure and transcendent power of divine inspiration. Conflating heart and lung functions makes plausible the metaphoric identification of blood and air in the body's passageways, and both brain and liver are permitted to retain their places in this integrated economy of spiritual and physical exchange. As Siraisi explains, the "usual solution" to the problem of dominance among the body's organs "was to introduce a conceptual hierarchy in which the heart ruled the brain in some ultimate or philosophical sense and the brain ruled the nervous system directly."[12] The governing dynamics within the court of the body were as much a part of corporeal rhetoric as were the structure and arrangement of the internal organs. The philosophical or spiritual coherence of the textually constructed body mattered intensely, not only to the ancients but to their early modern revivers. The illusion of life or motion in these textualized bodies relied upon strategically deployed metaphors which functioned much as the animated backgrounds did for anatomical illustrators like Calcar. The "scientific" mindset that distrusts this supporting substratum of metaphor in the anatomies was slow to make its appearance. In Shakespeare's time, poets, artists, and physicians might draw on each other's ideas without having first to traverse the vast desert of suspicion that separates the sciences and humanities in our own time.

Early modern theologians, natural philosophers, and professors of medicine found little reason to reject the rich legacy of systematic thought that posited a brisk exchange of life-giving materials occurring regularly in the heart. Humoral fluids, animal spirits, air, ideas, and feelings were, they asserted, sucked irresistibly into the heart from the extremities of the body and the ambient atmosphere. There they were acted upon and transformed by the characteristic heat of the heart into substances more pure and useful to the entire body. The heart is where the action is, where it all begins and where, eventually, it ends. It is the proactive source of many passions as well as the elastic receptacle of emotions originating elsewhere in the natural world. The heart, then, is a wonder of nature and the human measure of the changeable world in pre-modern as well as early modern discourses of natural philosophy.

---

[12] Nancy G. Siraisi, *Medieval and Early Renaissance Medicine: An Introduction to Knowledge and Practice* (Chicago: University of Chicago Press, 1990), 81–2.

A paradoxical feature of the heart and its functions, recognized from earliest times, is that it is both container and thing contained. It is ingeniously embedded within the human breast, as Vesalius explains at length in Book VI of the *Fabrica*, yet is also the container of visible material, notably blood, and invisible spirits. Its own invisibility, at least under normal circumstances, makes the motions of this rhythmically felt, constantly moving part of the interior body a frequent subject of imaginative representation. The heart appears in early modern verse and prose as fountain, furnace, book, castle, king, food, window on the soul, cesspool, storehouse, and in innumerable other guises. Each of these metaphors carries its own emotional weight, and identifying clusters of heart metaphors and their shifts over time can help to direct our attempts to define the affective power of heart references in changing cultural contexts.[13]

We may well wonder why there was such a multitude of metaphors for the heart, far more than for the liver, spleen, or other internal organs. Poets, natural philosophers, and theologians evidently kept trying to capture in images and analogies the functions of an organ that was largely unknown, though its distinctive shape could be encompassed in one hand. Like other metaphors, those for the heart tended to work only within a restricted area of discourse. They all broke down at some point, the connection between tenor and vehicle becoming increasingly tenuous, especially as more and more contradictory descriptions of the heart's mechanisms and purposes were published during the sixteenth century.

Consider, for example, the "book of the heart" in which biblical prophets and medieval lovers inscribed their faith and love. Such constant and intense feelings are ideal material for inscription in the heart's book, but the act of reading what was written there could come to seem too passive a function for such a vital and ever-moving part of the body. The pages of a book could memorialize religious and erotic fervor, but they could not sustain life in the way that the heart was said to. Other metaphors were needed for that. The heart as furnace, for one, lent biblical sanction to the idea of heat as the first principle of life. Images such as Daniel Cramer's of the heart-shaped retort (Fig. 12) captured the idea of purification by fire but none of the heart's suppleness or its motions. When Shakespeare uses the heart-furnace image, we find him

---

[13] On the history of affect, see the informative collection of essays, *Reading the Early Modern Passions: Essays in the Cultural History of Emotion*, ed. Gail Kern Paster, Katherine Rowe, and Mary Floyd-Wilson (Philadelphia: University of Pennsylvania Press, 2004).

quickly sliding into other, more vitalizing images, as in this passage from an early history play:

> I cannot weep; for all my body's moisture
> Scarce serves to quench my furnace-burning heart;
> Nor can my tongue unload my heart's great burthen,
> For self-same wind that I should speak withal
> Is kindling coals that fires all my breast,
> And burns me up with flames that tears would quench.
>
> (*3 Henry VI* 2.1.79–84)

Richard of Gloucester's elaborate rationale for not crying when he learns of his father's death is dense with Galenic physiology. A single heart image cannot sustain the psychic complexity that Richard strategically projects. The "furnace-burning heart" cannot be separated from the breath that fans the internal fires and the bodily fluids that fail to quench Richard's vengeful rage. His heart is the locus not of moral refinement or of life-sustaining love, but of bitter hatred and dynastic ambition. Wind, water, and fire figure the passionate turmoil that he wants his brother Edward to believe stirs him at this moment. The speech works simultaneously on physiological and metaphoric levels. Humoral dynamics reflect political dynamics in a metaphoric cluster that takes the heart as its center.

Metaphors of the heart often shift restlessly from biological and political processes to the world of humanly crafted objects, many of them architectural structures. The house or castle of the body, healthy or diseased, has as its central support an organ that displays the ingenuity and power of its ultimate designer, God. Defining the precise nature and purpose of such a foundational organ in early modern terms is a daunting task.

As is often the case in pursuing complex matters of definition, accounts of what the heart is *not* can add a good deal to more direct definitional methods. Hearts, for example, do not function like heads or hands. Indeed, prominent patterns of opposition between heart and head, heart and hand emerge so prominently in Western culture as to become proverbial.[14]

---

[14] Morris Palmer Tilley, whose collection of proverbs is by no means exhaustive, records some 270 heart proverbs under 41 different headings, many of them contrasting the virtues of the heart with the defects of other body parts, as for example, the courage of the heart with the cowardice of legs that run away from danger and the loyalty of the heart with the glibness of the tongue. Such sayings testify simultaneously to broadly shared cultural values and to remarkable diversity in the metaphoric application of the heart to everyday experience. See Tilley, *A Dictionary of the Proverbs in England in the Sixteenth and Seventeenth Centuries* (Ann Arbor: University of Michigan Press, 1950), 300–3.

The agonistic nature of the body's parts in early modern literature – the head against the heart, the belly against the big toe – has been explained as the result of the politicization of the body in the Middle Ages. See Jacques Le Goff, "Head or Heart? The Political Use of Body Metaphors in

The head was well established as the seat of rational thought long before the so-called Age of Reason. The post-Enlightenment semiotics of the head involved a crucial split between "brain" and "mind" that had no parallel in the language of the heart. The brain became the organ of analytical thought, while "mind" connoted a far broader range of human perception and agency. Descartes's interchangeable use of "soul" and "mind" encouraged the continued association of spirituality with head-work.[15] Heart-work in the Christian era, while it gradually lost many of its explicit Aristotelian associations with thinking, retained its rich association with the spirituality of the past because of its close association with the human suffering of Christ. As sinful mankind attacked and reviled Christ, piercing His heart and augmenting the most profound exemplum of passion imaginable, so each believer felt himself or herself to be vulnerable to agonizing doubts over the all-important question of individual salvation. The good works of one's intellect were no more efficacious in allaying these uncertainties than were the labors of one's hands. As Pascal explained,

[T]hose to whom God gave religion by the way of the sentiment of the heart are in fact most content and rightfully persuaded. But to those who do not have it, we can only offer it by way of reason, awaiting the time when God may give it to them through the feelings of the heart.[16]

The truth in one's heart for which reason could sometimes serve as a temporary place-holder, was the sole determining criterion for salvation within the theology of *sola fides*.

The doctrine of faith notwithstanding, one's moral stature in the community was measured by the quality of one's actions. The pure heart's virtues were visible through acts of charity performed on behalf of family, friends, and strangers. It was the performance of one's conviction of salvation that was available to be judged by one's peers. Since the heart's primary agent is the hand, one's handiwork was supposed to mirror the heart and soul of the elect. The difficulty was the all-too-frequent disconnection between the motions of the heart and those of the hand. The seeds of a general alienation of human will from manual agency became a prominent feature of early modern literature. A theatrically arresting case of this disconnection is the

---

the Middle Ages," trans. Patricia Ranum, in *Fragments for a History of the Human Body*, ed. Michel Feher, Ramona Naddaff, and Nadia Tazi (New York: Zone Books, 1989), 3: 13–26.

[15] See Scott Manning Stevens's provocative and incisive essay "Sacred Heart and Secular Brain," in *The Body in Parts: Fantasies of Corporeality in Early Modern Europe*, ed. David Hillman and Carla Mazzio (New York: Routledge, 1997), 263–82.

[16] Blaise Pascal, as quoted in Milad Doueihi, *A Perverse History of the Human Heart* (Cambridge, MA: Harvard University Press, 1997), 132.

alien instrumentality of Bosola in Webster's *The Duchess of Malfi* and the severed hand that Ferdinand delivers to his sister. While the Duchess's brothers madly attempt to bend their sister to their wills, to force her, in the words of a 1623 marriage sermon, to be no more than "an iron hand, or a wooden leg" doing only their bidding, her inner resistance frustrates their attempts at control and defines her heroic stature. Her manipulative brother Ferdinand appeals to the specious pall cast over his own heart by the young widow's desire to remarry:

FERDINAND　[T]hou has ta'en that massy sheet of lead
　　　　　　That hid thy husband's bones, and folded it
　　　　　　About my heart.
DUCHESS　　Mine bleeds for't.
FERDINAND　Thine? Thy heart?
　　　　　　What should I name't, unless a hollow bullet
　　　　　　Filled with unquenchable wild-fire?[17]

The icy, lead-shrouded heart denies the pitiful, bleeding heart, constructing it as a hollow cannonball filled with explosive, destructive passions.[18] But if the heart can be constructed as the seat of explosive affections, it can also be the quiet place of truth that survives apart from the turmoil and corruption of the world. The Duchess's calm dignity in the face of her corrupt brothers allows her to take action to satisfy the private desires of her heart through her secret marriage. While Ferdinand's mad dissimulations challenge the conventional assumption that the human will forges honest links between intention and action, the tenacity of the Duchess in her pursuit of marital and domestic happiness confirms the truth in her heart. Some anatomists in the period postulated the existence of a nerve extending from the heart to the fourth finger on the left hand, symbolizing the intimate affective bond between the loving heart and the part of the hand that wears the public token of marital fidelity, the wedding-ring. Later cultures, by contrast, have tended to gravitate toward the idea of a mental disjunction between human desires and actions. The matter of linking head and hand to heart as the instruments for conceiving and enacting the will was not at all settled in the early modern period, as the following examples, drawn from a pair of seventeenth-century

---

[17] John Webster, *The Duchess of Malfi*, ed. Brian Gibbons, New Mermaids, 4th edn. (New York: Norton, 2001), 3.2.112–16.

[18] Gail Kern Paster locates the source of Ferdinand's anti-social, indeed anti-human, urges in a humors-based conception of what it means to share species-continuing impulses with other people and other animals. His lycanthropic inversion of the wolf's body (he is smooth on the outside, hairy on the inside) denies the human warmth that would support the Duchess's desire for companionate marriage and progeny. See Paster, *Humoring the Body: Emotions and the Shakespearean Stage* (Chicago: University of Chicago Press, 2004), 160–4.

poets of the body and an influential theologian, will show. For them, the motions and affections of the sick or hardened heart were as likely to result in conflict as in truth.

One of the most remarkably sustained translations of early modern physiology into poetry is Phineas Fletcher's *The Purple Island* (1633). The interior conflicts depicted in the poem are played out in explicitly political terms, and the motions of the body are cast in the format of the popular travel literature of the day. The poet develops the extended conceit of exploring a remote, exotic place whose geographical details correspond with the anatomy of a person. The poetic text is typographically paralleled by a set of marginal annotations, alphabetically keyed to terms in the seven-line stanzas that name each anatomical part and explain its appearance and function within the political economy of the body. The traveling narrator, having just departed from "the Arch-citie *Hepar*" (the liver), visits the city of Kerdia, or the heart, before pushing on to "Head-citie." In Kerdia he discovers a palace that generates heat for the entire body-nation, so much heat that were it not for the cold wind rushing in from the nearby hills (that is, the lungs), the entire place would be consumed in fire.

> Within this Citie is the palace fram'd,
> Where life, and lifes companion, heat, abideth;
> And their attendants, passions untam'd:
> (Oft very hell in this strait room resideth)
> And did not neighbouring hills, cold aires inspiring,
> Allay their rage and mutinous conspiring,
> Heat all (it self and all) would burn with quenchlese firing.[19]

The sidenote informs us that "The Heart is the fountain of life and heat to the whole bodie, and the seat of passions." In Fletcher's account, those passions, like the furnace in which they reside, require cooling down through self-discipline. In this the heart differs from the liver, which is able to contain and control its own energies. The heart is not simply another stop along a well-regulated route through the interior canal; it is a high-risk location in all of us. While Fletcher doesn't quite have the physiology of the heart right (he perpetuates the Galenic notion of a porous wall between the halves of the heart and the idea that air is conducted directly into the heart), he perceptively incorporates both emotional and physical states into his own fictional geography. The dynamic that regulates the heart in the

---

[19] Phineas Fletcher, *The Purple Island*, Canto 4, Stanza 25, in *The Poetical Works*, ed. Frederick S. Boas (Cambridge: Cambridge University Press, 1909), 2: 50.

purple interior land of the body is what he calls "government," and its seat
is the heart.

> In middle of this middle Regiment
> *Kerdia* seated lies, the centre deem'd
> Of this whole Isle, and of this government:
> If not the chiefest this, yet needfull'st seem'd,
> Therefore obtain'd an equall distant seat,
> More fitly hence to shed his life and heat,
> And with his yellow streams the fruitfull Island wet.[20]

What keeps the island from being a blazing desert, as Fletcher's note
explains, is the presence in the pericardium of "an humour like whey or
urine, as well to cool the heart as to lighten the body." The metaphor of
climate within the body, especially the desirability of temperate climate,
shows a complex and subtle understanding of the body's mechanisms for
dealing with not only disease but also emotional turbulence or internal
conflict.[21] Such regulation was widely recognized as crucial to religious
exercise as well as to personal feelings of love and hate. Indeed, the entire
well-being of those who have experienced turmoil in what Francis
Anthony calls "the Emperie of the Heart in mans bodie" requires careful
attention to their spiritual health: "the first office of euerie good Physition
is, to haue speciall regarde, to maintaine and vphold the spirituall
functions of his diseased patient, which all haue their originall from the
heart."[22] Moderate Protestants in the 1630s were anxious to control
religious enthusiasm in an increasingly vocal set of radical sects. The
physical as well as spiritual excesses of the Diggers, Anabaptists, and
Family of Love, among others, were threatening the balance of the
Church of England. Moderating the affections of the individual heart
afforded the surest way to guard the authority of the collective church as
well as the health of the individual body.[23]

Secular authority, too, was represented metaphorically as subject to the
motions and affections of the heart, notably in John Davies of Hereford's

---

[20] Fletcher, *The Purple Island*, Canto 4, Stanza 15, 2: 48.
[21] Timothy Hampton, "Strange Alteration: Physiology and Psychology from Galen to Rabelais," in
Reading the Early Modern Passions, 272–93. Also see Schoenfeldt, *Bodies and Selves in Early Modern
England*, 2–12, on humoral regulation and balance and Jonathan Sawday's fine analysis of *The
Purple Island* in *The Body Emblazoned: Dissection and the Human Body in Renaissance Culture*
(London: Routledge, 1995), 170–82.
[22] Francis Anthony, *An Apologie, or defence of . . . a medicine called arum potable . . . for the
strengthning* [sic]*of the heart* (London: J. Leggatt, 1616), 7–8.
[23] On the ubiquity and impact of these sects see Paul Christianson, *Reformers and Babylon: English
Apocalyptic Visions from the Reformation to the Eve of the Civil War* (Toronto: University of
Toronto Press, 1978).

Microcosmos: The Discovery of the Little World, with the government thereof
(1603). Extended comparisons of the human body and the macrocosm were
commonplace in the early seventeenth century, which is to say, they were
generally accepted as true representations of the unity of physiological, civil,
and cosmological governance. The current critical habit of viewing whatever
is "commonplace" as dull and, hence, unresponsive to the immediate cultural
environment has resulted in poets like Davies being seriously underestimated
as chroniclers of their times.[24] Davies is careful to observe continuities,
despite variations in scale, across the political continuum from king to
subject. From Davies's perspective, the change of monarchs in England
called for a calming influence on the passions of the individual hearts of
Englishmen as reflected in the careful regulation of the King himself.

> The *Hart* with *Passion*, passion may each *part*,
> Which *Ioy* or *Sorrowe* with the *Hart* abides:
> So, *Kinges* their praise and *People* may subvert,
> If *Passion* over-rule their ruling *Art*.[25]

The poet's rhetoric of reiteration presents the disconcerting possibility
that the royal art of regulation may be "over-rule[d]" in a heart unable to
control its affects. But the new king's conviction of a divine corrective is
also available in Davies's account of the political economy of the heart.

> That *God*, whose powre no *power* can resist,
> Resists all *powers* that are too violent,
> And ever doth the *moderate* assist. (57)

The basic instincts of the heart, according to the poet, seek the virtuous, but
when it has been hoodwinked by sin, sometimes "From this desire of *Good*,
th' *affections* flie" (58). At this point in his poetic narrative of the body,
Davies's physical heart has taken on the functions of the soul: "The motiues
of the *Soule* these *motions* are, / Whose other names are called the *Affects*"
(59). In short, "The *Hartes affects*, produce the *Heades effects*, / Which make

---

[24] In his quest for Elizabethan accounts of a systematically ordered universe in *The Elizabethan World Picture*, E. M. W. Tillyard made a great deal of Davies's poem *Orchestra*, though his work has been decidedly out of favor for decades now. My claims on Davies's behalf are based not on innovative style or philosophical profundity but on the habit of seventeenth-century English poets of seeing macrocosmic effects rooted in microcosmic affects. On the proportional and analogical as aspects of later seventeenth-century thought, see Lisa Jardine, *Ingenious Pursuits: Building the Scientific Revolution* (New York: Doubleday, 1999). Jardine comments perceptively on the growing fascination with the telescope and microscope as instruments that brought into focus, metaphorically as well as literally, the very large and the very small. Her brief section "Autopsy – seeing with your own eyes" (110–13) considers Harvey's observations of the heart.

[25] Sir John Davies, *Microcosmos: The Discovery of the Little World, with the government thereof* (Oxford: J. Barnes, 1603), 54. Subsequent references will appear parenthetically.

the *Soule* and *Bodies* concordance" (78). Affective concord is the end toward which the properly moderated body is directed. This entails aligning one's emotions or felt motives with the physical motions of the body's organs and members.

It may at first seem odd that for Davies and other heroic poets such as Fletcher and Du Bartas the most congenial system for linking the noble actions of the body with the elevated intentions of the mind was a modified version of Galenic humors theory. In that system, appropriate regimens of diet, sleep, excretion, and exercise prepared the body to generate and process the four humors for maximum "concordance," in Davies's term, of soul and body. The motions of the heart were understood to be synchronized with both "the *Heades effects*" and with the digestive and evacuative functions of the "lower" body. This hardly seems to us the stuff of epic poetry, but the particular confluence of the physiological and the poetic makes a good deal of sense when we recall that the greatest challenge for the epic hero, from Odysseus onward, is to govern and discipline his own passions. Threats from without are minor by comparison.

When self-government is lacking and the passions rule, even in the case of the head of state, only divine integration of body and soul will save us, as John Calvin makes clear in his *Institutes* and *Commentaries*. The motions of the body tend ultimately toward corruption, and the affections are vulnerable to excesses that defy moral reason. According to Calvin, the heart whose passions run unchecked becomes a secret hiding place of vanities and falsehoods.[26] Such a hard and overcharged heart must be knocked to pieces and then reconstructed by the gathering action of God, according to Calvin's commentary on the phrase that he renders "unite my heart to fear thy name" (Ps. 86: 11):

[I]n the word *unite*, there is a very beautiful metaphor, conveying the idea, that the heart of man is full of tumult, drawn asunder, and, as it were, scattered about in fragments, until God has gathered it to himself, and holds it together in a state of stedfast and persevering obedience ... [U]prightness of heart is entirely the gift of God.[27]

The metaphor he notes in this passage is the same one that Cynthia Marshall explores in her book *The Shattering of the Self*.[28] Marshall argues

[26] John Calvin, *Institutes of the Christian Religion*, ed. John T. McNeill, trans. Ford Lewis Battles (Philadelphia: Westminster Press, 1960), 1: 554.

[27] John Calvin, *Commentaries (Commentary on the Book of Psalms)*, trans. Rev. James Anderson (Edinburgh: Calvin Translation Society, 1847), 3: 388.

[28] Cynthia Marshall, *The Shattering of the Self: Violence, Subjectivity, and Early Modern Texts* (Baltimore: The Johns Hopkins University Press, 2002).

that what early modern thinkers discovered was not a stable and integrated self available to all people but rather a radically *dis*integrated identity encountering a world of fluctuation and contradiction. Marshall's thesis is a useful corrective to some recent studies of the early modern self. From the insistent early modern rhetoric of the need for controlled and ordered self-assessment we may infer a generally felt experience of its opposite, namely instability and disorientation – a perception, that is, of emotional chaos that never quite achieves the goal of settled integrity.

The shattering and scattering of the soul finds an instructive analogy in the willful rebellion of body parts.[29] Like many preachers and teachers in the period, Calvin is especially distressed by the disjunction between tongue and heart, rhetorical posture and genuine faith. In the *Institutes* he denounces as Sophists those who speak contrary to their true affections.

[W]e detest these trifling Sophists who are content to roll the gospel on the tips of their tongues when its efficacy ought to penetrate the inmost affections of the heart, take its seat in the soul, and affect the whole man a hundred times more deeply than the cold exhortations of the philosophers![30]

"Affection" in this context is a far more profound experience than mere passing emotional attraction. The integrity of the Christian heart has, in Calvin's view, been too often undermined by the glibness of the ancients.[31] As Calvin repeatedly reworks the concept of the unified heart, we can see that he wishes to read the body as an instrument for interpreting the

---

[29] One is reminded of Menenius's famous fable that begins, "There was a time when all the body's members / Rebell'd against the belly" (*Coriolanus* 1.1.96–146), a tale rehearsed by Plutarch, Livy, Averell, Spenser, Sidney, Camden, Paracelsus, Boyle, and others. Hillary M. Nunn contrasts Shakespeare's tragic application of the Fable of the Belly to the far more positive moral of "social stratification" drawn in Helkiah Crooke's application of the fable in *Mikrokosmographia*. See Nunn's *Staging Anatomies: Dissection and Spectacle in Early Stuart Tragedy* (Aldershot: Ashgate, 2005), 41–8.

As John Rogers has shown, subsequent political theorists were forced to acknowledge that oligarchic societies suppress the fact that centralized authorities, like the belly, are not agents of production. In the middle of the seventeenth century, the model of William Harvey's theory of blood circulation was readily adaptable to a liberal economic system of material circulation without interference from the Crown. See Rogers, *The Matter of Revolution: Science, Poetry, and Politics in the Age of Milton* (Ithaca: Cornell University Press, 1996), 24–7.

[30] Calvin, *Institutes*, 1: 688.

[31] Calvin explains in his commentary on St. John that "*The* heart is sometimes in Scripture put for the seat of the affections; but here, as in many other passages, it denotes what is called the intellectual part of the soul." See *Commentaries (Commentary on the Gospel According to John)*, 2 vols., trans. Rev. William Pringle (Edinburgh: Calvin Translation Society, 1847), 2: 43.

The passage he is addressing reads: "He hathe blinded their eyes, and hardened their heart, that they shulde not se with *their* eyes, nor vnderstand with *their* heart, and shulde be conuerted, & I shulde heale them" (John 12: 40).

gospels. In glossing St. Paul's injunction "to increase and abound in love one toward another ... [t]o the end [that the Lord] may stablish your hearts unblameable in holiness before God" (1 Thess. 3: 112–13), he moves directly into the language of moral philosophy: "He [i.e. St. Paul] employs the term *hearts* here to mean *conscience*, or the innermost part of the soul."[32] At this stage in the history of the conscience, the term is still associated with social cooperation, with loving one another and integrating the loving self with the community of Christ on earth. The strong belief that all Christians have a conscience capable of drawing the same truths from God's eternal laws bound the community of the faithful together. By the middle of the seventeenth century in England, however, the term "conscience" would become associated with individual isolation as people sought rationales for distancing themselves from the monarch and the state church. The heart, still the repository of moral principles and love of God and one's fellows, in the highly dangerous political world of mid-century England, would become the inviolable inner preserve into which the authorities were barred from inquiring.[33]

Preaching in the Puritan stronghold of Beverley in 1642, John Shawe defends the integrity and inviolability of the inner person, the spirit located in the heart and functioning as the conscience:

[M]an consists of two essentiall parts (or in Scripture phrase, two men, inward man and outward man) body and soule, inside and outside; now the soule (or inside) according to its severall relations or Offices is called by severall names; from its nature is called a spirit, from its principall seate, the heart; from its enlivening the body, the soule; from one maine Office, the conscience; yet one and the same soule: as one man is both Father, Master, Husband yet the same Man: for I take not the spirit, for the purer and more spirituall part of the soule, *viz.* The

---

[32] Calvin, *Commentaries (Commentaries on the Epistles of Paul the Apostle to the Philippians, Colossians, and Thessalonians)*, trans. Rev. John Pringle (Edinburgh: Calvin Translation Society, 1851), 271. Calvin's association of the heart with the conscience was, as Scott Manning Stevens notes, a commonplace of early modern Christian discourse. The source of the Good "was not perceived by the intellect but, rather, by the conscience, which was thought to reside in the heart," and unlike Platonic/Galenic systems in which "the heart was considered to be the seat of the passions and hence the site of our affective sensibilities . . . Christianity brought to it the perceptive abilities of the conscience . . . This in effect allowed the heart to 'know' things in a way that the brain could not" (Stevens, "Sacred Heart and Secular Brain," 271).

[33] I owe this account of the historical change in the notion of conscience during the period in question to conversations with Camille Wells Slights. Studying the impact of covenant theology in the seventeenth century, Victoria Kahn points to "voluntary subjection" to God through the affections of the heart as a central theological concept in defining the relation of conscience to social action. See the section "The Law of the Heart" in her book *Wayward Contracts: The Crisis of Political Obligation in England, 1640–1674* (Princeton: Princeton University Press, 2004), 64–73.

understanding, and the heart for the lower part or affections, as some are pleased to speak.[34]

Shawe rejects the hierarchical arrangement that assigns only the "lower part or affections" to the heart, allowing it a central part in spiritual understanding and moral decision-making. So long as the heart remains soft and supple, it will sustain the wayfaring Christian. In a witty turn, Shawe appropriates the rhetoric of revolutionary warfare to his own preaching goals. Answering his own question, "How may we keep our hearts soft?" he pretends not to understand the language of the revolutionary tracts that were flooding the bookstalls and churches:

There are foure things much talked of now adaies, which in the sense they are spoken I much understand not, *viz.* Malignant parties. 2. Posture of defence. 3. Ordering of the Militia. 4. Trayning. But in a spirituall sense to keepe thy heart soft, take them thus:

1. Kill, and be daily opposing that malignant party, I meane thy lusts . . .
2. Get thy soule into a posture of defence, into the Rock Christ, the onely true defence . . .
3. Order the Militia, get up thy spirituall armor . . .
4. Train or exercise (but I mean) S. *Pauls* exercise daily . . . (*A Broken Heart*, 35)

Only by transforming the strategies of the war, then, can the individual Christian protect the integrity of the heart.

Rightness of conscience and soundness of heart can never be taken for granted, given the conflicting truths perpetually present in the heart. Treatises on the doubting conscience and the hardened heart were stock-in-trade for English publishers. Such English casuists as William Perkins, William Ames, Robert Sanderson, Jeremy Taylor, Thomas Barlow, and Richard Baxter explore the joint work of heart and mind, reconciling human desire with divine law, not just in a few but in all actions.[35] The bulk of their cases of conscience and instruction on how to address difficult cases deals not with peaceful or "right" consciences acting in harmony with divine command-ments but rather with erring, scrupulous, and doubting consciences. The most challenging cases of all are those raised by men who knowingly sin but then convince themselves in their wayward hearts that self-justification is just one tortured argument away, men like Shakespeare's Duke Angelo and King

---

[34] John Shawe, *A Broken Heart, or the Grand Sacrifice. As it was laid ovt in a sermon preached at St. Maries in Beverley . . . 1642* (London: s.n., 1643), 14. Subsequent references will appear parenthetically.

[35] See Camille Wells Slights, *The Casuistical Tradition in Shakespeare, Donne, Herbert, and Milton* (Princeton: Princeton University Press, 1981).

Claudius. They adamantly deny the wisdom of Solomon, cited by Jeremy Taylor in *Ductor Dubitantium: or the Rule of Conscience*: "It is safer to walk on plain ground, than with tricks and devices to dance upon the ropes."[36] The heart has its ways not only in love but in hateful self-delusion.

In England, poets joined the Protestant theologians in revising and consolidating earlier views of the heart that formed the basis of their knowledge of interior experience, the motions and affections that constituted the awareness of self. They devised an array of terms that would shape and communicate encounters with the self, especially the self in love, for the next hundred years. No poet did this more successfully than Shakespeare.

Shakespeare was fully aware that scrutinizing and catechizing the heart had traditionally been a major preoccupation of the love poet, most notably cast in the Italian verse form of the sonnet. His own Sonnet 62, "Sin of self-love possesseth all mine eye," shows us the poet turning inward to test his own affections and self-perceptions against a more profound, conflicting reality that is "grounded inward in [his] heart." It is a poem about self-correction and about blurring inner/outer boundaries by rash acts of identity assertion. In this case a lover asserts the identity of his inner self with that of his beloved, thereby creating a hugely inflated ego. This philosophically and physiologically complicated move is "grounded" in his heart, where love and self conjoin as "self-love." The feelings that flourish in this ground – in the heart's rich soil – may either be purely self-regarding, or they may extend to embrace a radically transformative Other. The question we are left with after the couplet's assertion of the identity of self and beloved is whether what we have been witnessing is genuine profundity or witty sophistry.

> Sin of self-love possesseth all mine eye,
> And all my soul, and all my every part;
> And for this sin there is no remedy,
> It is so grounded inward in my heart.   4
> Methinks no face so gracious is as mine,
> No shape so true, no truth of such account,
> And for myself mine own worth do define,
> As I all other in all worths surmount.   8
> But when my glass shows me myself indeed,
> Beated and chopp'd with tann'd antiquity,
> Mine own self-love quite contrary I read;
> Self so self-loving were iniquity.   12

---

[36] *The Whole Works of the Right Rev. Jeremy Taylor*, ed. Reginald Heber (London, 1828), II: 422.

> 'Tis thee (myself) that for myself I praise,
> Painting my age with beauty of thy days.

What begins as the sin of self-love, rooted firmly in the heart, ends as praise of the youthful beloved, enabled by a "contrary" reading of the signs of sin and of the poem itself. The final breakthrough is both religious and amorous, with the sonnet form itself forging a realignment of inner and outer selves.

Helen Vendler identifies "self" as the sonnet's "Key Word," and cites the Prayer Book's "grafted inwardly in our hearts" and the biblical "Thou shalt love the Lord thy God with all thy heart, and with all thy soul, and with all thy mind" (Matt. 22: 37) as functioning intertexts.[37] The speaker's assertions of divine supremacy are denied by the sin that *appears* to be dominating "all mine eye . . . and all my every part" (perhaps punning on eye/I) in the first quatrain. What apparently is required to redeem the possessed speaker is nothing less than an exorcism to root out the devil so firmly, if not irremediably, "grounded inward in my heart." The sin of pride reverberates through the second quatrain's assertion that "I all other in all worths surmount." Ironically, an outward sign – the speaker's image in a looking-glass – is able to dislodge the inner conviction of sin with a "contrary" reading of the situation. The speaker confesses that his reflected self is not beautiful but instead "Beated and chopp'd" (weather-beaten and chapped with age), and he narrowly avoids the "iniquity" of self-love. Although, as Stephen Booth acknowledges, the grammatical sense of the poem's self-correcting conclusion "cannot be precisely glossed,"[38] the parenthetical juxtaposition of beloved and lover – "thee (myself)" – stands for a perception of identity that transfers the epideictic thrust of the poem from aging poet to youthful friend: " 'Tis thee (myself) that for myself I praise, / Painting my age with beauty of thy days." It's not so much that the exorcism or cleansing of the heart has been achieved as that it wasn't finally needed, once the self had been correctly, that is contrarily, "read." A number of serious critics of the Sonnets, among them Philip Martin, have not been moved to accept the sudden redefinition of self-love as true love at the end of Sonnet 62:

The couplet does, I think, feel a bit glib, and on its own lacks the resources needed to give enough imaginative force to the idea that the beloved is a second

---

[37] Helen Vendler, *The Art of Shakespeare's Sonnets* (Cambridge, MA: Harvard University Press, 1997), 293. I am convinced that there is much to be gained by reintroducing sacred thinking into the aggressively secular readings that have dominated recent interpretations of the Sonnets.
[38] Stephen Booth, *Shakespeare's Sonnets* (New Haven: Yale University Press, 1977), 243.

self . . . Does Shakespeare intend the weakness of the couplet: is he deliberately showing the lover's comforting self-delusion or is he falling into it himself? I am inclined to think the latter. The way out of the poet's predicament is proffered in too smooth and facile a manner.[39]

I would agree that Martin's rejected proposition (that the speaker is being caught out and exposed as self-delusional – like T. S. Eliot's Othello *"cheering himself up"*[40]) is not convincing. That level of unawareness simply isn't compatible with the "I" of the Sonnets. Nor, however, do we need to follow Martin in accusing Shakespeare of deceiving himself with "facile" rationalizations in an attempt to avert a genuine moment of self-discovery.

A more plausible explanation of the couplet of Sonnet 62 involves the speaker's honest confrontation with an idealized image of his beloved into which he himself can grow. The growth may entail moments such as this, when one is caught out in the act of self-regard by the internalized other who sees and judges one's behavior, but the result, as Lars Engle has argued, provides a way to avoid "paralyzing guilt" and indicates instead a kind of moral enrichment based on a keen awareness of the larger community. As Engle concludes about another of Shakespeare's "shame" sonnets (number 122), "Such an internalized other helps constitute the idiosyncratic, self-exploratory, resistant interiority Shakespeare . . . claims as a necessary resource not only for the just pleasure of persons but for the general social good."[41]

Reading the language of the heart is never easy, and the heart in love is especially difficult to decipher. Exposing the temptation to "paint" the body and all its parts in the colors of another's youthful beauty, mistaking subject for object, is painful even when successful. As Booth and Vendler suggest, the object of praise turns out to be not quite the speaker himself "but rather the young-man-in-himself, a cosmeticized inner self, painted with the young man's beauty."[42] To this rereading or contrary reading I would add that the all-important container and transformer of this layered self is the heart, the organ of affection and truth. Only in the act of scrutinizing the heart can the self peel aside the layers of self-assurance that have been hiding the truth from view.

---

[39] Philip Martin, *Shakespeare's Sonnets: Self, Love and Art* (Cambridge: Cambridge University Press, 1972), 48.

[40] T. S. Eliot, *Selected Essays* (New York: Harcourt, Brace, 1950), 111.

[41] Lars Engle, " 'I am that I am': Shakespeare's Sonnets and the Economy of Shame," in *Shakespeare's Sonnets: Critical Essays*, ed. James Schiffer (New York: Garland, 1999), 185–98, quotation from p. 196.

[42] Vendler, *The Art of Shakespeare's Sonnets*, 294.

The self-reflexive, self-corrective exercise I have been tracing in Sonnet 62 is a persistent theme of the Reformation, and Shakespeare put it to work repeatedly – in *The Rape of Lucrece*, in the Sonnets, in *Hamlet*. His characters seem so alive partly because they consciously arrange themselves on a scale that extends from nearly total self-assurance to abject self-abnegation. The dramatized experience of characters observing and evaluating themselves in the process of engaging with the world constitutes much of the humanity of the poems and plays. Not just major tragic figures such as Hamlet and Lear exhibit this penetrating kind of self-awareness. At the beginning of Act 3 of *All's Well That Ends Well*, a French lord, designated only as the second of two, responds with finely tuned modesty to the Duke of Florence's request for an interpretation of the French king's refusal to support the ongoing Florentine war:

> Good my lord,
> The reasons of our state I cannot yield
> But like a common and an outward man
> That the great figure of a council frames
> By self-unable motion, therefore dare not
> Say what I think of it, since I have found
> Myself in my incertain grounds to fail
> As often as I guess'd. (*All's Well* 3.1.9–16)

The most arresting phrase in his answer to the Duke is "self-unable motion," which modern editors understandably find challenging to gloss.

Is the lord referring to "his own inadequate conjectures (*motion* = motion of the mind, thought)" as the Riverside editor says, or is he explaining his demur "by analogy of individual, and hence insufficient, motives," as the Arden 2 editor suggests?[43] The idea is particularly complicated because it invokes, in highly compressed form, an entire physiological conception of how the self functions, or fails to function. A single person, the Second Lord says, cannot comprehend within himself the complexities of a decision framed by an entire council. The endeavor would be overwhelming, as it nearly was for Shakespeare's most "unable" private man thrust into public life, Vice-Duke Angelo in *Measure for Measure*. Faced with an emotional crisis in his first private meeting with the attractive novice Isabella, Angelo, speaking in soliloquy, explains the internal motions that render his heart "unable for itself."

---

[43] The editors in question are, respectively, G. Blakemore Evans and G. K. Hunter.

> Why does my blood thus muster to my heart,
> Making both it unable for itself,
> And dispossessing all my other parts
> Of necessary fitness?
> So play the foolish throngs with one that swounds,
> Come all to help him, and so stop the air
> By which he should revive; and even so
> The general subject to a well-wish'd king
> Quit their own part, and in obsequious fondness
> Crowd to his presence, where their untaught love
> Must needs appear offense. (*Measure for Measure* 2.4.20–30)[44]

Angelo's heart, like Hermione's in *The Winter's Tale* (3.2.150) is "o'ercharg'd" with a humoral influx caused, in this case (though certainly not in Hermione's) by overweening lust. The overloading of the heart reflects the full spectrum of moral response, from Angelo's uncontrolled desire for the virginal novice Isabella to the mortified sexual virtue of the royal mother in *The Winter's Tale*. Nor are sexual passion and its complications the only emotional stimuli that regularly overwhelm the heart. The violent "motions" of the heart provide a measure of all aspects of human vulnerability, as Thomas Wright explains in *The Passions of the Minde in Generall*:

> [F]or what other reason, in feare and anger become men so pale and wanne, but that the blood runneth to the heart, to succour it? ... [W]hat causeth their motions to the heart; they themselves, as it were, flie vnto the heart? ... I answere, that (in mine opinion) the partes from whence these humours come, vse their expulsive vertue, sending the spirites choler, or blood, to serve the heart in such necessity ... [T]he heart also affected a little with the passion, draweth more humors, & so encreaseth.[45]

While there is undeniable power within the heart-centered self, there is also potentially overpowering vulnerability. Shakespeare was as much aware of this dichotomy as were the Church Fathers, reformers such as Calvin and Luther, and other, more directly analogical poets such as Davies and Fletcher.

Looking into the heart became the dominant paradigm for the meditative act of self-scrutiny in the early modern period. What was revealed in the profoundest of these meditations was the heart discovering how it knew

---

[44] The local referent of these lines may be King James's terror of crowds, as many editors explain, but the urge to repel curious gawkers is certainly familiar to anyone who has used, or even heard, the standard phrase, "Stand back. Give him air."

[45] Thomas Wright, *The Passions of the Minde in Generall* (London: V. Simmes, 1604), 33–4 and 36.

what it knew. For all the current clamor about Shakespeare's residual Roman Catholicism, there is little compelling evidence in his poems and plays that his habits of mind in writing fictions draw their strength from the intercessions of priests, the Church Fathers, the Virgin Mary, or the saints. His work is just as likely to reflect the introspective turn of mind employed by the Reformers to locate the self within the sufferings and triumphs recorded in the Psalms and parables. He more often explores the deep space of the self than the chronologically protracted history of the Roman Catholic tradition. The acts of self-reflection that characterize his dramatic as well as his lyric output place philosophy at the service of poetry. Recounting the motives of love in Sonnet 62, Shakespeare recognizes that the mistaken self-perception is as valuable to share as the revised, improved one: if we learn anything from Shakespeare's aggregated works, it is that self-knowledge, like being in love or anatomizing the body, is a work-in-progress with no settled conclusions taking the day. The sonneteer and playwright is as much a part of this ongoing process as is the explorer in John Davies of Hereford's *Microcosmos*, the cartographer of Fletcher's *Purple Island*, or the soul-prober of Calvin's *Commentaries*. Each of these writers is working in philosophical as well as narrative modes. Each at some point finds the heart the most compelling place to locate affect and thought as they pursue abstract truths through personal experiences of loss and reclamation. Perhaps Shakespeare is the best equipped of the trio of English poets I have been examining to embrace the self-mortification at the heart of Calvin's convictions, but his sonnets also move beyond the corrosive effects of perceived error. His program is Sidney's: "Fool, look in thy heart and write."

Viewing one's own heart was not only difficult in a literal way that did not escape the notice of early modern poets, it was fatal. Traitors were made to gaze upon their own corrupt hearts, yanked from their breasts by the executioner, but the next moment, they were dead. Dante, as we will see in Chapter 4, experiences a kind of spiritual death and rebirth as he watches, transfixed in his dream, while the naked figure of his beloved Beatrice feasts on his heart. The moment in the *Vita Nuova* is absolutely terrifying. It is as much an image of cannibalism as of adoration. Seeing the heart outside the body is possible only because this is a dream, but the dream is a disturbing mix of nightmare and prophecy of one of the world's great loves. Terror and ecstasy are figured in the fusion of early modern anatomy and amatory symbolism.

When we try to assess just what all the thinking and writing about the heart contributed to early modern culture, we see immediately that the organ could never exist apart from the prevailing systems of thought that alone made sense of this crucial, invisible, and unregulatable part of the body. Chief among these systems of thought were the philosophical, physiological, anatomical, theological, political, and poetic. Philosophers from Aristotle to Hobbes found in the heart the origins of human-ness and human society. Not only animal heat but also the ability to make moral discriminations and to feel affections for one's fellows were viewed as functions of the heart. The physiological systems developed by Galen, perpetuated and refined by physicians throughout the Middle Ages, and radically transformed by the followers of Paracelsus in early modern England arranged patterns of humoral transfer and balance around the heart. These systems relied not on the electrical pulses measured by an ECG or systolic-diastolic motions of the heart or even the circular movement of the blood caused by cardiovascular propulsion in Harvey's model, but rather they depended on the vital attractive force that moved blood and *spiritus* into the center of the body. The anatomists of sixteenth-century Europe, men like Vesalius working in Padua, Berengario in Bologna, and Banister in London, opened this system to view and enabled the correction of false hypotheses about how the inner mechanisms of the body function. These revisions in turn affected the way that love poets and religious thinkers conceived of the interior self.

The carefully recorded proto-scientific and poetic activity that I have been reviewing did not end but rather redirected and reinvigorated the tradition of heart-based metaphors that began with the Bible. Revamped metaphors and renewed physiological observations flowed into a discourse of the inner self that has been treated as the purview of spiritual biographers. The most influential of the Church Fathers, Augustine of Hippo, is generally credited with instituting a highly textual conception of human consciousness in *The Confessions*. He distinguishes between the external body and the inner person, whose moral history is inscribed in the heart.[46] Protestant thinkers embraced both the inner/outer distinction and the notion of divine inscription in the heart. At the time of the Reformation, Luther was largely responsible for rescuing the heart from the Protestant iconophobes by making it the conceptual repository of the image of Christ in the faithful, while Calvin made the heart the active agent in sinful man's suffering and repentance. In Calvinist theology, the sinner's heart is broken and scattered in acts of transgression, then made whole again by God. The notion of internalizing the Word of God and the City of God achieved its doctrinal shape in the writings of Augustine and a quite

---

[46] See Eric Jager, *The Book of the Heart* (Chicago: University of Chicago Press, 2000), 27–43.

different shape in the New World settlements and congregations of English Puritans, but its polity was consistently modeled on the relationship of the heart to the body. William Harvey's methodology as well as his model for the circulation of the blood helped to shape political philosophy in the later seventeenth century through the work of Thomas Hobbes and others.[47] Finally, the metaphoric uses of the heart expanded well beyond its medical, theological, and political applications into the narratives constructed by the poets and playwrights of the period. These narratives form the subject of the next chapter.

[47] On the political applications of Harvey's scientific theory see I. Bernard Cohen, "Harrington and Harvey: A Theory of the State Based on the New Physiology," *Journal of the History of Ideas* 55 (1994): 187–210. The use of such organicist political metaphors in England dates back at least as far as John of Salisbury (1159), according to Jacques Le Goff's essay "Head or Heart?" (17).

CHAPTER 4

The narrative heart of the Renaissance

It is extraordinarily difficult to imagine living in an age whose strategies for coping with the vagaries of the human body were so different from our own. Heart transplants and quadruple bypasses were unimaginable to people living in Renaissance England, people who had only the most rudimentary grasp of preventive medicine, corrective surgery, epidemiology, and biochemistry. Although much had been written about various parts of the body – notably, for my purposes, the heart – there was little diagnostic consistency and still less agreement about remedies when something went wrong. When Renaissance anatomists began to revive and extend the ancients' protocols for dissecting the human body, when natural philosophers began to reconceive the systemic functions of our internal organs, and when Protestant theologians began to redefine the heart as a locus for spiritual inwardness, society had to undergo a series of profound mental and cultural adjustments. These adjusted conceptions and circumstances were amply reflected in the prominent positioning of the heart in English Renaissance narratives. Only by reconstructing a fine web of theological, anatomical, philosophical, political, and poetic systems of thinking can we hope to gain a true sense of the contributions of the heart narrative to early modern knowledge culture.

Often enough the heart had its own story to tell about the experience of being human in a proto-scientific age. As we have seen in previous chapters, those stories were solidly grounded in the legacy of ancient philosophers, medieval artists, and Renaissance medical practitioners, but they went far beyond these beginnings to register the collective trauma of an age increasingly dedicated to anatomizing the human body and the mysteries of the heart. The impact of the anatomical Renaissance on the narrative discourses of the period was often terrifying, though there were also sustaining comforts to be found in the heart stories of the past. To become familiar with these narratives and their distinctively Renaissance retellings is to understand something of what it meant to have a heart – that is, to be human – in a world increasingly perturbed by the advent of modern medical science.

Renaissance England inherited a distinguished classical tradition of representing the heart as the mainspring of life and nature's best evidence that the gods had lavished all their care on humankind. The most influential texts of natural philosophy all single out the heart for special comment.[1] For Plato the heart was the source of life-producing heat and passion, and its action was made to conform in the Platonic system to the will of the gods and the three parts of the soul. Aristotle located the vital functions of the animal soul in the heart, which, for him, was far and away the most important of the organs, the first to be created and the last to die. Galen followed Plato in locating spiritual and emotive vitality in the heart, though he assigned the rational and nutritive functions to the brain and liver, respectively. A complicating factor in the Galenic scheme is that blood is always being burned up and replaced, while other fluids vie for ascendancy in the humoral body. According to Robert A. Erickson, the result was "a fragile, unstable, vulnerable body."[2] Nevertheless, this model, so often represented by natural philosophers of the ancient, medieval, and Renaissance periods, generally joins heart and soul in a harmonious union. This philosophical tradition that harmonized heart and soul, though marked by disagreements and distinctions, was not directly contradicted by the writings of the Renaissance anatomists from Vesalius and Fabricius to Harvey.

Besides being innovators in the field of anatomical knowledge and medical procedure, the Renaissance anatomists thought and wrote with great care about the relation of their own discoveries to past philosophical systems. They were deliberately repeating, reviewing, and reinterpreting the anatomical experiments of the classical past.[3] Their public demonstrations of dissection, performed on human and animal subjects, provoked intense curiosity. In some quarters this curiosity produced deep respect for doctors of anatomy and medicine who trained at such centers as Padua and Leiden, then practiced in London. A significant segment of the English populace,

---

[1] The relevant primary texts include Plato's *Timaeus*, Aristotle's *Physics*, Galen's works on respiration and the arteries, The Hippocratic Writings (especially *De corde*), and Lucretius' *De rerum natura*. For careful surveys of this tradition see Andrew Cunningham, *The Anatomical Renaissance: The Resurrection of the Anatomical Projects of the Ancients* (Aldershot: Scolar Press, 1997), 10–36, and Robert A. Erickson, *The Language of the Heart, 1600–1750* (Philadelphia: University of Pennsylvania Press, 1997), 1–24.

[2] Erickson, *The Language of the Heart*, 10. Gail Kern Paster describes the humoral body, the basis of most Renaissance physiology, as "porous" and "leaky." See *The Body Embarrassed: Drama and the Disciplines of Shame in Early Modern England* (Ithaca: Cornell University Press, 1993), 23–63.

[3] See Cunningham, *The Anatomical Renaissance*, 167–84 and 258–68.

however, responded to invasive anatomical procedures with fear and revulsion. Municipal governments throughout Europe had for many years enforced strict controls on the protocols of dissection in an attempt to curb such reactions, but the poetry, and especially the drama, of the English Renaissance suggests that such controls were never entirely efficacious.[4] The art of the dissectionist, whether practiced by the university professor or the common barber-surgeon, never quite escaped derogatory comparisons with the art of the magician. While body studies in the period were part of what Keith Thomas calls "the decline of magic," there remained a strongly negative cultural residue in this branch of knowledge.[5] Interfering with the motive forces within the noblest of God's creations, whether physically or spiritually, was always a sensitive business, and the stories that persisted in the philosophical, medical, theological, and poetic discourses of the heart in England provide an important measure of the widely perceived threat to personal integrity associated with the anatomical Renaissance.

In the Christian tradition, the heart is the most prominent metaphor for human spirituality, as we have seen. The biblical heart is searched, purified, and uplifted. It is the chief repository of the knowledge of God and the chief instrument of the higher love. The injunction to "love the Lord thy God with all thy heart" is repeated in Deuteronomy, Matthew, Mark, and Luke. It also features prominently in the Book of Common Prayer. As noted previously, Bernard of Clairvaux's devotions had helped to establish the Devotion of the Sacred Heart within the Church of Rome as early as the twelfth century. The most direct access to Christ's heart provided by scriptural and early iconographic traditions was through the wound made in His side at the time of the Crucifixion. For a devout Catholic, kneeling before a crucifix, this most conspicuous of the Savior's wounds was not just a window of observation but a door for entry into the divine flesh. As we noted in Chapter 2, the fatally penetrated Sacred Heart of Jesus was complemented in Catholic iconography by representations of the agonized heart of the *Mater dolorosa*, dispensing life-giving milk, tears, and blood from the breast of the Mother of God. Images of this kind proved to be inspiring to Catholic believers but upsetting to Protestant reformers in early modern England, where there was a concerted effort to transform the heart from a place of explicit suffering into a site of individual meditation.

---

[4] On the rules for acquiring corpses for dissection, licensing anatomical demonstrators, and proceeding systematically with the entire procedure, see Andrea Carlino's study, *Books of the Body: Anatomical Ritual and Renaissance Learning*, trans. John Tedeschi and Anne C. Tedeschi (Chicago: University of Chicago Press, 1994).

[5] See Keith Thomas, *Religion and the Decline of Magic* (New York: Scribners, 1971).

In order to gauge the traumatic impact of anatomical instruction and practice on late sixteenth- and early seventeenth-century England, I will look particularly at narratives that involve cutting the heart and shedding lifeblood. I begin with a fourteenth-century text that captures the brutal, negative impact of cardiectomy. Boccaccio's *Decameron* includes the story of the incestuously driven Prince Tancredi sending his daughter Ghismunda the heart of her clandestine lover, Guiscardo, in a golden chalice. The betrayed girl adds her copious tears and a vial of poison to her lover's blood, drinks the fatal mess, and mounts her bed to await death, pressing his heart to her breast. The spectacle is exceedingly grisly, parodically religious, and deliberately eroticized. It suggests, among other things, a strange devotion to the erotics of the innards and the futility of suppression in the affairs of the heart.[6]

The story was well known to late Elizabethan audiences, having been composed in dramatic form by the "Gentlemen of the Middle Temple," performed before the Queen, and revised for print by Robert Wilmot in 1592 as *The Tragedy of Tancred and Gismund*. In the second scene of Act 5, the distraught Gismund repeatedly addresses the heart she holds in the golden goblet as "my sweet heart" and "mine owne deare heart" (sig. G4ʳ) in her effort to reconstitute the metaphoric identity of lovers' hearts that has been destroyed by the literalism of her father's murderous anatomy of Guizard. She is able to rejoin her beloved only by consuming the "harty draught" (sig. H1ᵛ) of tears, heart's blood, and deadly poison from the goblet.

The compelling point for me is that these narratives, and many like them in the early modern period, turn on the struggle to conceal but also to reveal, to protect but also to display and touch inner spaces that are at once sacred and sexual. The display of the bleeding heart which occurs in such Elizabethan plays as *Cambises* reaches orgiastic levels of display in the theater of Jacobean and Caroline England. Extravagant, often mad, forms of inwardness in this drama seem to require equally extravagant acts of evisceration that are at once titillating and repugnant. These works reflect more than a taste for theatrical sensationalism. They are complex responses to a narrative tradition encompassing sacred and secular hearts and to the quest for new anatomical knowledge.

The literature of the late Middle Ages and the early Renaissance is replete with images of the adored and agonizing heart. Poets invested the

---

[6] See Giovanni Boccaccio, *Decameron*, trans. John Payne, revised and annotated by Charles S. Singleton (Berkeley: University of California Press, 1982), 1: 302–3. This is the first story of the fourth day. Other interpretive possibilities include father-daughter incest and a displaced castration fantasy. See Alberto Moravia, *L'uomo come fine e altri saggi* (Milan: Bompiani, 1964), 135–58.

heart with metaphoric life apart from and far beyond that of the rest of the body. There is ample evidence in *Tristan and Isolde*, Dante's *Vita Nuova*, and Petrarch's *Canzoniere* that during the period from the twelfth to the fourteenth century the heart emerged as a fully detachable sign of amorous passion, one capable of sustaining, sometimes simultaneously, both the negative associations of the Boccaccio passage that we have just looked at and positive, inspirational texts. For example, the opening of the third paragraph-section of the *Vita Nuova* presents a dream vision in which a lordly, white-robed figure offers Dante's heart to Beatrice so that she may eat it:

> I seemed to see in his arms a person asleep, naked except that she seemed to me lightly wrapped in a crimson cloth; one whom I, regarding with great attention, recognized as the lady of the salutation [i.e. Beatrice], who the day before had deigned to greet me. In one of his hands he appeared to hold something all aflame, and he seemed to say to me these words: "Vide cor tuum" ["Behold your heart"]. And after he had waited awhile, he appeared to waken her who slept; and he so constrained her in his way that he made her eat this thing ablaze in his hand, which she consumed hesitatingly.[7]

After the lady ascends to the heavens, Dante wakes feeling inspired to write a sonnet addressed to those poets who have written of love. The vision of the beloved constrained to eat of the poet's flaming heart is presented as terrifying and baffling. At the same time, the themes of annunciation, ascension, and inspiration woven into the story lend a decidedly uplifting tone to Dante's dream and its aftermath. The sacrifice of the lover's heart in the ritual eating of flesh is, as Milad Doueihi argues, Dante's initiation into the mysteries of his poetic vocation.[8] What moment could be more positive than this in the poet's spiritual autobiography? Still, the terror of heart excision and consumption casts something of a pall over the episode and indicates a tragic direction that English poets and playwrights were to pursue with what at times seems ghoulish persistence.

The terrible act of cutting the heart is often associated metaphorically with the brutal honesty required by religious self-scrutiny. The ritual act

---

[7] Dante Alighieri, *Vita Nuova*, trans. Dino S. Cervigni and Edward Vasta (Notre Dame: University of Notre Dame Press, 1995), 49–51.

[8] Doueihi's *Perverse History of the Human Heart* (Cambridge, MA: Harvard University Press, 1997) is almost exclusively concerned with the narrative trope of the devoured heart from Dionysus and the Titans through such French versions as the early thirteenth-century *Lai d'Ignaure*, the late thirteenth-century *Roman du châtelain de Couci et de la Dame de Fayel*, and Jean-Pierre Camus's "Le cœur mangé" (1616), culminating in a section of the book called "Incarnation, Sacred Heart, and the Eucharist." He associates the passage I have quoted from the *Vita Nuova* specifically with the Annunciation (56–62).

of purifying the flesh can encompass the editorial act of expunging all unworthy matter from what was commonly referred to as the book or tables of the heart.[9] In so far as the heart is the place where faith is reproduced and inscribed, it resembles the organ of sexual generation.[10] Extravagant metaphoric gestures of breaking or incinerating the sinner's heart were analogous in some ways to Christ's suffering on the cross. The spiritual narrative that the Passion epitomizes is both torturing and tortured. It embodies the kind of complex metaphor that Donne used in his poems to expand the boundaries of religious and amatory experience, and in the biblical context it has special force. The idea of circumcising the heart that we encountered in Chapter 1 conveys with extraordinary immediacy the need for lacerating honesty and ritual marking in explorations of the spiritual self. The pain of this procedure in the case of Christ's circumcision is felt in his mother's heart, according to the Jesuit poet Robert Southwell: "The knife that cutt His fleshe did perce her hart, / The payne that Jesus felt did Marye tast."[11] The symbolic suppression of the desires of the flesh continues to involve the presence of the flesh.

A parallel narrative of the suppression of individual desire, this time in the service of the state, unfolds on the early modern English stage. Marlowe's Tamburlaine feels compelled to penetrate any body that gets in his way. He commands his horsemen to drive their spears through the four

---

[9] Helena uses a puzzling image in *All's Well That Ends Well* (1.1.91–6) that involves imprinting Bertram in her "heart's table." Being the "hind [i.e. hart/heart] that would be mated by the lion," Helena bears the emotional scars of the lion's claws all too willingly and seems to be the instrument of her own torment.

[10] See Erickson, *The Language of the Heart*, 49–52 on the subject of biblical heart-inscription and 200 on the ejaculatory power of the heart.

[11] Robert Southwell, "The Circumcision," in *The Complete Poems of Robert Southwell, S.J.*, ed. Rev. Alexander B. Grosart [1872] (reprinted Westport, CT: Greenwood Press, 1970), 130. Southwell's younger contemporary Robert Herrick links the circumcision of Christ to a ritual exchange of gifts between Savior and saved at New Year in "To his Saviour. The New yeers gift" (*The Complete Poetry of Robert Herrick*, ed. J. Max Patrick (New York: New York University Press, 1963), 496):

> That little prettie bleeding part
> Of Foreskin send to me:
> And Ile returne a bleeding Heart,
> For New-yeers gift to thee.
>
> Rich is the Jemme that thou did'st send,
> Mine's faulty too, and small:
> But yet this Gift Thou wilt commend,
> Because I send Thee *all*.

Though diminished to the size of the baby Jesus' foreskin, the poet's bleeding heart still represents the totality of his being and hence is a commendable ritual offering.

Damascan virgins; he mummifies the dead Zenocrate; and he exchanges the following threats with the caged, starving Bajazeth:

BAJAZETH   I could
                    Willingly feed upon thy blood-raw heart.
TAMBURLAINE   Nay, thine own is easier to come by. Pluck out that
                    And 'twill serve thee and thy wife.
                                        (*Tamburlaine, Part I* 4.4.11–14)[12]

Such utterances supplement the physical violence of the play as the unrestrained tyrant of the East extends his military might with non-stop threats of yet more bloodshed. The sneering invitation to Bajazeth to turn his warrior's heart into a convenient meal is just one of a series of heart attacks that continues into the second part of the play: "our murdered hearts have strain'd forth blood" (*Tamburlaine, Part II* 2.4.123); "rip thy bowels and rend out thy heart" (3.5.121); "our bleeding hearts, / Wounded and broken" (5.3.161–2); "our hearts, all drown'd in tears of blood" (5.3.214). The heart is the target of violent action in all of these phrases. In Marlowe, the state demands from its adherents as well as its enemies the ultimate sacrifice of heart's blood. A major crisis arises for Tamburlaine in *Part II*, when one of his primary adherents, his son Calyphas, reveals pacifist tendencies and is branded his father's chief enemy. The ambivalence of the heart – stalwart in battle; tender in affection, remorse, and suffering – takes its toll on a tyrannical father who can understand only half the story. When he slays his flesh and blood, his own end is not far away.

A similar situation involving a father's aggression against his own child arises in *Titus Andronicus*, when Rome's most revered military hero commands his ravished, tongueless, handless daughter:

> get some little knife between thy teeth,
> And just against thy heart make thou a hole,
> That all the tears of thy poor eyes let fall
> May run into that sink, and soaking in,
> Drown the lamenting fool in sea-salt tears. (*Titus Andronicus* 3.2.16–20)

Lavinia eventually perishes from such a thrust to the heart, administered by her father in Act 5, the fatal mixture of blood and tears shed on behalf of honor and the state having taken its toll. A somewhat different ritual of state becomes an orgy of blood-lust in Ben Jonson's *Sejanus His Fall* (1603) when the heart of the fallen Roman prince is claimed by the mob

[12] Christopher Marlowe, *Tamburlaine the Great, Parts I and II*, ed. John D. Jump, Regents Renaissance Drama Series (Lincoln: University of Nebraska Press, 1967). Subsequent references will appear parenthetically.

as a souvenir, along with his liver and toes (5.805–32). The despised heart of Tiberius's former favorite and almost-son loses all distinction among his other, equally inconsequential body parts in this ritual run amok. Even in plays not concerned with the romantic potential of the heart, betrayal of and by parental affection overtakes military and political prowess and devours the heart. The honor of the state swallows up individual agency, and the heart's truth is destroyed. This pattern is also worked out, for example, by George Chapman in *Bussy D'Ambois* (1604) and by John Ford in *The Broken Heart* (1627–31). The drama becomes a rich breeding-ground for spectacularly destructive invasions of the inner sanctum of the stoic heart.

Actual invasions of the human breast were carried out by soldiers, murderous outlaws, executioners, and those skilled in anatomy. As guns became the weapon of choice for invading armies and outlaws, the executioners and anatomists were left to practice the rituals that to some extent insulated their respective professions.[13] The anatomists carried out their studies in public arenas, exploring interior spaces that had formerly been represented only metaphorically but which were now being revealed literally in dissection theaters and illustrated graphically in such influential texts as Vesalius's *Fabrica* and in the so-called anatomical fugitive sheets. This graphic material, though at times aestheticized by the classical poses of the dissected bodies, still contained an element of the grotesque reminiscent of the brutal flayings and eviscerations performed by state executioners and torturers.

While it is impossible to say with any certainty that the poet Edmund Spenser was directly influenced by the anatomists of his time, he made the fevered pursuit of knowledge harbored within the human heart central to the story of Britomart's daring rescue of Amoret from the enchanter, Busirane, in Book III of *The Fairie Queene*. The defilement and subsequent

---

[13] Carlino's *Books of the Body* studies in detail the regulation of anatomical procedures by law and ritual practice in Renaissance Rome. He concludes that "The norms governing the practice of public anatomies in the *Studium Urbis* in the sixteenth century, the criteria followed for the selection of the subjects of dissection, and the procedures and acts before, during, and after the desecration of their remains, emerge as a series of prudent strategies implemented to limit the circumstances under which anatomical demonstration could be legitimately allowed. Public anatomy in Rome, as in other Italian university seats, was a rigid academic ceremony. The ritual surrounding dissection seems to have served to domesticate and curb the anthropological risks of the operation" (3–4). Carlino's assertion can be challenged by evidence from the most influential of the body books that he studies, Vesalius's *Fabrica* (1543), in which a set of historiated capitals depicts a group of *putti* fetching a cadaver from the gallows and robbing a grave to provide fresh corpses for the dissection table. While academic protocols might reassure the populace to a degree, certain allied practices smacked of magic, sacrilege, and horror.

rescue are prepared for by the processional figure of a "dolefull Lady" with "deathes owne image figurd in her face" (III.xii.19), called back to life only to be further tormented by Despight and Cruelty.[14] The lady's "brest all naked, as net ivory" (Stanza 20) has been laid open and her heart placed in a basin and pierced with a "deadly dart":

> At that wide orifice her trembling hart
> Was drawne forth, and in silver basin layd,
> Quite through transfixéd with a deadly dart,
> And in her bloud yet steeming fresh embayd:
> And those two villeins, which her steps upstayd,
> When her weake feete could scarcely her sustaine,
> And fading vitall powers gan to fade,
> Her forward still with torture did constraine,
> And evermore encreaséd her consuming paine.
> *(The Fairie Queene* III.xii.21)

Here certainly is the body in pain – silenced, subjected to the penetrating gaze of all who choose to look, upheld by her cruel captors simply to prolong her suffering. Britomart witnesses all this suffering, then encounters an identical spectacle in the form of the imprisoned Amoret just ten stanzas later, on the second day of her vigil in Busirane's enchanted house. She watches in horror while the enchanter "figures" his spells to enslave the virgin Amoret to his lusts:

> And her before the vile Enchaunter sate,
> Figuring straunge characters of his art,
> With living bloud he those characters wrate,
> Dreadfully dropping from her dying hart,
> Seeming transfixéd with a cruell dart,
> And all perforce to make her him to love. (III.xii.31)

The spell-binder writes his mysterious characters in Amoret's heart's blood, but we are initially assured that her innermost being is proof against his blandishments: "A thousand charmes he formerly did prove; / Yet thousand charmes could not her stedfast heart remove" (Stanza 31). Britomart finally intervenes and gains the upper hand, in the process being wounded herself in her "snowie chest" (Stanza 33).[15] Before she can deliver Busirane's death

---

[14] I quote from *Edmund Spenser's Poetry*, ed. Hugh Maclean, 2nd edn. (New York: Norton, 1982). Subsequent references will appear parenthetically.

[15] The full line is "Unawares it [Busirane's knife] strooke into her snowie chest, / That little drops empurpled her faire brest." Rendering the wound diminutive, as Titus does when he tells Lavinia to "get some little knife" and "just against thy heart make thou a hole" (*Titus Andronicus* 3.2.16–17), is a standard ploy used in heroic poetry to diminish and aestheticize violent assaults on the female heart.

blow, Amoret enjoins her to spare his life, "For else her paine / Should be remedilesse, sith none but hee, / Which wrought it, could the same recure againe" (Stanza 34). Under the female knight's careful scrutiny and threat of execution, Busirane retrieves his book of spells and begins "his charmes backe to reverse" (Stanza 36), deconstructing the false charms of his forcible seduction and mending the wounds in Amoret's virgin flesh and her fainting (though still pure) spirit. By rehearsing his "bloudy lines" of "sad verse," Busirane is made to recant the unholy power of his former incantations to a god of love somehow made incarnate in the maiden's heart.

Spenser's enchanter acts out of a curious combination of hostility and fervent adoration which, I would argue, exposes the dangerous motives that can underlie attempts to delve into the heart's secret knowledge. Lacking faith that love can be moved by conventional rhetorical means such as praise or petition, he assaults the resisting center of passion in Amoret. His ritual incantations over her heart, involving imprisonment and the writing of arcane text with her blood, must have been efficacious in some way, since he is required to undo what he has achieved, to relieve the pain he has inflicted, to release her from the contract he has inscribed in her heart's blood. Discussing the potential dangers of the word as Spenser represents them, Kenneth Gross speaks of a "deadly symbiosis that reading and writing entails."[16] Through the invasion of Amoret's heart, the inner secret of love is legibly written. Once it has been so materialized, it can be figured out – traced, that is – with Busirane's magic figures. Composed in this way, the power of figures becomes terrifying, mesmerizing, arresting. The horror and arousal are as intense in Spenser's reader as in his would-be iconoclast, Britomart. The warning seems to be directed against the erotics of iconography itself, especially as it is embodied in Busirane's allegorical statue of Cupid: "Ah man beware, how thou those darts behold" (III.xi.48).[17] The blind boy can strike the viewer blind; the words inscribed by the phallic dart are as treacherous as the image itself.

Is it possible, then, that Busirane's vicious attack on the shrine of Amoret's heart is Spenser's allegorical recapitulation of the struggle over iconographic representation, especially Catholic icons of the tortured heart? It is certainly the case that the struggle for dominance of the symbolic heart had engaged the minds of some of the most powerful men

---

[16] Kenneth Gross, *Spenserian Poetics: Idolatry, Iconoclasm, and Magic* (Ithaca: Cornell University Press, 1985), 169.

[17] Gross comments, "In line with much Reformation theology, Spenser suggests that the image is not so much deceptive in itself as it is made deceptive by its worshipers, who are themselves turned from true worshipers into fetishists as empty as their object" (161).

of the preceding generation, men such as Somerset and Cranmer, who were major players in the Protestant iconoclasm debates of the sixteenth century. Spenser's explicit depiction of the operation that reveals Amoret's heart links the traumas of the new anatomical science with the superstitious iconography of the Old Religion.

Makers of public policy through the ages have feared that icons themselves, rather than the deities and ideologies to which they give visible shape, would become objects of worship. Nothing is so disturbing to the iconophobe as the possibility that the absent spirit and all-too-present image, the *invisibilia* and the *materia*, might be conflated, thereby generating a force more compelling than their own. Thus, in various times and places, from eighth-century Byzantium to seventeenth-century Bedfordshire and beyond, the statuary, reliquaries, and iconic paintings of the Christian church have been subjected to iconoclastic assaults. There was strenuous opposition in post-Reformation England to projecting classical and Catholic forms of the heart image into what was advertised as a thoroughly spiritualized age. Early in the English Reformation, there was an attempt to codify and enforce the distinction between "abused" religious images that are sacrificed to in idolatrous fashion and those that serve a purely commemorative function in a sacred setting. Like any image, the heart could either remain at a safe remove from actuality and spirituality, or it could become directly, dangerously interactive with the worshiper, a real, pulsing presence. The distinction between acceptable and abused images was formulated under Henry VIII and propagated by Thomas Cromwell. Subsequently it was reasserted in the reign of Edward VI and promulgated by Somerset and Cranmer, though under the combined pressure of radical reform and greed for resaleable church plate, vestments, and ornament, the distinction soon became eroded and *all* iconic treasures subjected to seizure by the government.

Iconoclasm creates its own revisionist story even as its interventions and erasures are being carried out. Authorities with the power to destroy icons are telling their own story, often silently, invisibly. In an age when literacy accompanied privilege, iconoclasm was a peculiarly class-based form of censorship. At the time of the English Reformation, the iconoclastic impulse took shape around the argument that poor, simple, illiterate folk – the *rudes* – were particularly at risk from the poisonous misdirection of religious icons.[18] Because this large segment of the population had no direct

---

[18] David Freedberg, *The Power of Images: Studies in the History and Theory of Response* (Chicago: University of Chicago Press, 1989), 399.

access to the written word of God, to the textualized Christ of the highly logocentric reformed Church, they *had* to rely on icons and images. It was never thought to be the clergy or ministers of the state but always the underclasses who were subject to the seductive power of "popular" icons, because their idolatrous enthusiasm was not subject to the interpretive constraints of the printed word. Of the various forms of imagery available to the devout – picture, pictogram, ideogram – the phonetic sign and its controlling grammars were seen as the least explosive (though by no means always safe) form of doctrinal instruction.[19] According to this way of thinking, the uneducated succumb to the temptation to fetishize an icon of, say, the heart of Jesus, whereas those capable of *reading* the world aright have access to the true meaning of the Passion through the revealed Word.[20] The artistic production of the Church of Rome had already coopted such potent icons as the Sacred Heart to serve as instruments for instructing the unlettered masses. The enormous task facing the reformers was not only to destroy those tainted images but to discredit the iconic habit of mind even as it preserved imaginative vitality within its own textual-figural procedures.[21]

A significant alliance was forged in seventeenth-century England between traditional iconoclasts and enemies of stage-playing.[22] If the house of God needed to be purged of dangerously misleading religious images, the house of Satan, the divine mimic, needed to be plucked down and its actor-writers silenced. Having amassed marginal annotations from sixteen Church

---

[19] See W. J. T. Mitchell, *Iconology: Image, Text, Ideology* (Chicago: University of Chicago Press, 1986), 7–52.

[20] John Phillips, *The Reformation of Images: Destruction of Art in England, 1535–1660* (Berkeley: University of California Press, 1973), 82–100. Note particularly his quotation from Bishop Gardiner concerning the attack on the nobility in Germany following a period of intense iconoclasm (90).

[21] This complex process is traced by Thomas H. Luxon in *Literal Figures: Puritan Allegory and the Reformation Crisis in Representation* (Chicago: University of Chicago Press, 1995). For a full account of how Lutherans dealt with the problem by relocating the image of Christ crucified in the hearts of the faithful, see Joseph Koerner, *The Reformation of the Image* (London: Reaktion Books, 2004). John Donne, caught between the new religion and the old, announces in "The Dampe" that an autopsy of his body will reveal a lady's iconic "Picture in [his] heart" and will send a fatal "sodaine dampe of love" (lines 4–5) through the hearts of his inquisitive friends as it had through his own. See Ernest B. Gilman, *Iconoclasm and Poetry in the English Reformation* (Chicago: University of Chicago Press, 1986), 135.

[22] On the opposition between religion and the thriving theater industry of the period see Jonas A. Barish, *The Antitheatrical Prejudice* (Berkeley: University of California Press, 1981). Huston Diehl has argued, on the other hand, that though the idols of the medieval Church were vigorously attacked on the Elizabethan and Jacobean stage, the tragedies of the period were not "hostile to Protestantism" and reformed religion was not "inherently antitheatrical." *Staging Reform, Reforming the Stage: Protestantism and Popular Theater in Early Modern England* (Ithaca: Cornell University Press, 1997), quotation from p. 5.

Fathers, a dozen emperors, four Church Councils, as well as from King James and Queen Elizabeth, William Prynne (that indefatigable compiler of authorities) concludes that all right-thinking men must

absolutely condemne, *as sinfull, idolatrous, and abominable the making of any Image or Picture of God the Father, Son, and holy Ghost,* or of the sacred Trinity . . . [as well as] the very *art of making Pictures and Images, as the occasion of Idolatry,* together with all Stage-portraitures, Images, Vizards, or representations of Heathen Idols, &c.[23]

By condemning the act of making such heathen idols in church or on the stage, Prynne adds the often ignored agency of the artist to the iconoclast's call to action. The makers of these iconic abominations, not just the objects themselves, require purging and scourging. What might seem at first blush a vast difference between the eighth-century scriptural-doctrinal debates over icons in Byzantine churches and the anti-theatrical campaigns of Caroline England in fact emerges as a continuous strand of concern over the power of visual representation. Here again is Prynne, sounding for all the world like St. Gregory or the early Martin Luther:

[It is] a hainous sinne contrary to the expresse words of the second Commandement, to paint or make any Picture, any Image of God; because the invisible incorporiall God, (whom no man hath seene at any time, nor can see; betweene whom and any Image, Picture, or creature there is no similitude, no proportion,) cannot be expressed by any visible shape or likenesse whatsoever, (his Image being onely spirituall and invisible like himselfe,)[24]

What is at issue from the ancient Church to the early modern stage is the immediacy, the high and potent visibility, of the bodies in question.[25]

Tracing the trajectory of the violated heart into the seventeenth century, we find even more radical forms of iconoclasm than in Spenser. Traditional values are regularly mocked and desecrated in the English drama of the period. John Fletcher's bizarre play *The Mad Lover* uses the threat of cutting into the heart to dismantle Marlovian heroic values along with Spenserian courtly ones. A bragging soldier named Memnon returns triumphant from the wars and offers the youthful Princess Calis his heart on a plate – or, rather, in a cup. At first this "mad" lover insists that his heart contains true love made visible: "I would you had it in your hand sweet Ladie / To see the

---

[23] William Prynne, *Histrio-mastix. The Players Scourge* (London: E. A. and W. I. for Michael Sparke, 1633), 901.

[24] Prynne, *Histrio-mastix*, 895.

[25] The playwright John Webster was a master of generating theatrical excitement from the quasi-iconic treatment of actors' bodies, ranging from a severed (wax) hand in *The Duchess of Malfi* to the fatal poisoned-portrait kissing scene in *The White Devil*.

truth it beares ye" (1.2.89–90).[26] Before long it has been transmuted into a token of "the honour and the valour of its owner" (3.2.62). But honor and valor are precisely the virtues rendered irrelevant in a post-war world where lust for the princess-prize drives out any sense of military loyalty.

Fletcher's play oddly blends the anatomical and medical with the farcical in its representations of the heart. While Memnon's messenger is delivering a message to the princess about the gift of his commander's heart, she callously asks her attending ladies, "what should we doe wo't? dance it?" The suggested alternative is to "Drie it and drinke it for the wormes" (2.3.16–17). The proposal to dance a jig with the bloody heart or to use it to concoct a traditional home remedy for intestinal parasites indicates the material depths to which the romantic image has declined.[27] Calis's attendants jokingly recommend that, since the weather is unusually warm, the extracted heart should be perfumed, wrapped in a napkin, and preserved in a gold goblet to retard spoilage, chief enemy to the anatomically curious from time immemorial. Memnon, the would-be heart donor, becomes a figure of ridicule, even as he tries to construct himself as the ecstatic high priest, sacrificing himself on the altar of love (3.4.58–60).[28] Just before the surgeon is contracted to perform the cardiectomy, Memnon's brother convinces him to

---

[26] *The Mad Lover*, ed. Robert Kean Turner, in *The Dramatic Works in the Beaumont and Fletcher Canon*, Fredson Bowers, gen. ed., vol. 5 (Cambridge: Cambridge University Press, 1982). Subsequent references will appear parenthetically.

[27] In his "anatomical duel between Aristotle and Galen" Alexander Ross gives his prescription for curing heart worm: "I have read of one whose heart being opened, there was found in it a white worm with a sharp beck, which being placed on a table, and a circle of the juice of Garlick made about it, died, being overcome with that strong smell." *Arcana microcosmi: or, the hid secrets of man's body discovered* (London: T. Newcomb, 1652), 74. The particular worm he discusses is doubtless the one pictured and discussed at length by Edward May in *A most certaine and true relation of a strange monster or serpent found in the left ventricle of the heart of Iohn Pennant . . .* (London: G. Miller, 1639). May construes Pennant's problems as spiritual as well as medical. See Fig. 22 in the present study.

[28] Derision is likewise heaped on a man attempting to communicate his love in the anonymous English tragedy *Arden of Faversham* (1592). A jealous lover rants about a love token sent by an artist to his beloved:

> But he hath sent a dagger sticking in a heart,
> With a verse or two stolen from a painted cloth,
> The which I hear the wench keeps in her chest.
> [. . .]
> I'll send from London such a taunting letter
> As she shall eat the heart he sent with salt
> And fling the dagger at the painter's head.

Arden of Faversham, ed. Martin White, New Mermaids (New York: W.W. Norton, 1982), Scene 1, lines 152–60. The phrase "painted cloth" suggests that both verse and heart have been plagiarized from a cheap, vulgar wall hanging. The detail of saucing the heart with salt is a particularly vicious touch. I am grateful to Jessica Slights for this reference.

substitute another man's heart. The anatomically extravagant gesture is thus cynically emptied of romantic significance. While Fletcher avoids the horror of displaying the removal of Memnon's heart, he permits the literal treatment of human interiority to obliterate the tenderness of the lover and the courage of the soldier, both formerly located in the heart.

When he wrote *The Mad Lover*, Fletcher knew he could represent the potent mix of horror and absurdity in his main character simply by literalizing the gestures of generations of heart-struck lovers. Embedded in the heart image he found the most potentially disturbing indicator of the self in extremity, including the extremities of terror, eroticism, and foolishness. Memnon goes mad in his heart, not his head. That is what makes his story the perfect vehicle for Fletcher's complex analysis of the collapse of heroic and generic purity. What is hidden at the secret heart of this play is not an integral self but a travesty of conventional gesturing, a bittersweet glimpse of a once great but now shrivelled heroic heart. This literalized heart represents for Fletcher not just a comic turn but also a tragic loss, the loss of a world adequate to its heroes and, hence, the loss of the heroes themselves.

The pattern of evisceration as a show of power diminished to a spectacle of futility reaches its apex in John Ford's *'Tis Pity She's a Whore* (1633). Annabella's heart is the target of grotesque emotional and, finally, physical abuse. It is identified with the fraternally impregnated womb, ripped out of the murdered girl and presented by her brother on dagger-point as fit fare for a banquet:

> You came to feast, my lords, with dainty fare;
> I came to feast too, but I digg'd for food
> In a much richer mine than gold or stone
> Of any value balanc'd; 'tis a heart,
> A heart, my lords, in which is mine entomb'd.[29]

At the moment of Giovanni's phallic thrust into his sister's heart, the horizontal structures of kinship and the vertical structures of power collide. Annabella's heart/womb/tomb has fallen prey not only to the sin of incest but to the imperial conqueror who comes to worship at and finally to destroy the rich, illicit shrine of the female heart.[30]

---

[29] John Ford, *'Tis Pity She's a Whore*, ed. N.W. Bawcutt, Regents Renaissance Drama Series (Lincoln: University of Nebraska Press, 1966), 5.6.24–8.

[30] Surgical assaults on the womb were sparked by an insatiable curiosity about what goes on in there, especially during pregnancy, a curiosity still only partly satisfied in our own time by ultrasound technology. The gravid woman is a frequent subject of the anatomical fugitive sheets which allowed the viewer to lift a flap of paper representing the belly to see inside the figure's womb. A representative example, engraved by Cornelis Bos (1539), is used as frontispiece in Andrea

In considering the kinds of cultural work being accomplished by these violent acts of evisceration, it is worth asking whether they present a moral perspective on the fragility of the body and the need to defend it against assault. Alternatively, we may ask whether playgoers are simply being confronted with the spectacle of the flesh *in extremis*, undergoing final torments such as no one would wish to suffer but which many would enjoy observing from a safe distance. Asking such questions suggests that there may be other options at work, redistributing among the audience the power resident in the idea of the disembowelled heart.

A common strand of ritualized public spectacle connects the tragic acts of heart cutting that we have been considering. In each case the rituals run directly counter to the transcendence of spirit over flesh that characterizes ritual enactments of Christian suffering. These tragic rendings of the heart have more in common with the satirist's impulse to interrogate the human condition by anatomizing it than with the celebratory gestures and incantations of the priest re-enacting or memorializing the sufferings of Christ. Rather than a top-down reading of the heart icon – one in which the suffering of lower subjects is assigned meaning through divine mediation – these tragic instances present us with an inferior being (a deranged father, an incestuous brother, etc.) absconding with a radically desacralized heart.[31] In so far as their surgical acts function as aids to moral scrutiny in their tragic worlds, they do so from a position of no plausible authority. The only aspects of the interior self revealed by these acts are the perpetrators' own morally questionable desires to possess or, failing that, to dominate another's heart. At this point in the history of the heart an intensely anti-romantic hostility toward the female body seems to dominate dramatic writing.

The act of excavating the heart in this drama does not always guarantee moral discoveries. Much as the moral and ecclesiastical authorities of the

---

Carlino's *Paper Bodies: A Catalogue of Anatomical Fugitive Sheets, 1538–1687*, trans. Noga Arikha (London: Wellcome Institute, 1999).

[31] According to Corrine Coop-Phane, Professor of Epistemology at the Université de Paris, the desacralization of the heart in modern medical discourse sounds a similarly negative note in the ear of a largely optimistic public: "Pour devenir une science et une technique efficaces, la cardiologie, comme bien d'autres spécialités médicales, a dû payer le prix d'une désacralisation que l'opinion publique, pour laquelle le cœur reste non seulement le signe de la vie mais aussi le symbole de la générosité humaine, semble avoir du mal à admettre." (As has happened with many other medical specializations, the price paid for cardiology's development into a real and technically efficient science has been the desacralization of the heart, a development ill-received by a general public for whom the heart remains not only the sign of life but also the symbol of human generosity.) Corrine Coop-Phane, "L' âme au cœur," *M/S: médecine science* 14 (1998): 1089–96, quotation from 1095, translation by Jamie Reid-Baxter.

time wished the hearts of their charges to be the residence of God's word, delving into the human breast sometimes revealed a vacuous or hopelessly corrupt heart. Villains of the Richard III variety are represented as heartless in moralized history as well as drama. Lacking the seat of moral reason, they cannot be assailed by virtuous motions, except perhaps as a despairing afterthought. At the other end of the spectrum are those characters of such stoic resolve that they can never be dis-heartened. John Ford's Calantha in *The Broken Heart* remains outwardly implacable while her heart, incapable of change, is crushed within her. But by far the vast majority of stage representations of the heart under siege show a moral proving ground which is neither vacant nor adamantine. The heart is precisely not the place of stability but the center of torment and turmoil.

What we have noted thus far about the alarmingly negative impact of dissection procedures on narratives of personal integrity in early modern England tells only part of the story. The cynical demetaphorizing of the heart in the plays we have been examining was counterbalanced by a fresh and vibrant response to the anatomically revealed heart in the corpus of English Protestant poetry. A characteristically Protestant sense of the inner self was fed by the increasingly detailed knowledge of the interior of the body. Precise information about what were called "the motions of the heart" provided metaphoric material for poets seeking to describe the inward-looking spirituality of Protestantism. The rules for minding the little shop of the soul – the human microcosm – were rewritten with greater emphasis on individual interiority and less on the role of the priest and the sacraments. Not surprisingly, the heart was at the center of this new sense of interiority.

The distinguished line of English Protestant poets who generated an intense feeling of vitality around the spiritualized heart includes such figures as Edmund Spenser, John Donne, George Herbert, Aemelia Lanyer, and John Milton. I have already had some things to say about the first two poets, and the work of the latter two contains surprisingly few (though intense) references to the heart. The reason for this is likely generic, as the lyric poem became the preferred form for revealing the inward secrets of the heart. On these grounds, I will turn my attention next to the poetry of George Herbert before considering a less canonical but entirely representative seventeenth-century poet, Christopher Harvey – not to be confused with the anatomist, William Harvey.

Herbert's heavily heart-inflected poems can tell us a great deal about the place of the heart in mainstream Anglican thought of the early seventeenth century. The poet's mind seems to be moved to intensely intellectual speculation by the image of the heart. His way of working through problems of love, confession, and meditation on the name of God are precisely focused within the penitent heart and take on a characteristically Protestant coloring. While there are strong continuities in his poems with the violence and visceral immediacy of Catholic iconography, the poet's strategies of abstraction and detachment create a rather different impact from late medieval treatments of the heart.

The poem "Love unknown" is a "long and sad" tale of a sinner's heart hurled shockingly into the triple trauma of Baptism, Holy Communion, and the Order for the Burial of the Dead. It is a liturgical parable of a soiled, hard, and dull heart being cleansed, softened, and quickened by the sacrifice of Christ's blood and the sacraments of the Church of England. Arnold Stein calls the poem "a full exercise in fantasy," and it is precisely that imaginative and storytelling quality that helps to distinguish its reading of the penitent heart from that of its Roman Catholic precursors.[32]

Each of the three central encounters with divine "Love unknown" in the poem of that name stuns the speaker, who had expected to make far more banal offerings to his landlord (God) than his own sensitive heart.[33] He first places his heart in the midst of a "dish of fruit," but the Lord's "servant,"

> Quitting the fruit, seiz'd on my heart alone,
> And threw it in a font, wherein did fall
> A stream of bloud, which issu'd from the side
> Of a great rock: (lines 12–15)[34]

Sudden and violent though the action is, it is also heavily mediated by the biblical narrative and typology of Moses striking the rock to produce life-giving water (Exod. 17: 6 and Num. 20: 8), Christ's cleansing blood streaming from the wound in his side, and the Rock of the Church – all of which lead to the washing away of original sin in the baptismal font.[35] The heart's blood, however, is here primarily a liturgical vestige in a highly abstract "tale" of personal salvation.

---

[32] Arnold Stein, *George Herbert's Lyrics* (Baltimore: The Johns Hopkins Press, 1968), 205.

[33] As Chana Bloch points out, Herbert's speaker appears at best confused, at worst slow-witted, because he is still learning to know God. A possible alternative title for the poem might be "Love Unrecognized." See Bloch's *Spelling the Word: George Herbert and the Bible* (Berkeley: University of California Press, 1985), 212–14.

[34] *The Works of George Herbert*, ed. F. E. Hutchinson (Oxford: Clarendon Press, 1941), 129.

[35] The emblematic image clusters surrounding Baptism, Communion, and Burial in "Love unknown" are all part of what Ira Clark calls a "personal neotypology" for Herbert. Old Testament legalistic types of New Testament love are, he argues, the basis of Herbert's representation of his own faith. See Clark's early essay "'Lord, In Thee the Beauty Lies in the Discovery': 'Love Unknown' and Reading Herbert," *ELH* 39 (1972): 560–84.

The same may be said for the second and third encounters in "Love unknown." When the sinner brings an offering from his "fold" to be cast into the "boyling caldron" (line 27) fired by a "spacious fornace flaming" (line 26) and inscribed around its edge with the word "*AFFLICTION*," he is astounded that "the man, / Who was to take it from me, slipt his hand, / And threw my heart into the scalding pan" of "holy bloud" (lines 33–5, 41). The blood (of Christ) is then surreptitiously slipped into the speaker's cup by a "friend," and the Eucharistic ritual is complete. The poetic strategies for bringing the sinner's heart to God are more like those of the intellectual emblematist Daniel Cramer in "Probor" (Fig. 12) than the physically shocking imagery of Juan Correa's *Alegoría del Sacramento* (Fig. 15).[36]

When Herbert's speaker seeks to retire from the pains of life, he finds his bed stuffed with "thoughts, / I would say *thorns*" (lines 51–2) that not only torment him but also quicken his heart into new life through death. Despite the speaker's surprise when he finds pain and renewal where he had simply embraced lethargy, his tone is calm and reflective, and the result of this heart attack, like the two earlier ones, is peaceful consolation. In Herbert's words, "all my scores were by another paid" (line 60). The speaker's problem, as his friend and the interpreter of his threefold encounter says, is that "*Your heart was dull*" (line 56). Giving in to such sluggishness, despite three warnings, was the lapse indulged in by the Disciples in the Garden of Gethsemene as recounted by Matthew, Mark, and Luke. Christ, who knows the secrets of our hearts, never sleeps; nor, at the last day, shall we, as the Order for the Burial of the Dead reminds us.[37] While the first Adam was as dull and obtuse as Herbert's speaker, "the last Adam was made a quickening spirit" (1 Cor. 25: 20, as quoted in the Order for the Burial of the Dead). The thorns of life that both torment and "*quicken*" (line 66) the sleeping/dying sinner are the punishment of old Adam (Gen. 3: 17–18) and the reinvigorating stimulus of Christ's passion. Significantly, the site of all this activity in the poem and of its scriptural precedents is the individual Christian's heart as defined by the offices of the Church.

---

[36] In *Love Known: Theology and Experience in George Herbert's Poetry* (Chicago: University of Chicago Press, 1983) Richard Strier, who goes further than I would in banishing Catholic sensibility and tradition from Herbert's poetry, asserts that the narrator of "Love unknown" is not sinful but childish (161). While I agree that the speaker is childishly ignorant of what his Lord has sacrificed for him and petulant about the rejection of his own sacrifices, the pricking of his tender conscience throughout the poem (which Strier himself foregrounds) suggests that we are dealing with a sinning adult's, not an innocent child's, heart.

[37] *The Book of Common Prayer, 1559: The Elizabethan Prayer Book*, ed. John E. Booty (Charlottesville: University Press of Virginia for the Folger Shakespeare Library, 1976), 312.

A somewhat different take on the lyric expression of spiritual interiority is available to us in Herbert's poem "Confession." The Reformation de-emphasised auricular confession in an effort to limit the powers of the priesthood and to engage the sinner in a more direct conversation with God. In Herbert's poem, this involves reviewing the speaker's feeble strategies for escaping the plagues and "torture[s]" sent by God to afflict his "tendrest parts," in particular, his heart (lines 11–12). The skills of the perverse builder (a kind of antitype of Christ the carpenter) have been used to construct a series of tills within boxes within chests within the closet within his heart (lines 2–5). This Chinese strongbox ploy fails to exclude God's attacks upon the heart-*cum*-conscience, and the paradoxical truth emerges that "Onely an open breast / Doth shut them out, so that they cannot enter" (lines 19–20). Stein credits Herbert, "a master of analytical detachment," with effecting an intense conversion of "intimate experience … into impersonal exp-ression."[38] While it is certainly the case that the poet analyzes in great detail his efforts to enclose the secrets of his heart and thus to exclude God's troubling presence there, I find most compelling Herbert's personal engagement in this poem with the body – especially the heart – in pain.

A third poem, and the last I will look at in detail, uses language itself (Latin and English) as the architect's materials for constructing the place of worship and spiritual consolation. "JESU" is the name of the poem and the name that is "deeply carved" in the altar of the speaker's heart, but the "frame" containing God's name has been smashed to pieces. Once re-collected, however, the bits of the "broken heart" spell "*I ease you*" as well as "*JESU*" (lines 9–10). Herbert has managed, emblematically, to embody the Old Testament's concern with breaking down the hardened heart and the New Testament's emphasis on Christ's reconstructive solace. This brief lyric has more to do with strenuous mental gymnastics (akin to acrostic poems) than with visceral impact. It treats the heart as the repository of the idea and experience of salvation. The habit of mind that leads Herbert to convert religious anxieties into concrete images of the heart is one he shares with the Protestant emblem-makers of the seventeenth century and their Catholic forerunners.

One of these forerunners was the sixteenth-century Jesuit priest, martyr, and poet Robert Southwell. In one of Southwell's best known poems, a "prety Babe all burninge bright" appears on a very particular "Winter's night."[39] The poem reconfigures the heat associated by natural

---

[38] Stein, *George Herbert's Lyrics*, 89.
[39] Robert Southwell, "The Burning Babe," in *The Complete Poems of Robert Southwell, S. J.*, 109–10.

philosophers with the heart as something extra-natural. The floating, flaming apparition of the fiery baby discourses on its own suffering, present and future. Its tears, which should quench the flames that engulf it, instead feed them. "[W]oundinge thornes" fuel the sacred heart's fire, which is called simply "Love." The entire scene is so vividly imagined and so intensely and precisely explained by the divine apparition that the poem itself seems to glow. The eventual suffering of Christ is adumbrated in the first night of His life: as we learn in the poem's last line, "it was Christmas-daye."

The symbolism of this visionary poem lies in a direct line with the ecstatic saints' personal narratives of the late Middle Ages. The poem's details derive not from medical or anatomical texts but from a stock of religious writing which, while embracing the material body, transforms it according to the guidelines of the Church of Rome. Southwell's flaming heart of Jesus is of the kind that might be exchanged for the reader's sinful one in the manner of St. Catherine or Sister Marguerite-Marie.[40]

Another prominent voice of the Counter-Reformation in England, one subtly attuned to the symbolic communicative power of the Sacred Heart, was Richard Crashaw (1613–49). Crashaw wrote three poems on the image of St. Teresa of Avila in which he presents a special sense of the viewer's interaction with the divine image and the holy word. In "The Flaming Heart," he deliberately revises the Catholic iconographic tradition that represented the saint beside an angel from the ranks of the seraphim who holds a flame-tipped dart with which he pierces Teresa's heart and inscribes God's Word within her.[41] Crashaw begins his poem insisting that Teresa herself, author of a divinely inspired autobiography, is the true writer of the

---

[40] Compare Figs. 8 and 9 above.

[41] Bernini's is the most famous rendering of the transverberation of St. Teresa. His sculpture, produced in the mid-seventeenth century for the Cornaro Chapel in the church of Santa Maria della Vittoria in Rome, does not show the saint's heart but rather focuses the moment of ecstatic union with God in her face.

Graphic heart emblems appear twice in the original volumes of Crashaw's poems. The emblems derive from Jesuit collections published in Antwerp in 1606 and 1640, respectively. One shows the book of the heart, with a hinge on one side, a lock on the other, and verses recommending "the Word" as the key to the heart. See *The Poems English, Latin and Greek of Richard Crashaw*, ed. L. C. Martin (Oxford: Clarendon Press, 1957), 236. The other depicts a weeping Magdalene from whose torso emerges a winged heart (308).

As scholars have long recognized, the iconographic mode came easily to Crashaw. See Robert T. Peterson, *The Art of Ecstasy: Teresa, Bernini, and Crashaw* (New York: Atheneum, 1970). Diana Treviño Benet has argued that Crashaw rejects both the emphasis of the German Reform Church on the Word and that of the Roman Catholic Church on painted images in favor of a direct and passionate approach to the saint's inner ecstasy. See "Crashaw, Teresa, and the Word," in *New Perspectives on the Life and Death of Richard Crashaw*, ed. John R. Roberts (Columbia: University of Missouri Press, 1990), 140–56.

scene, not the male seraphim, who simply stands by to admire her word-working. Readers of the misleading picture and the corrective poem need to be instructed in how to "read it right" lest the genuine holiness of the saint be lost to view:

> Well meaning readers! You that come as freinds
> And catch the pretious name this peice pretends;
> Make not too much hast to' admire
> That fair-cheek't fallacy of fire.
> That is a SERAPHIM, they say
> And this the great TERESIA.
> Readers, be rul'd by me; & make
> Here a well-plac't & wise mistake.
> You must transpose the picture quite,
> And spell it wrong to read it right;
> Read HIM for her, and her for him;
> And call the SAINT the SERAPHIM.[42]

The "fiery DART," which Crashaw explicitly associates with the saint's pen, "fill'd the Hand of this great HEART" (lines 35–6). As the poem proceeds, Crashaw recuperates the painting by moving beyond the male/female opposition, asserting the ultimate power of the iconic heart to reconcile all differences through love: "Oh HEART! the æqual poise of loues both parts / Bigge alike with wounds & darts" (lines 75–6).

Christopher Harvey's volume of lyrics, entitled *Schola Cordis* (1647) and called *The School of the Heart* on the title page of the 1664 edition, derives, like Crashaw's, from a Jesuit emblem collection, Benedict van Haeften's *Schola Cordis* (1629), but Harvey owes his distinctively Protestant English readings of the heart to the "displacement of image by language."[43] Sketching out the transition from Old to New Testament typologies, Harvey's God outlines the failure of commandments written in stone and proposes the heart as the new, lively site of inscription:

> My Law of old
> Tables of stone did hold,
> Wherein I writ what I before had spoken,
> Yet were they quickly broken:
> A signe the Covenant
> Contain'd in them would due observance want.
> Nor did they long remaine

---

[42] Crashaw, "The Flaming Heart," lines 1–12.
[43] Ira Clark, *Christ Revealed: The History of the Neotypological Lyric in the English Renaissance* (Gainesville: University of Florida Press, 1982), 67–8.

Coppy'd again.
But now I'll try
What force in flesh doth lie:
Whether thine heart renew'd afford a place
Fit for my Law of grace.[44]

In these lines, a virtual gloss on Ezekiel 11: 19, the personalized word of God replaces not only Moses' tabular icons but also the iconography of the bleeding heart, so evident, as we have seen, in the Counter-Reformation poetry of Southwell and Crashaw.[45] Gone, too, is the violence of the tragic stage spectacles of Marlowe, Shakespeare, and Ford.

Harvey's source volume by the Dutch monk van Haeften had been shaped in its purpose, form, and content by Catholic meditative traditions which also, as Louis Martz and others have argued, contributed substantially to seventeenth-century English religious lyrics. But Harvey disturbed the three-part meditative structure of van Haeften's emblem collection, removed the lengthy "*Lectio*" sections in which glosses from the Church Fathers had been instructively cited, and changed the original Vulgate texts to accord with the King James Bible. As Michael Bath points out, van Haeften's internal

---

[44] Christopher Harvey, *Schola cordis, or the heart of it selfe, gone away from God . . . in 47 Emblems* (London: for H. Blunden, 1647), 106. The related image of the sinner's stony heart that must be broken down and rebuilt by God constitutes the central, supporting section of George Herbert's concrete poem, "The Altar" (1633), here cited from *The Works of George Herbert*, ed. F. E. Hutchinson (Oxford: Clarendon Press, 1941), 26:

> A broken ALTAR, Lord, thy servant reares,
> Made of a heart, and cemented with teares:
> Whose parts are as thy hand did frame;
> No workmans tool hath touch'd the same.
>> A HEART alone
>> Is such a stone,
>> As nothing but
>> Thy pow'r doth cut.
>> Wherefore each part
>> Of my hard heart
>> Meets in this frame,
>> To praise thy Name:
> That, if I chance to hold my peace,
> These stones to praise thee may not cease.
> O let thy blessed SACRIFICE be mine,
> And sanctifie this ALTAR to be thine.

The following poem in *The Church*, "The Sacrifice," invokes the biblical comparison of the "stonie rock" from which Moses drew life-giving water (Deut. 8: 15) and the hearts that Christ must "trie" for living truth (lines 122–3).

[45] Crashaw's poem "The Flaming Heart," for example, conflates the male and female organs of sexual generation with the bleeding heart of St. Teresa.

meditations become, in the English version, "the object of externalised allegorical play" carried out in the Mannerist mode:

> The two figures of Cupid and Anima throw [the heart] about, they pile dishes on it, shut it in a chest, cut it in half, hammer it, squeeze the world inside it, pour water out of it, burn it, bathe it in sweat, sound its depth with a plumb line, and squeeze it in a winepress.[46]

All these changes notwithstanding, the Protestant and Catholic emblem-makers are not, as Bath rightly argues, so radically different as some scholars believe. Both traditions combine the exegetical with the meditative in ways that point to continuity rather than contradiction between the two faith communities in the matter of imagining the spiritual functions of the heart. Their work combines the sacred with the secular, and their tone is at once playful, didactic, and inspirational.[47]

Christopher Harvey's hearts are coddled and bathed, preparing the path of pure, personal redemption that John Bunyan's pilgrim was to follow. Bunyan explicitly reworked the idea of the broken heart in his late devotional work *The Acceptable Sacrifice or Excellency of the Broken Heart: showing the nature, signs and proper effects of a contrite spirit* (1689). The broken heart is not the cause of a lover's death, as it is in plays by Shakespeare, Ford, and others, but the precondition for accepting God's imprint. "This broken heart," Bunyan says, "is . . . a pliable, and flexible Heart, and prepared to receive whatsoever impressions God shall make upon it, and is ready to be moulded into any frame that shall best please the Lord."[48] It is auspicious, then, that Christian's wife in the second part of *The Pilgrim's Progress* (1685) finds "the Caul of her Heart [rent] in sunder" as though by lightning.[49] Robert Erickson has brilliantly unpacked the "caul" metaphor for us:

> The "caul" was literally the pericardium, the thin membranous sac surrounding the heart, but it was also the term for the amnion or inner membrane enclosing the fetus before birth, and it could even mean a woman's hair net. The caul of

---

[46] Michael Bath, *Speaking Pictures: English Emblem Books and Renaissance Culture* (London: Longman, 1994), 178. One is reminded by this account of the torments so gleefully inflicted on her lovers' hearts by Frau Venus (Fig. 21 above).

[47] Bath, *Speaking Pictures*, notes (84) the "program of loyal Protestantism which underpins the political ideology" of another influential collection, Geffrey Whitney's *A Choice of Emblemes and Other Devices* (Leiden: F. Raphelengius for C. Plantin, 1586), but he also stresses that, as John Manning has shown, the fusion of profane and divine love in the period was a largely Counter-Reformation-inspired project. See John R. Manning, "Whitney's *Choice of Emblemes*: A Reassessment," *Renaissance Studies* 4 (1990): 155–200.

[48] John Bunyan, *The Acceptable Sacrifice* (London: for G. Larkin, 1689), sigs. A4^{r-v}.

[49] *The Pilgrim's Progress* , ed. James Blanton Wharey, rev. by Roger Sharrock (Oxford: Clarendon Press, 1960), 178.

the heart was then a birth metaphor and a woman's word. It enclosed a pun on God's "call" of the heart to regeneration. But the "caul of the heart" was often interpreted as a symbol of the hard, unregenerate heart and was thus analogous to the foreskin that had to be removed for acceptance into the male theocratic community. Hence the image of the caul of the heart was found in everyone and not confined to one gender.[50]

Bunyan's strategy of double-gendering the heart, then releasing it from its restraining containers, suggests a libidinal release. At the same time, spiritual discipline, not sexual indulgence, remains the characteristic behavioral mode of *The Pilgrim's Progress*. The imagery of the heart serves both ends. Erickson goes on to argue that even the scientific work of William Harvey on the heart develops an elaborate ejaculatory metaphor to figure the systolic propulsion of blood through the circulatory system: "The unmistakably phallic – even masturbatory – characteristics of Harvey's depiction of the heart recall the phallic, life-giving power of the seminal God."[51] But the erotics of the heart are just one aspect of Harvey's methodical observations of the heart in *De motu cordis*.[52]

Harvey's book is a dissertation that stops short of being a disputation. While his conclusions differ vastly from those of Aristotle, Galen, Mondino, and Vesalius, he always manages to convey an attitude of respect for the earlier studies from which he learned so much. His approach combines rhetorical tact (since disrespect would alienate many readers), political expediency (dedicating the work to Charles I, "the heart of the state" [3]), and intellectual deference (acknowledging that earlier methodologies produced important, if flawed, results).[53] Harvey's small book is charged with excitement and ideas. On the basis of his direct observation that "the heart

---

[50] Erickson, *The Language of the Heart*, 44.

[51] Erickson, *The Language of the Heart*, 76. Compare Harvey's assertion that "the contained blood escape[s] in spurts at each movement or pulsation during the contraction of a heart which has undergone a penetrating wound of the ventricle." *Movement of the Heart and Blood in Animals (De motu cordis)*, trans. Kenneth J. Franklin (Oxford: Blackwell Scientific Publications, 1957), 27–8. Subsequent references will appear parenthetically.

[52] Harvey's methodological concerns are evident, for example, at the start of Chapter 6 of *Movement of the Heart and Blood*, where he stresses the importance of studying not one but many species of animals.

[T]hose persons do wrong who while wishing, as all anatomists commonly do, to describe, demonstrate and study the parts of animals, content themselves with looking inside one animal only, namely, man – and that one dead. In this way they merely attempt a universal syllogism on the basis of a particular proposition (like those who think they can construct a science [*disciplinam*] of politics after exploration of a single form of government, or have a knowledge of agriculture through investigation of the character of a single field). (44)

[53] See Peter W. Graham, "Harvey's *De motu cordis*: The Rhetoric of Science and the Science of Rhetoric," *Journal of the History of Medicine* 33 (1978): 469–76.

empties during its contraction" he concludes, "Hence the heart movement which is commonly thought to be [its] diastole is in fact [its] systole" (28). His emphasis on the pumping action of the heart and the crucial postulation of a connection between arteries and veins at the body's extremities led him to a clear explanation of what had previously only been suspected – that the blood circulates continuously through the body.

Harvey's conclusions rest on firsthand observations of many species, alive as well as dead, and are bolstered by the judicious use of an array of dynamic metaphors. His heart science cannot work without poetry, and his pleasure at revealing the divine perfection of the human form is everywhere evident. He declares at one point that "Nature, perfect and divine, making nothing in vain, has neither added a heart unnecessarily to any animal nor created a heart before it had a function to fulfil" (107). He compares the "harmoniously and rhythmically" synchronized movements of auricle and ventricle to the rapid, continuous movement of a flintlock gun striking the spark, igniting the powder, and shooting the ball (39). He then compares the periodic pulsations of the heart to a horse swallowing water, occurring "with successive gullet movements, each one causing a sound and an audible and tangible thrill" (40). He records a thrill of a different kind to dramatize the heart's life-and-death function:

In an experiment carried out upon a dove, after the heart had completely stopped moving and thereafter even the auricles had followed suit, I spent some time with my finger, moistened with saliva and warm, applied over the heart. When it had, by means of this fomentation, recovered – so to speak – its power to live, I saw the heart and its auricles move, and contract and relax, and – so to speak – be recalled from death to life. (35–6)

The concluding poetic phrase in the Latin version reads "*et quasi ab orco revocari, videbantur*" or, literally, "as if summoned back from the depths, so it seemed." While he is clearly anxious about the possibility of sacrilege in his act of revivification, Harvey is irresistibly stirred by his proximity to the secrets of life initiated and sustained by the motions of the heart.

If correcting basic misapprehensions about the movement of the blood through heart, lungs, veins, and arteries required minute observation and a keen conceptual mind, penetrating the depths of human emotion involved the transfer of these mental qualities into broader cultural realms. The idea of the heart as the center of human identity and love remained vibrant throughout the English Renaissance. In much the same way that the classical idea of the heart as seat of the soul and chief example of divine ingenuity persisted through the anatomical Renaissance, the hearts of Renaissance lovers, holy and profane, continued to figure prominently in the works of Spenser, Marlowe, Shakespeare, Fletcher, Ford, Harvey, and Bunyan. As Scott Manning Stevens remarks, "the heart, as a symbol, could absorb the shock of its own realistic representation."[54] Even when plucked out, mocked, and desecrated, the heart remained a mysterious and compelling metaphor for the affective life of the period.

The heart also continued to be a pivotal symbol in religious poetry of the later seventeenth century. As Robert Erickson has shown in convincing detail, John Milton builds his epic of the Fall around our first parents' sharing "One heart, one Soul in both" and Christ's consoling love written "upon thir hearts."[55] Eve, as he aptly puts it, is Adam's "heartmate and his soulmate."[56] But the angel Raphael carefully explains to Adam that his marital bond is only a shadow of a higher love, a first step on the Platonic ladder that will lead him away from the beasts toward God:

> Love refines
> The thoughts, and heart enlarges, hath his seat
> In Reason, and is judicious, is the scale
> By which to heav'nly Love thou may'st ascend,
> Not sunk in carnal pleasure, for which cause
> Among the Beasts no Mate for thee was found.
> (*Paradise Lost* VIII, 589–94)

This proper form of love "enlarges" the sympathies of the heart and is informed by the heart's "Reason." The residence of the poem's opposing intelligence in the Serpent is ambiguously placed by Satan:

> in at his Mouth
> The Devil enter'd, and his brutal sense,
> In heart or head, possessing soon inspir'd
> With act intelligential. (IX, 187–90)

The point of possession of the Serpent's brute senses, whether heart or head, appears to be a matter of indifference. The false reason with which it is endowed will work on the corruptible thinking of Eve's heart.

---

54 Scott Manning Stevens, "Sacred Heart and Secular Brain," in *The Body in Parts: Fantasies of Corporeality in Early Modern Europe*, ed. David Hillman and Carla Mazzio (New York: Routledge, 1997), 275.

55 See especially Erickson, *The Language of the Heart*, 139–46, and *Paradise Lost* IX, 967 and XII, 489. I quote from *John Milton: Complete Poems and Major Prose*, ed. Merritt Y. Hughes (New York: Odyssey Press, 1957). Subsequent references to Milton will appear parenthetically by the name of the work and book and line numbers.

56 Erickson, *The Language of the Heart*, 140.

Even Satan is aware that true communication requires perfect accord between the heart's desires and the speaker's words. He uses this awareness to flatter the Son in *Paradise Regained*:

> I see thou know'st what is of use to know,
> What best to say canst say, to do canst do;
> Thy actions to thy words accord, thy words
> To thy large heart give utterance due, thy heart
> Contains of good, wise, just, the perfect shape.
>
> (*Paradise Regained* III, 7–11)

Word, act, and intent are perfectly harmonized within the "large heart" of Christ.

Milton is well aware, however, that conventional thinkers, such as the Chorus in *Samson Agonistes*, are capable of equivocating about the moral wiggle-room between the heart's intentions and the hand's actions: "Where the heart joins not, outward acts defile not" (*Samson Agonistes* 1368). But Milton's "hero of conscience" is having none of this kind of sloppy moral reasoning.[57] He denies that Aristotle's notion of constrained, unwilled acts being blameless can be applied in his case, since he is not being physically dragged off to the Temple of Dagon but only commanded to attend. "Commands," he says, "are no constraints" (line 1372). He remains free to follow the dictates of his heart, those "rousing motions" (line 1382) that bring his final destructive action into line with his intention to find a way out of bondage to the Philistines. The poem ends on a note of "peace and consolation . . . / And calm of mind, all passion spent" (lines 1757–8).

The furious passions of *Samson Agonistes* may seem remote from the lyric exuberance of Milton's early Sonnet I, "O Nightingale," whose song fills "with fresh hope the Lover's heart" (line 3). But that same note of heart hope is sounded a quarter of a century later (1655) in his Sonnet XXII, "To Mr. Cyriack Skinner upon his Blindness." Three years of blindness have caused no abatement "Of heart or hope" in the poet (line 8). His refusal to lose heart sets the stage for the reassurances at the end of *Samson Agonistes* and is a useful reminder that the heart was not relegated to the mundane physical task of circulating blood in the wake of William Harvey's paradigm-altering work on its motions.

Most historians of science hold that Renaissance anatomical studies of the heart constitute a revolutionary departure from the traditions of natural philosophy, eventually replacing the seat of emotion and intellect with a

---

[57] See Camille W. Slights, "A Hero of Conscience: *Samson Agonistes* and Casuistry," *PMLA* 90 (1975): 395–413.

mechanical pumping station devoid of spiritual significance. Another conclusion, the one favored by Andrew Cunningham in *The Anatomical Renaissance*, emphasizes continuity with the natural philosophers and the predominance of "pious motives" (206) in the anatomical enterprise. The evidence provided by writers of the English Renaissance shows clearly that both views persisted through the seventeenth century. As medical practice developed out of anatomical theory and demonstration, popular culture responded with a combination of anxiety and relief. Far from losing its importance as a human signifier, the heart continued to be a focal point for the intellectual and emotional turmoil of the age.

"My heart upon my sleeve": early modern interiority, anatomy, and villainy

The year before Elizabeth I acceded to the throne of England, Lord Stourton employed five men to kidnap William Hartgill and his son John, beat them senseless, and slit their throats over a matter of property. William Farre, the man who actually did the throat-cutting, reportedly recoiled from the deed immediately, saying, "Ah my Lorde! This is a pytiouse sight: hadde I thought that I now thincke, before the thing was doon, your hole land could not have woon me to consent to soch an acte," to which Stourton replied, "What, fainte harted knave! ys yt anny more then the rydding of two knaves that lyving were trooblesome both to Goddes lawe and man's?"[1] The accusations of faint-heartedness and knavery are worth pausing over. The charge of knavery, entailing social as well as moral condescension, is complicated by being applied to both perpetrator and victim of the atrocities and is rendered thoroughly ironic in the mouth of the lord who authorized them. The charge of cowardice and irresolution, figured as a flaw located conventionally in the innermost recesses of Farre's being, in his heart, signals the need for further moral and legal probing of all involved in the murder as being themselves deeply "trooblesome both to Goddes lawe and man's." In the event, both Stourton and his servants were convicted and hanged within months of the incident. The case presents an array of concepts that can be helpful in sorting out the ways that crime writers and those concerned with representing villainy on stage explored the interior make-up, especially the hearts, of those who transgress and, occasionally, rediscover "Goddes lawe." Chief among those writing about the place of God's law in the heart of man in early modern England were divines and anatomists. In what follows, I will draw

---

[1] As reported from *The Wiltshire Archaeological and Natural History Magazine* of 1864 by Martin Wiggins in *Journeymen in Murder: The Assassin in English Renaissance Drama* (Oxford: Clarendon Press, 1991), 12.

on their insights in order to reconstruct the cultural context in which stage villains were endowed with a degree of psychological complexity that rivals that of the heroes they are pitted against.

I will argue that playwrights of the period used the language of anatomical and spiritual interiority – specifically the language of the heart, figured as the seat of human identity, vulnerability, and corruption – to define a world that is anathema to their villains. Most stage villains insist that they have a vacuum where others have a conscience, a deep-seated sense of the divine, tender fellow-feelings, and a heart. They refuse to acknowledge their own interiority in order to exploit others'. Vicious characters of Iago's sort self-consciously set out to subvert a conception of interiority based on anatomical theories and spiritual beliefs that were being actively promulgated during the sixteenth and seventeenth centuries. Even the most engaging of their fraternity fail in this, however, because the narratives and images of hidden interior lives that they seek to repudiate are precisely the ones they require to carry out their secret plots. They trade in the vulnerabilities of faith and the body.

An identifiable shift in conceptions of the villain's self took place between the Middle Ages and the early modern period. In pre-modern times, before the body, with its stipulated designation of outside and inside, came to stand for the subject, villains were defined by positionality rather than personality. As a result, they tended to be doubles of the heroes in medieval romances. In the case of *Sir Gowther*, for example, the titular hero himself moves seamlessly from demon to saint with no alteration of his personal style. Literally the spawn of the devil, the infant Gowther bites the nipples off his mother and kills five wet nurses. Later, he incinerates a nunnery and all its inhabitants. His virulent misogyny continues until he confesses to the Pope and is assigned a rigorous penance that involves taking no food that hasn't been brought to him by a dog. In the saintly latter period of his life, he exercises exactly the same forms of violence he had before, but now his victims are the enemies of Christianity.[2] Like Sir Gowther, medieval villains generally lack the reflexive wit and psychological depth to disguise themselves in the way that an Archimago or an Iago does. As Elizabeth Hanson says in *Discovering the Subject in Renaissance England*, moving into the sixteenth century takes us beyond the dominant medieval corporate sense of self into a realm of experiential

---

[2] *Sir Gowther*, in *Six Middle English Romances*, ed. Maldwyn Mills (London: Dent, 1973), 148–68. I am indebted to my colleague Yin Liu for directing me to *Sir Gowther* and to Kevin Whetter for helping me to understand it within its appropriate generic and temporal context.

science and legally protected selves.[3] These redefinitions of self are at the core of our fascination with villains in early modern plays.

Arguably the most mesmerizing stage villain of all is Iago. He sneers at what a dull, honest, transparent ass Othello is, and he mocks the very thought of showing anybody his own inner self:

> For when my outward action doth demonstrate
> The native act and figure of my heart
> In complement extern, 'tis not long after
> But I will wear my heart upon my sleeve
> For daws to peck at: I am not what I am. (*Othello* 1.1.61–5)

When he says "native act," he means what is proper specifically to himself. The "figure of my heart" is an emblematic representation of himself as he really is. While he lives, the world will never see his heart nor learn its secret intentions. During his moments of conspiracy and soliloquy we learn that Iago has fallen into what Francis Bacon calls the habit of dissimulation and, worse, simulation. In Bacon's words, the dissimulator "let[s] fall Signes, and Arguments, that he is not, that he is," and the simulator "pretends to be, that he is not."[4] Later, when Othello threatens, "By heaven, I'll know thy thoughts," Iago turns him aside by distinguishing between shared knowledge and secret thoughts: "You cannot" know my thoughts, he answers, "if my heart were in your hand, / Nor shall not, whilst 'tis in my custody" (3.3.162–3).[5] Othello is groping in the dark when he looks to Iago for "close dilations, working from the heart" (3.3.123), not realizing that Iago carefully denies access to his interior self for fear of becoming as susceptible to manipulation, humiliation, and punishment as his victims are. Iago concludes the speech from which I've drawn the title of the present chapter with the words, "I am not what I am" (1.1.65), chillingly negating God's act of self-naming in Exodus

---

[3] Elizabeth Hanson, *Discovering the Subject in Renaissance England* (Cambridge: Cambridge University Pess, 1998), 11.

[4] Francis Bacon, "Of Simulation and Dissimulation" in *The Essayes or Counsels, Civill and Morall* (1625), ed. Michael Kiernan, the Oxford Francis Bacon (Oxford: Clarendon Press, 1985), 21. Stephen Greenblatt's analysis of Iago's behavior in terms of empathy with and displacement of the hero resembles Bacon's description of simulating a virtue. See *Renaissance Self-Fashioning: From More to Shakespeare* (Chicago: University of Chicago Press, 1980), 222–57.

[5] An engraving of the anatomy theater at Leiden University in 1609 depicts the anatomist Peter Pauw holding what may be the heart of his subject-cadaver in his left hand. One symbolic implication of such a possibility is that the anatomist has penetrated to the profoundest knowledge of his subject. Iago finds such a possibility anathema. He rejects the goals of natural philosophy (i.e. formulating and sharing knowledge) in order to pursue a rhetoric of innuendo and indeterminacy, what Madeleine Doran calls "Iago's if." See Doran's essay, "Iago's 'if': An Essay on the Syntax of *Othello*," in *The Drama of the Renaissance: Essays for Leicester Bradner* (Providence, RI: Brown University Press, 1970), 53–78.

3:14, "I AM THAT I AM." This was also the mantra of the straightforward comic book hero, Popeye the Sailor Man, who said it with a Brooklyn accent: "I yam whad I yam." But there appears to be no stable, unified self in Shakespeare's villain, no "I yam," only layers of mask and pretense and surfaces. Who is he, and what does he desire? There is evidence in the play, however contradictory, that Iago wants Othello's wife, Roderigo's money, Cassio's position, the Duke's respect, and Emilia's obedience. But these motives don't quite make the sum of Shakespeare's character. With Iago, we experience something like the disillusionment of the Renaissance anatomists attempting to cut to the truth under the skin of their subjects. Devon Hodges and Jonathan Sawday have argued that anatomists such as Modino, Fabricius, Columbo, Vesalius, and Banister looked into the body for evidence of divine mystery at the most profound level of the soul but found instead only progressive layers of surface.[6] They found no prime mover inside each of us, unless it be the heart.

The issue, as always in the study of staged interiority, is whether it is possible to draw anything authentic from within a dramatic character, especially one as defensively self-aware as Iago. My own view, based on studying a variety of villains in close conjunction with the anatomy textbooks that helped to shape early modern thinking about the structures and uses of the body's interior parts, is that the complex moralization of both drama and dissection allows far more information to be communicated than can be contained by even the most secretive villains. Truths – if not *the* truth – about an Iago or a Richard III bleed around the edges of the masks they create for popular consumption. Richard's vows to protect others – his brother, his wife, his cousins, his king – repeatedly reveal his urge to murder them. The impulse underlying everything that "honest" Iago does is to *dis*honor everyone around him. The special relationship that dramatists, like anatomists, develop with their audiences in the pursuit of disguised truth is deepened rather than obscured by their representations of those who seek to destroy the truth.

The deep desire to expose those who only pretend to profess the truth is equally evident in the anatomy handbooks of the period. As Nancy G. Siraisi argues in her reading of the teleological common ground shared by the two most famous anatomists of the pre-modern and early modern period, Galen and Andreas Vesalius, this branch of natural philosophy was both negatively and positively moralized. On the negative side she lists the depiction of the

---

[6] Devon L. Hodges, *Renaissance Fictions of Anatomy* (Amherst: University of Massachusetts Press, 1985), 15, and Jonathan Sawday, *The Body Emblazoned: Dissection and the Human Body in Renaissance Culture* (London: Routledge, 1995), 11.

skeleton as symbol of universal decay and dissection as the final act of exposure and punishment of criminals. To these I would add the implied critique of those wealthy and influential spectators attending anatomical dissections for idle curiosity or cheap thrills and also the popular fear that the anatomists were desecrating the temple of the Holy Spirit. These are the same negative morals embodied in Iago. He presents a cynical picture to Roderigo in the play's opening scene of the (nearly) universal corruption to which mankind is subject. In the final scene he refuses to take part in a public spectacle of confession and contrition, swearing "From this time forth I never will speak word" (5.2.304). His defiant vow of silence puts him in the way of another public, physical form of spectacle, torture ("Torture will ope your lips" (5.2.305)). The opening of his lips may well entail the drawing (disembowelment) and quartering of his criminal body. Gratiano and Lodovico can think of no grimmer threat for the secretive villain than having his innards exposed to the prying eyes of the Venetian populace.[7] There may also be some solace for the victims of villainy in the act of dissection. Baffled by what makes such ungrateful characters tick, King Lear proposes, "Then let them anatomize Regan; see what breeds about her heart. Is there any cause in nature that make these hard hearts?" (*King Lear* 3.6.76–8). The enormous hope invested in the skill of the anatomist is futile, however. Answers to the question of evil are not forthcoming.

The counterpoise to this negative moralization of anatomy and tragedy is that those who produce both kinds of discourse are celebrating the divine splendor of the human mind and the human form, even at their most vulnerable. Here, for instance, is Vesalius on the achievement of the "*Opifex rerum*," the Maker of all things, when it came to constructing a flexible cage to contain the vital organs:

One must admire the skill of the supreme Creator of the world in constructing the thorax, not entirely from bone nor entirely from flesh, but from muscle and bone alternately . . . [I]f the thorax consisted wholly and solely of bones, the

---

[7] In *Discipline and Punish: The Birth of the Prison*, trans. Alan Sheridan (New York: Pantheon Books, 1977), Michel Foucault famously puts the case for interpreting public execution and other forms of punishment as spectacular demonstrations of the power of the state mechanism at work. His evidence comes from a slightly later period, and scholars have found counter-evidence suggesting contemporary rejection of this form of political moralizing. The careful regulation of public dissection in the early modern period, however, suggests some such ideological imperatives at work.

Vesalius described having "dissected [a] girl's uterus for the sake of the hymen" during one of his autopsies. See C. D. O'Malley, *Andreas Vesalius of Brussels, 1514–1564* (Berkeley: University of California Press, 1965), 63. Howard Marchitello proposes this account as a possible model for the spectacle of male domination and exploitation of the female body in *Othello*. See Marchitello's "Vesalius' *Fabrica* and Shakespeare's *Othello*: Anatomy, Gender and the Narrative Production of Meaning," *Criticism* 35 (1993): 529–58.

movements of the chest which we require mainly for breathing in would be completely abolished; and if, on the other hand, it was formed solely of muscles to produce these movements, the muscles, having nothing outside to control them, would collapse upon the lungs and heart.[8]

The parts of the human frame and the uses for which God designed them are the subject of Vesalius's highly ambitious and influential book, and he is as critical of those who misconstrue that divine plan as the tragedian is of villains who twist the truth out of shape for their own ends. Vesalius is outraged, for example, that Galen misrepresents the masterful join between skull and spine:

> What, if the truth be told, could be more disgraceful than to impute to Nature, who is much more precious to me than Galen is, extreme carelessness in what is actually the most brilliant joint in the whole body? Nature has done nothing to deserve such treatment! ... What joint, I ask you, is there in the whole body, in which the head of one bone moves in the socket of another in such a way that the head loses contact with the socket? None, of course, except, if we believe Galen, the joint between the head and the first vertebra. (*Fabrica*, 153)

The writer's outrage that anyone, particularly the "prince of anatomists," should so twist the truth and deprecate God's purposeful design for human life is palpable in this passage. Such occlusion of God's truth is nothing less than villainous, and the failing is not just technical but spiritual as well. The intimate link between the functions of the body's parts and its spiritual vitality brings us back to the centrality of the heart in all this.[9] As Vesalius puts it in Chapter 4 of the *Epitome* of his *Fabrica*, "Of the organs which are created for rekindling the natural heat within us and for the restoration and nourishment of our spirits, the heart is considered by far the most important part of the agitative faculty."[10] Such sentiments likewise inform the most important breakthrough in seventeenth-century body science, William Harvey's *De motu cordis*, whose dedication to Charles I begins, "The heart of animals is the foundation of their life, the sovereign of everything within them, the sun of their microcosm, that upon which all growth depends, from which all

---

[8] Andreas Vesalius, *On the Fabric of the Human Body Book 1* (1543), trans. William Frank Richardson and John Burd Carman (San Francisco: Norman Publishing, 1998), 207. Subsequent references will appear parenthetically.

[9] In his stimulating book *Bodies and Selves in Early Modern England: Physiology and Inwardness in Spenser, Shakespeare, Herbert, and Milton* (Cambridge: Cambridge University Press, 1999), Michael C. Schoenfeldt argues that Galen's theory of humors facilitated a material-psychological experience of the inward self, an experience that required discipline lest the body overrun its boundaries. This discipline, he insists, is profoundly moral. He draws literary evidence for his argument mainly from lyric and epic poetry, but it is equally borne out by early modern stage villainy.

[10] *The Epitome of Andreas Vesalius* (1543), trans. L. R. Lind (New York: Macmillan, 1949), 57.

power proceeds."[11] The heart had been considered the center of nobility and the target of inward corruption since classical times, and early modern students of anatomy honored that tradition.

From the time of Plato to the Renaissance, the heart changed in its purported functions, but it never lost its premier position among the organs. In the Platonic scheme, as we have noted earlier, the heart was the source of the passions and of the heat that distinguished all living things. The vitality of the animal soul was, for Aristotle, uniquely situated in the heart. Galen adhered to this tradition, though he assigned crucial physiological functions to the brain and liver. The lifeblood of the humoral system, a system that persisted well into the eighteenth century, was thought to be created in the heart. Without its perpetual renewal, the body, and especially the male body, would cease to have its essential characteristic of heat. Exposing the heart to view through vivisection of snakes, frogs, dogs, pigs, and apes and through postmortem dissection of human bodies during what Andrew Cunningham calls the anatomical Renaissance demonstrated its rhythmic pulsation and helped to correct such erroneous assumptions as a permeability of the septum between the chambers of the heart and the existence of a bone in the heart. While such procedures should have acted to demystify the metaphorical heart, they did no such thing.

In 1639, with the impact of the anatomical Renaissance already well established, Edward May published *A most certaine and true relation of a strange monster or serpent found in the left ventricle of the heart of Iohn Pennant*, including an illustration of a monstrous heart worm that had to be surgically removed and subdued within a magic circle of garlic (Fig. 22). May traces the genesis of the evil "serpent" to Pennant's state of spiritual despair. A similar narrative of despair marking the heart of its victim involved one of Queen Elizabeth's maids of honor, Mistress Ratcliffe, who, grieving the death of her brother, "voluntarily [set] about to starve her selfe." Upon her death, "her Mae^tie being [present?] commaunded her body to be opened and founde it all well and sounde, saving certaine stringes striped all over her harte."[12] The results of these forensic autopsies attest to the moral dimension of early

---

[11] William Harvey, *An Anatomical Disquisition of the Motion of the Heart and Blood in Animals [De motu cordis]*, trans. Robert Wills (London: J. M. Dent & Sons, 1907), 3. Harvey's microcosmic placing of the heart within the body is part of a continuous tradition of metaphors for the sovereign majesty of the organ. For example, in 1548 Thomas Vicary, enumerating the "partes that be inwardly," speaks "fyrst of the Hart, because he is the principal of al other members, and the beginning of life: he is set in the middest of the brest seuerally by him selfe, as Lord and King of al members." *A Profitable Treatise of the Anatomie of Mans Body* (London: H. Bamforde, 1577), sigs. H4^v–J1^r.

[12] From *The Letters of Philip Gawdy*, quoted by Michael Neill, "'What Strange Riddle's This?': Deciphering *'Tis Pity She's a Whore*," in *John Ford: Critical Re-Visions* (Cambridge: Cambridge University Press, 1998), 156.

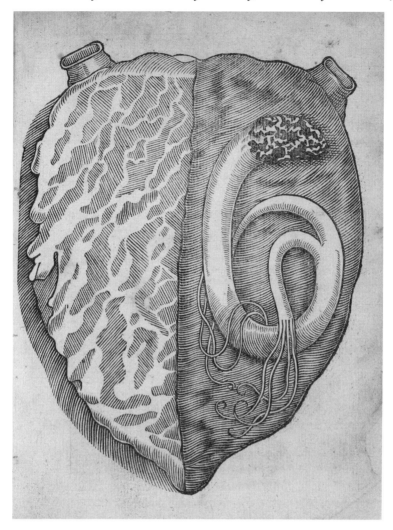

Figure 22. Heart worm. Edward May, *A most certaine and true relation of a strange monster or serpent found in the left ventricle of the heart of Iohn Pennant* (London: G. Miller, 1639), sig. A4^r, reproduced by permission of the Folger Shakespeare Library, Washington, DC. Shelfmark STC 17709. The coiled worm was surgically removed and subdued within a magic circle of garlic during Pennant's autopsy.

modern heart science. Something far more sinister than the word of God was thought to be inscribed in the hearts of sinners, and the practice of dissection was enlisted in its discovery.

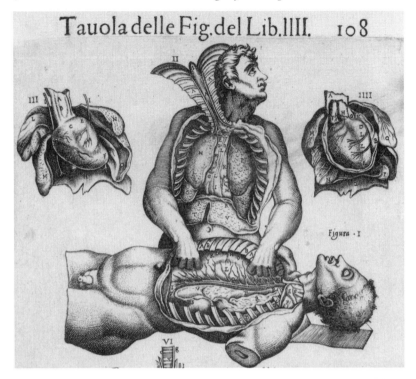

Figure 23. Self-dissecting anatomist. Juan Valverde de Hamusco, *Anatomia del corpo humano* (Rome: A. Salamanca, 1560), Lib IIII: 108, reproduced by permission of the Wellcome Library, London. Shelfmark 6476/D. The interior of the anatomical demonstrator himself has been revealed, and a heart has been drawn on either side.

A happier act of self-discovery is depicted in the *Anatomia del corpo humano* by the Spanish anatomist Juan Valverde de Hamusco (Fig. 23). In this illustration, the anatomist seems as pleased to retract his own sawn-off sternum as that of the cadaver on which he is demonstrating. He is flanked by two views of the heart in this act of self-revelation, almost as though he wears his heart on his sleeve. There is a remarkable degree of self-consciousness in the early modern anatomical texts that Andrea Carlino has called books of paper bodies. This textualization of the body created a powerful iconography that was brought into play not only in the university training of medical practitioners but also in dramatic and religious works of the period.[13] Further

---

[13] Recent studies by William Worthen, Janet Dillon, and Elizabeth Sauer have gone a great way in breaking down the unnecessary boundaries between performativity and textuality. See also William W. E. Slights, "Textualized Bodies and Bodies of Text in *Sejanus* and *Coriolanus*," *Medieval and Renaissance Drama in England* 5 (1991): 181–93.

work on the early modern history and culture of interiority requires study in all of these areas.

There was general agreement in the period that activities of the conscience were closely related to those of the heart. It was there that one made choices that were either consonant with or contrary to the law of God and there that those choices were retained for future inspection. The Reverend Robert Welstead instructed his congregation that:

by the heart you may not vnderstand that fleshly substance in mans body, which *Philosophers* obserue to be *Primu[m] viuens, & vltimum moriens*, although in that sense the word bee sometimes vsed in Scripture . . . but that more spirituall part of man, which is, as it were, the heart of that heart, that is, the soule, with all the powers, and faculties thereof, the minde, will, and affections and that which is in a sort compounded of them all, the Conscience: which because it keeps its chiefest residence, and exercises its most principall operations in and by the heart, is vsually in Scirpture [*sic*] knowne by that name[14]

The anchor for such lessons was always the Word, which spoke to the very heart of the physical heart, that is, to the soul. No intermediary interpreted the laws of God, only the individual conscience, which was located in the heart. As Samuel Page put it, our moral being is stored in "the book of our conscience" that "was called of old, our in-wit."[15] Meditation allowed the faithful to read what was stored in that interior book. According to the reformed churches of England, then, inventories of the heart were carried out not by a priest in the confessional but by one's self in moments of meditation and prayer. The heart was also scrutinized by an all-seeing God. Like clergymen, early modern anatomists and dramatists were keenly aware of the scriptural tradition of regular heart inspections as they are recorded in both Old and New Testaments. King David's instructions to his son Solomon, for example, are very particular on this point:

And thou, Salomón, my sone, knowe thou the God of thy father, and serue him with a perfit hearte, and with a willing minde: for the Lord searcheth all hearts, and vnderstandeth all the imaginacions of thoughtes: if thou seke him, he wil be founde of thee; but if thou forsake him, he wil cast thee of for euer. (1 Chron 28: 9)

Not only is the heart the object of moral scrutiny, it is also the organ that promotes (or ignores) spiritual health. Medical metaphors for spiritual well-being are a striking feature of the religious iconography of the early modern period. They are deeply implicated in the language and practice

---

[14] Robert Welstead, *The Cure of a Hard-Heart. First preached in diuers sermons* (London: W. Stansby for S. Man, 1630), 4–5.
[15] Samuel Page, *The Broken Heart: or, Davids Penance* (London: T. Harper, 1637), 10.

Figure 24. "Miracvla Christi." Hendrik Goltzius, 1578, engraving, 23.7 × 18.3 cm, reproduced by permission of the Wellcome Library, London. Library reference no. ICV No7857. Christ the physician holds a glass heart filled with animals for dissection, while a gravely ill woman catches His healing blood in a cup.

of curing diseased body parts, particularly the heart. An engraving by Hendrik Goltzius (Fig. 24) shows Christ the healer holding in his left hand a cross become caduceus (emblem of physicians) and in his right a heart-shaped glass container of animals from the anatomy laboratory, notably a pig and a frog. The healing blood from the crucified Christ's side-wound spurts into a cup held by a mortally ill woman. The anatomical and the moral work hand in hand in this reassuring picture. Into this scene, the authors of stage tragedy introduced the group of morally corrupt or, at best, ambiguous characters with whom I am primarily concerned here. So much of the language of moralized anatomy and medicalized theology had been absorbed into sixteenth-century culture that the most vehement denials by villains of an accessible interior life come across as a desperate defense against the inevitable. Their interior spaces will be probed and their motives discovered. The quest for interiority had become irresistible.

Interiority has been a lively topic of inquiry in early modern studies for some time now. The case for the crucial importance of interiority to early modern literature was made by Anne Ferry two decades ago in her book *The "Inward" Language*. She pointed to the "separation between 'what must show' and what is in the heart."[16] These ideas were further refined by Katharine Maus in *Inwardness and Theater in the English Renaissance* (University of Chicago Press, 1995) and highlighted the political bad faith of villains who divorce their outward appearances from the heart's truth. To this I would add that, while villains fall into widely varying categories, each one holds at arm's length a community from which he or she feels profoundly alienated.

Working from a brief taxonomy of stage villainy, we can gauge the degree to which these characters are aware of, and fiercely protective of, an inner self. Consider four distinct types of villains: the tool-villain, the demon-villain, the ambi-villain, and the hero-villain.[17] The first group includes assassins for hire, frequently men with low social status and little understanding of the moral complexity of the actions into which they have been thrust. Sometimes they are named simply by their plot function: third murderer. The assassin for hire has little to hide by way of inner secrets. The demon-villains, such as Iago, Richard III, and Flamineo in John Webster's *The White Devil*, are preternatural spoilers who are constitutionally unable to permit anyone around them to experience contentment. They are endowed with enormous rhetorical skills with which they deflect the attempts of other characters to discover their goals and motives. What I have called the ambi-villains are characterized by an initial commitment to evil, a subsequent change of heart, and an eventual crisis of self-recrimination. Like the real-life villain

---

[16] Anne Ferry, *The "Inward" Language: Sonnets of Wyatt, Sidney, Shakespeare, Donne* (Chicago: University of Chicago Press, 1983), 28.

[17] Eugene M. Waith uses the term "tool-villain" in his eminently sensible essay, "Concern for Villains," *Renaissance Drama* n.s. 24 (1993): 155–70, though he uses it in a somewhat looser way than I do. I will explain "ambi-villain" in due course.

William Farre with whom I began this chapter, these villains are profoundly ambivalent about the morality of their actions. Their moments of inner enlightenment and reversal occur too late to save their victims but in time to engage the moral faculties of an audience that watches in horror as the consequences of troubling "Goddes lawe and man's" play themselves out on stage. Finally, the hero-villains articulate their motives and ambitions in agonizing detail. Their overreaching and underachieving find expression in their intense acts of self-analysis. Even as they pursue their goals with heroic energy, they are carrying out acts of self-dissection that lay bare the colossal imperfections of their hearts.

Readers will have noticed that the four categories of villainy I have just outlined not only overlap, they also leave out a great many stage knaves. Where, for instance, might Marlowe's Barabas or Shakespeare's Edmund of Gloucester fit into this taxonomy? But by considering exemplars from each group, we can usefully identify several stages of interiority and the cultural assumptions they represent. Consider first the tool-villain named Black Will from *Arden of Faversham*. Will is a villain-for-hire and a notorious oath-breaker. He wears the bloody badge of violence on his face, and he is eager to disembowel Arden, for a price:

> Tush, I have broken five hundred oaths!
> But wouldst thou charm me to effect this deed [i.e. murdering Arden],
> Tell me of gold, my resolution's fee;
> [. . .]
> Seest thou this gore that cleaveth to my face?
> From hence ne'er will I wash this bloody stain
> Till Arden's heart be panting in my hand.[18]

The tool-villain's motives are purely external: gold alone confirms his resolution to be a villain. For Black Will the heart holds no secrets. It is simply a piece of meat which, when ripped from Arden's body, will serve as economic exchange for his gold. Indicative of his ignorance of the body is the verb "panting," which conflates the pulsations of the heart with the rhythms of respiration, a common error of early anatomies that Vesalius had been at pains to correct. Black Will simply equates the bleeding heart of his victim with the "bloody stain" on his own forehead. The equation reminds us that we are dealing here with a bumbling, comic villain, a veritable Cloten. His head gets bloodied while he lurks near a shop, waiting to assassinate Arden. The shopkeeper, closing up for the day, lowers his shutters and accidentally

---

[18] *Arden of Faversham*, ed. Martin White, New Mermaids (New York: Norton, 1982). Quotation from Scene 3, lines 82–99.

clonks Will on the head, allowing Arden to escape once again in the ensuing confusion. At this stage, action trumps interiority. Much the same can be said in the case of what I have called the demon-villains; however, their careless rejection of the heart as the seat of conscience serves, as we shall see, to heighten the suffering of their victims.

Shakespeare's Aaron in *Titus Andronicus* offers a parody of the grave-robbing anatomist. He forces others to look into their hearts and confront painful emotions that they have tried, for their own self-preservation, to forget.

> Oft have I digg'd up dead men from their graves,
> And set them upright at their dear friends' door,
> Even when their sorrows almost was forgot,
> And on their skins, as on the bark of trees,
> Have with my knife carved in Roman letters,
> "Let not your sorrow die, though I am dead."
>
> (*Titus Andronicus* 5.1.135–40)

Rather than a confession, this is a taunt. Unlike an anatomist labelling an illustration of a cadaver for the benefit of his students, Aaron has inscribed the grim message of *memento mori* directly onto the flesh itself for his own sadistic pleasure. Lust for the conquered Queen Tamora and an Iago-like resentment of the conquering hero Titus are simply the proximate causes of his life-long, heart-felt bitterness. John Webster's demon-villain Flamineo rivals Aaron in the extent of domestic grief he causes. He pimps for his sister, Vittoria; he stabs his brother to death in front of their mother; he poisons a duke; he seduces, then beats up the black slave Zanche. Then he arranges an elaborate deception to expose the viciousness of his sister and his lover. He proposes a triple suicide, giving Vittoria the pistol to take her turn first. Instead, she shoots him, and the two women viciously attack his prostrate body.

VITTORIA   [T]hy sins
          Do run before thee to fetch fire from hell
          To light thee thither.
FLAMINEO   O I smell soot,
          Most stinking soot, the chimney is a-fire –
          My liver's parboiled like Scotch holy-bread;
          There's a plumber laying pipes in my guts, it scalds;
          Wilt thou outlive me?
ZANCHE   Yes, and drive a stake
          Through thy body; for we'll give it out
          Thou didst this violence upon thyself.[19]

---

[19] John Webster, *The White Devil*, ed. Christina Luckyj, New Mermaids, 2nd edn. (New York: Norton, 1996). Quotation from 5.6.137–45. Subsequent references will appear parenthetically.

Vittoria happily ushers her brother's spirit to hell, and the superstitious Zanche believes the only way to kill this devil is to drive a stake through his heart. Flamineo, overacting the part of the dying man, turns his gaze inward and discovers not a contrite heart but a boiler plate of liver and an incompetent surgeon fumbling with his internal plumbing. But he is not dying: "the pistols held no bullets" (5.6.148), and he has tricked the women into acting out their own murderous intentions.

The ambi-villain retains a strong sense of an inner self by combining intensely private anti-social motives with sympathy for his victims and moments of self-loathing. One of the most fascinating of these villains is the vicious and repentant Bosola in Webster's *The Duchess of Malfi*. Before displaying the inner turmoil of a man with a wounded conscience, he torments the Duchess with wax figures of her husband and children, apparently murdered, and casually tosses the wax husband's severed hand into her lap, laughing ghoulishly at her terrified response. Then, like Lord Stourton (or Browning's Duke of Ferrara), he gives commands and watches as the lovely young Duchess is strangled to death by his henchmen. Like William Farre, however, he repents his actions, pledging in all sincerity that he would give his own heart's blood to restore her to life.

> I would not change my peace of conscience
> For all the wealth of Europe –
>   [DUCHESS *moves*]
>   She stirs! Here's life!
> Return fair soul from darkness, and lead mine
> Out of this sensible hell! She's warm, she breathes!
> Upon thy pale lips I will melt my heart
> To store them with fresh colour. [*Kisses her*][20]

The melting heart and ruby lip are familiar tropes from Renaissance love poetry. In turning from villain to would-be lover, Bosola has added a fresh dimension to stage villainy. The audience engages with his emotional turmoil and is prepared to extend its sympathies to include even the chief architect of suffering in the play. He is, after all, a person with a soul, though not such a fair one as the Duchess had. He is as convincing a figure of openness as he had been a figure of secrecy, but he embodies these two contrasting principles of dramatic character sequentially. In this play, as in so many imaginative works of the early modern period, the world of the heart embodies and articulates the antithetical qualities of spiritual and sexual experience.

[20] John Webster, *The Duchess of Malfi*, ed. Brian Gibbons, New Mermaids, 4th edn. (New York: Norton, 2001). Quotation from 4.2.330–5.

Hero-villains like Macbeth must be both covert villain and publicly suffering hero at once. Macbeth's false face must be seen to hide a once-true heart, one amply endowed with courage and passion, however lacking in loyalty. He offers only half of this perception to his wife following his "If it were done" soliloquy: "False face must hide what the false heart doth know" (1.7.82). Lady Macbeth's heart becomes the object of medical scrutiny in the sleep-walking scene. The doctor speaks of her condition with a kind of medical and metaphoric precision generally overlooked in editorial glosses:

DOCTOR   The heart is sorely charg'd.
GENTLEWOMAN   I would not have such a heart in my bosom for the dignity
              of the whole body. (*Macbeth* 5.1.53–6)

The term "charged" conveys the idea that her heart is heavily burdened with troubles and also that it is loaded with an explosive charge, like a flintlock gun, ready to explode. The metaphor is used by William Harvey in *De motu cordis* to describe the violence of systolic movement (37–8). Lady Macbeth's heart is not in what the anatomists would have described as its natural state; it is so tainted that it infects the "dignity" or regal status of the queen's "whole body." Following close upon these lines, Macbeth acknowledges at the start of his famous speech about falling into the sear, the yellow leaf, "I am sick at heart" (5.3.19). In what follows, he converts his confession of illness into a moving plea for sympathy:

> [T]hat which should accompany old age,
> As honor, love, obedience, troops of friends,
> I must not look to have; but in their stead,
> Curses, not loud but deep, mouth-honor, breath,
> Which the poor heart would fain deny, and dare not. (5.3.24–8)

His has become a "poor" heart, one lacking the courage to reject flattery and to defy opposition. In this moment he, like Lady Macbeth, garners the sympathy of the audience. What allows Shakespeare to meld villain and hero is his precise anatomy of the heart, which reveals an enormously vulnerable interior place in his ambitious villains. Our view of the heart in agony provokes a desire, not to emulate or to condemn, but somehow simultaneously to sympathize with and to distance ourselves from the infected organ. This double response reflects the ambivalence with which our society as well as Shakespeare's regards the heart as a symbol of interiority. It is the seat of health and of disease, the tablet on which God inscribes His Word but also the secretive place where that Word is defied.

For years I have noticed that my students are eager to find explanations for the evils of Richard III, Aaron, Iago, Jachimo – for the whole gallery of

Shakespeare's villains. In this age of the socially constructed self, they are likely to maintain that villains are villainous because they are physically challenged (hunch-backed) or blacks trapped in a white world or Jews trapped in a Christian one or someone unfairly passed over for promotion or a poor, scorned courtier. These sympathetic outpourings for Shakespeare's creepiest characters are sometimes oversimplified, but they have a certain validity. The impulse to search out motives reveals something about how we like our villains. Samuel Taylor Coleridge notwithstanding, we don't like watching them because they are "motiveless malignit[ies]" that lack a complex inner self, but because they seem to have hugely mixed-up motives and selves, what Cynthia Marshall conceives of as shattered selves.[21] By working toward the radical incoherence of all but the simplest of the stage villains, my students are often able to locate forms of interiority that some professional critics assume could not have existed before the age of late modernity.

I began by positing as a kind of baseline for interiority God's clear and simple assertion, "I am that I am." But this is not an invitation to explore the inner make-up of God. It is a stonewalling tautology. Further questioning appears to be foreclosed, as it is when Iago declares, "Demand me nothing; what you know, you know: / From this time forth I never will speak word" (*Othello* 5.2.303–4). But I believe we can know a great deal about Iago, and the Bible brims with injunctions to learn to know God. In each case, there is far more to understand than a simple sailor man's good heart and the injunction to eat our spinach.

---

[21] See *Coleridge's Shakesperean Criticism*, ed. T. M. Raysor (Cambridge, MA: Harvard University Press, 1959), 1: 49. Sylvan Barnet explains that Coleridge is at pains to define Iago's inner corruption as anything but an element of his humanity, because otherwise the beloved Bard would have had to experience the human emotions himself that he depicts in his villain. See Barnet's "Coleridge on Shakespeare's Villains," *PMLA* 7 (1956): 10–20. On the prominence of the discontinuous self see Cynthia Marshall, *The Shattering of the Self: Violence, Subjectivity, and Early Modern Texts* (Baltimore: The Johns Hopkins University Press, 2002).

CHAPTER 6

Shakespeare and the cardiocentric self

HERMIA [*Starting up.*] Help me, Lysander, help me! do thy best
To pluck this crawling serpent from my breast!
Ay me, for pity! what a dream was here!
Lysander, look how I do quake with fear.
Methought a serpent eat my heart away,
And you sate smiling at his cruel prey.
(*A Midsummer Night's Dream* 2.2.145–50)

KING RICHARD O villains, vipers, damn'd without redemption!
Dogs, easily won to fawn on any man!
Snakes, in my heart-blood warm'd, that sting my heart!
Three Judases, each one thrice worse than Judas!
Would they make peace? Terrible hell
Make war upon their spotted souls for this! (*Richard II* 3.2.129–34)

JULIET O serpent heart, hid with a flow'ring face!
Did ever dragon keep so fair a cave?
Beautiful tyrant! fiend angelical!
Dove-feather'd raven! wolfish ravening lamb!
Despised substance of divinest show! (*Romeo and Juliet* 3.2.73–7)

The most stunning forms of betrayal in Shakespeare's early work are
captured by images of a serpent eating, stinging, or otherwise tormenting the
heart of an abandoned lover.[1] The association of the serpent with duplicity
and betrayal is as old as the book of Genesis, and its habit of insinuating itself
into the heart of its victims where it is nurtured by innocent heart's blood
was proverbial by the late sixteenth century. The image, if not unusual, is
arresting in the mouth of the terrified Hermia, the infuriated Richard II, and

---

[1] To the passages above may be added King Lear's complaint that, after cutting his train in half,
Goneril "strook me with her tongue, / Most serpent-like, upon the very heart" (2.4.160–1).
Contemporary naturalists held that the serpent's venom was delivered through its tongue.

the brokenhearted Juliet, all of whom made their debut on the London stage in the 1595–6 theater season.

The stinging pain of their fury and shame, to which I will return in a moment, is just one of the emotional experiences that Shakespeare embodied in the anatomical/religious imagery of the heart. Another thematically coherent set of images explores the suffering associated with pride, self-indulgence, and eventual contrition. These images of the dolorous, bleeding, bursting, weeping heart are, like the serpent-heart ones, spread across the full generic range of Shakespeare's work. The heart's repentance, when it comes, comes in distinctly religious forms, characterized by meditations on self-abnegation and anatomically precise descriptions of the body in pain.

In my search for a distinctively Shakespearean heart, I will consider the alienation of heart from tongue, eye, and hand, sure signs of a tragically disintegrating self. While it is common to talk about the "inner" lives of Shakespeare's characters, the fact is that surface and interior keep collapsing into one another in the early modern language of body and soul. The emotional lives of the characters are the product not only of their dialogues and monologues but also of their bodily postures on the stage.

Hermia's initial posture in 1.2 is supine and vulnerable as she tries to shake off the terrible nightmare of a serpent eating her heart away as her disdainful lover, seated nearby, observes the scene with a smile that is as cruel as the serpent's act of preying on the innocent sleeper. Freudians have, of course, had a field day with Hermia's dream and its aftermath, and rightly so, but my own concern is with the religio-humoral context of her waking terror. Her nightmare of losing her loving protector in the night wood focuses on the rapidly changing passions of her heart, which have replaced the thrill of elopement and deferred sexual experience with the terror of abandonment. She "quake[s]" with terror and soon confesses, "I swoon almost with fear" (2.2.154). The sudden, fearful chilling and shrinking of her heart has caused her blood to concentrate around that organ, leaving her limbs shaky and her head giddy in the Galenic version of a body in a state of shock. As Nicolas Coeffeteau explains in his *Table of the Humane Passions* (1621), a person in the grip of terror will "call back the blood and heate vnto the heart, as to the place where feare doth exercise her tyranny, therewith to defend themselues."[2] The "crawling serpent" that Hermia was cradling at her breast has robbed her of her vitality, not by stinging but by eating her heart in the manner of the medieval narratives of

---

[2] Nicolas Coeffeteau, *A Table of the Humane Passions*, trans. Edward Grimestone (London: N. Oakes, 1621), 21.

the *cœur mangé*. She has become the unhealthy victim of a love with decided satanic shadings. The feeling most painfully associated with this heart attack is shame, the shame of Lysander's dishonorable withdrawal under the influence of Puck's magic flower juice but also the imagined shame of the failure of Hermia's power to attract and retain a mate. While Lysander's passive spectatorship at the scene of the maiden in deep distress is shameful, so too is Hermia's desperate, indecorous pursuit of such a cad.

Like Hermia, King Richard II invokes the trope of snakes attacking his heart to express the shame of betrayal. The warmth of his "heart-blood" has spawned the vicious favorites Bushy, Green, and the Earl of Wiltshire, who have poisoned his entire system with their foul humors.[3] Returning to England from the hostilities in Ireland, Richard misses the warm welcome he had anticipated. All his supporters, young and old, male and female, have, according to Scroop's report, been transformed by Bullingbrook's military might into "hearts harder than steel" (3.2.111). Richard picks up the heart image as he transforms his own nascent fears of betrayal into fury directed against those he most loved and trusted: "Snakes, in my heart-blood warm'd, that sting my heart!" The narrative source of the image may well be Aesop's fable of the peasant who warmed a freezing serpent at his breast, only to be fatally stung by it, as Audrey Yoder notes, but the visceral force of Shakespeare's image derives from a close humoral reading of the body betrayed at its life-generating core by a substance that is both physiologically and psychologically corrosive.[4] The first reptilian betrayer in the Garden of Eden is displaced by a second one, and that one is multiplied exponentially by three, each of whom is "thrice worse than Judas" in Richard's self-projection into the role of the denounced Christ. Without dropping a metrical beat, Richard alters his rage into an equally unChristlike self-pity once Scroop explains to him that the villainous trio have made their peace not with Bullingbrook but with their Maker on the executioner's block:

> Let's talk of graves, of worms, and epitaphs,
> Make dust our paper, and with rainy eyes
> Write sorrow on the bosom of the earth. (*Richard II* 3.2.145–7)

The venomous heart has been replaced by the dolorous heart.

Juliet's "serpent heart, hid with a flow'ring face" registers no physiological symptoms because, like Richard and unlike Hermia, she is describing not her

---

[3] Bagot escapes Richard's curse, just as he has escaped the executioner's axe. See Charles R. Forker's "Longer Note" on 3.2.122 in the Arden 3 edition of *King Richard II* (London: Thomson, 2002), 493.

[4] Audrey Yoder, *Animal Analogy in Shakespeare's Character Portrayal* (New York: King's Crown Press, 1947), 18, 117–18.

own heart but the heart of her supposed betrayer, Romeo. Her nurse, though, feels the bodily chill of the rejection and calls for aqua-vitae to revive her (3.2.88–9) after Juliet calls for the damnation of her own personal Satan, her "fiend angelical." Here, as in the other two serpent-heart outbursts, we find ourselves standing to one side of the speakers' rage and self-pity, judging the betrayed as severely as the betrayer, since we know the extenuating circumstances and misread ambiguities that cloud the situations. Indeed, Juliet's highly contrived string of oxymorons ("Dove-feather'd raven! wolfish ravening lamb! " and so on) and Richard's Christ-complex have most often been read as disagreeable signs of immaturity and self-dramatization. But the case is never so simple where the emotions of the heart, especially love and shame, are in question. Our sympathies are never entirely disengaged. Hermia will be made to feel all the imagined inadequacies of a teenager in love; Richard will experience the shame of alienating all but a handful of his subjects; and Juliet will pay with her life for having dishonored her family with a Montague. All three have misconstrued the present circumstances, and all will feel bewildered and ashamed when they are undeceived. Juliet's "O what a beast was I to chide at him! " (3.2.95) and Richard's plunge into "sad stories of the death of kings" (3.2.156) follow immediately upon their mistaken denunciation of serpents' hearts, and in the next scene where she appears, Hermia speaks almost entirely in bewildered questions, ending "I am amaz'd, and know not what to say" (3.2.144). If the divinity of passion and the reliability of discipleship suddenly lose their attraction for Juliet and Richard, there are good reasons for the skepticism lying beneath their immediate errors of perception. It is the case that Romeo has been grossly provoked into killing Tybalt, and Bushy, Green, and Wiltshire have not been received into the enemy's camp, but it is equally true that both Juliet and Richard have been seduced by a naïve view of love and loyalty. The phantom acts of betrayal will be followed by other, real ones, and the heroes will eventually learn to repent the self-indulgent faith that falls victim to a heart paralyzed by fear and sorrow.

When Richard hears the bell that he imagines tolls for him in his Pomfret Castle prison cell, the sounds become groans striking on his dolorous heart. By this point in the action, Richard has been deposed and thoroughly derided. His humiliation or "bafflement" is complete;[5] his heart has become a mechanical register of lonely hours and his physical body reduced to the

---

[5] On the shaming ritual known as "baffling" or "bawchling" see William W. E. Slights, "Ain't It a Shame: History and Psychology in *Richard II* Criticism," in *Re-visions of Shakespeare: Essays in Honor of Robert Ornstein*, ed. Evelyn Gajowski (Newark: University of Delaware, 2004), 243–59, esp. 248–50.

level of the manikin or "Jack" who mindlessly strikes the bell on old clocks to record the passing of hours and fractions of hours. His dull heart is as full of sorrow as his days are of meaningless minutes.

> Now, sir, the sound that tells what hour it is
> Are clamorous groans, which strike upon my heart,
> Which is the bell. So sighs, and tears, and groans
> Show minutes, times, and hours; but my time
> Runs posting on in Bullingbrook's proud joy,
> While I stand fooling here, his Jack of the clock. (5.5.55–60)

He feels foolish and ashamed. The out-of-time music he had heard earlier cannot ease his heart's pain the way it should.[6] There is no relief in this for Richard's afflicted heart but total abnegation in the hope of salvation. The Groom, who interrupts his self-despising meditation, heightens and shares his sense of grief and yearning for a better world, saying that it grieved or "ern'd [his] heart" to watch Bullingbrook's triumphal entry into London mounted on Richard's "roan Barbary" (5.5.76–80). He also remarks on the terrible disjunction between what he is permitted to say in the current political environment and what he truly feels: "What my tongue dares not, that my heart shall say" (5.5.97). The heart has its own silent eloquence, preserving secret sentiments in troubled times.[7] Earlier innocent expectations of joy and hope are strangled in the heart by fear and sorrow.

While Shakespeare cannot be credited with devising a systematic plan of the human passions, there is abundant evidence that he injected vitality and subtlety into a scheme with a distinguished heritage among philosophers, theologians, and medical writers. In Platonic thought the passions or

---

[6] The Nurse's servant Peter in *Romeo and Juliet* comments on this function of music when he requests that the musicians play "Heart's Ease," part of which goes:

> When griping griefs the heart doth wound,
> And doleful dumps the mind oppress,
> Then music with her silver sound
> [. . .]
> With speedy help doth lend redress. (4.5.126–8, 143)

The song requested by Queen Katherine in *Henry VIII* associates the curative powers of music on the heart with the magical charms of Orpheus: "In sweet music is such art, / Killing care and grief of heart" (3.1.12–13). Many early treatises extol the medicinal virtues of music. See, for example, R. Brockleby, *Reflections on Ancient and Modern Musick, with the Application to the Cure of Diseases* (London, 1749).

[7] The drama of the period is filled with examples of lovers whose hearts are isolated from the world at large and from the rest of their bodies. Body parts that should communicate internally and externally – tongues, eyes, even blood – feel cut off. For example, the blood, which should carry true messages from the heart to the beloved, fails to do so in *The Spanish Tragedy* and *'Tis Pity She's a Whore* when letters literally written in blood are not believed by their recipients.

affections are sudden, short-lived eruptions that disrupt the natural disposition, producing exactly the kind of explosive interpersonal dynamic favored by dramatists.[8] The classification of the passions acquires a distinctly moral flavor when Aristotle defines these sudden, powerful inclinations and revulsions in terms of external objects that are either good – and hence to be pursued and embraced – or evil – and hence to be feared and shunned.[9] This moral component to passionate human behavior, whether the intemperate attraction of lovers or the sudden fury of villains, likely entered early modern thought through the influence of Cicero, whose *Tusculan Disputations* outline four primary passions: delight (*laetitia*), distress (*aegrituda*), lust (*cupiditas* or *libido*), and fear (*metus*).[10] We have been observing in the speeches of Hermia, Richard, and Juliet the ways that a combination of present grief and projected fear can suddenly replace the good impulses of joy and desire, turning love to hate. This is a familiar narrative pattern, and the ethical precision of the characters' articulation of their passions owes its form to the Ciceronian model.

St. Thomas Aquinas constructed his own scheme of the passions on Aristotle's categories of the "concupiscible" and the "irascible," dividing the former into six types of passionate responses to immediate pleasure and pain and the latter into five ways of pursuing less easily achievable objects of desire.[11] The arduous pursuit of the good and avoidance of evil are thus bound to human feelings and define an inner, spiritual discipline. While early modern treatises on the passions such as Timothy Bright's *A Treatise of Melancholie* (1586), Thomas Wright's *The Passions of the Minde in Generall* (1601), and Sir John Davies's *Nosce teipsum* (1599) tended to

[8] Plato *Laches* (191), Loeb Classical Library, trans. W. R. M. Lamb (London: William Heinemann, 1924), 49. Defining courage with the dubious help of Laches, Socrates insists that any definition must include "all who are not merely courageous against pain or fear, but doughty fighters against desires and pleasures." In the *Timaeus* (69), he specifies that "the heart, which is the junction of the veins and the fount of the blood which circulates vigorously through all the limbs" was created to be "the chamber of the bodyguard, to the end that when the heat of the passion boils up," the reason can bring "relief for the leaping of the heart." See the *Timaeus*, Loeb Classical Library, trans. Rev. R. G. Bury (London: William Heinemann, 1929), 181–3.

[9] Aristotle, *Ethics* (1105b20). In H. Rackham's translation the category of "emotions" is expounded as follows: "By the emotions, I mean desire, anger, fear, confidence, envy, joy, friendship, hatred, longing, jealousy, pity; and generally those states of consciousness which are accompanied by pleasure or pain." See the *Nicomachean Ethics*, Loeb Classical Library (London: William Heinemann, 1968), 87.

[10] Cicero, *Tusculan Disputations*, trans. J. E. King, Loeb Classical Library (London: Heinemann, 1927), Bk IV, 7, 14–15, and 611. In his *Arte of Logick* (London: W. Stansby, 1617; 1st edn. J. Windet, 1599), Thomas Blundeville asks, "*Which be the chiefe passions or affections of the minde?*" and answers, "The chiefe affections be these foure, ioy, lust, sorrow, feare" (32). The Player-King in *Hamlet* notes the precarious balance of the predominant passions: "Grief joys, joy grieves on slender accident" (3.2.199).

[11] St. Thomas Aquinas, *Summa Theologiae*, 1a2ae, Q. 25, 4 (London: Blackfriars, 1964), 19: 55–9.

return to the four-part Stoic arrangement of the passions, they never lost their deep concern for the moral valences of human desire and behavior.[12] Nor did they lose the conviction that the passions belong to the heart.

The woodcut title page of Edward Grimestone's 1621 translation of Nicolas de Coeffeteau's *A Table of the Humane Passions* (Fig. 25) is dominated by a heart containing the title and authorship details. Ranged beneath the heart are four women representing Pleasure (holding a bird), Paine (holding her aching tummy and head), Hope (leaning on her emblematic anchor), and Feare (hugging herself in terror). Coeffeteau explains that when the "spirits which we cal Vitall" are disrupted by these four passions, "the whole body feeles it selfe mooued, not onely inwardly, but also outwardly," always leaving "some visible trace."[13] These outward and visible signs (paleness, blushing, agitation, and so on) entered the rhetoric of early modern theatrical passion, though many such alterations in appearance could not actually be seen by spectators until the age of the cinematic close-up. Shakespeare's audience would have known, however, that the language of bodily perturbation referred to a sudden alteration, "contrary to the lawes of nature," that "transports the heart beyond the bounds, which nature hath prescribed it, and doth agitate it extraordinarily."[14] Writing in 1559, Thomas Blundeville explained with great precision and an elaborate table, that "Ioy is a sweet and delectable motion of the heart, wherewith it is stirred and delighted, whilest it enioieth some good that is present, or (at the least) seemeth good."[15] With his final phrase, Blundeville leaves open the possibility of a future "alteration" that might further disturb the balance of the affections, perhaps in the direction of fear, which, he says, "is a greeuous motion, causing the heart to shrinke together, whilest it flieth some euill that is to come." Symptomatically fear is expressed as "heauinesse, shame, terrour, sownding [i.e. swooning], and such like."[16] Here are the emotions, motives, and physical reactions of the body in extremity, the stuff of high drama.

No system such as the tetrapartite Ciceronian one for classifying the passions was ever received prescriptively or statically by a playwright. For the early modern dramatists and philosophic vitalists,[17] the heart was an

---

[12] Susan James, *Passion and Action: The Emotions in Seventeenth-Century Philosophy* (Oxford: Clarendon Press, 1997), 4. See also Rolf Soellner, "The Four Primary Passions: A Renaissance Theory Reflected in the Works of Shakespeare," *Studies in Philology* 55 (1958): 549–67.

[13] Coeffeteau, *Table of the Humane Passions*, 16–17.

[14] Coeffeteau, *Table of the Humane Passions*, 18.

[15] Blundeville, *Arte of Logike*, 32.

[16] Blundeville, *Arte of Logike*, 33.

[17] On seventeenth-century vitalism see John Rogers, *The Matter of Revolution: Science, Poetry, and Politics in the Age of Milton* (Ithaca: Cornell University Press, 1996), 8–38.

Figure 25. Title page. Nicolas Coeffeteau, *A Table of the Humane Passions*, trans. Edward Grimestone (London: N. Oakes, 1621), reproduced by permission of the Folger Shakespeare Library, Washington, DC. Shelfmark STC 5473. The heart containing Coeffeteau's title dominates the four female figures representing the chief passions: (left to right) Pleasure, Paine, Hope, and Feare.

interactive organ that both produced emotion and reacted in size and motion to stimuli from the external world. The heart never settled long into joy, hope, sorrow, or fear (at least not the first two), instead responding with indecision and ambivalence to a world of mingled good and ill. The passions are never single and simple but exist in a constant state of tension, with sometimes one, then another predominating, or else some new combination. Like consciences and acts of penance, these conditions of the heart are a source of constant debate and uncertainty. Inner self-conflict was presented as a source of vitality and evidence of having an active soul.

Late in his playwriting career Shakespeare uses an extended act of penance as the way out of a crisis of conscience that began with an excruciating heart attack. When Leontes confides in soliloquy that "I have *tremor cordis* on me," he goes on to specify that his strong reaction to watching the exchange of intimacies between his wife and his best friend is painful, not joyful: "my heart dances, / But not for joy; not joy" (*The Winter's Tale* 1.2.110–11). The jealous "Affection" or sudden alteration that seizes his mind and body and overwhelms him (line 137) "stabs the center" of his being, his heart (line 137). Here is a form of disease that Leontes can do nothing to counter. He is held in the grip of uncontrollable rage and, later, of his abject sorrow for the devastation caused by his misapprehension. The effects of *affectio* spread outward from the royal center of the realm like ripples in a pond, apparently killing a faithful wife, actually killing an auspicious young prince, banishing a true friend and a loyal servant, and abandoning an innocent baby to near-certain death. Antigonus, charged on oath to destroy the infant, finds himself unable to grieve as he should but afflicted by a bleeding heart that is reminiscent of the Catholic iconography of the suffering sinner:

> Poor wretch,
> That for thy mother's fault art thus expos'd
> To loss, and what may follow! Weep I cannot,
> But my heart bleeds; and most accurs'd am I
> To be by oath enjoin'd to this. (*The Winter's Tale* 3.3.49–53)

Antigonus, of course, has got it wrong. Perdita's *mater dolorosa* is without spot of sin, but still the hearts bleed in an orgy of shame and regret.

The combination of tearful repentance and heart's blood recurs in Act 5 during the Third Gentleman's narration of Leontes' reconciliation with his long-lost daughter. At the point in the proceedings where the king "confess'd" the judicial murder of her mother, we are told of the carefully engineered emotion that overtook not just the Gentleman but everyone watching the scene.

One of the prettiest touches of all, and that which angled for mine eyes (caught the water though not the fish), was when, at the relation of the Queen's death (with the manner of how she came to't bravely confess'd and lamented by the King), how attentiveness wounded his daughter, till (from one sign of dolor to another) she did (with an "Alas!"), I would fain say, bleed tears; for I am sure my heart wept blood. Who was most marble there chang'd color; some swounded, all sorrow'd. If all the world could have seen't, the woe had been universal. (5.2.82–92)

There are extraordinarily complicated narrative strategies at work in this speech, starting with the slightly condescending aesthetic judgment he passes on one "pretty" touch in Perdita's performance of filial "attentiveness," her heart-wrenching explicative, "Alas." The speaker's angling metaphor ("caught the water though not the fish"), expressed in a parenthetical editorial insert, suggests that he was almost but not quite hooked. He is not just the storyteller; he is also the guarded critic of his own story, which, he has admitted earlier, is "like an old tale, still" (5.2.61). He uses parentheses again almost immediately to insert his characterization of the king's own narrative manner as he "confess'd and lamented" his terrible, murderous deed. Each player evidently displayed the actor's gestures of inward grief as the scene progressed "from one sign of dolor to another." But then our storyteller pulls back again from complete identification with the business of re-enacting the pitiful scene of loss and the intervening period of separation: "I would fain say [the princess did] bleed tears." But he rejects that version of events when he realizes that it was his own "heart [that] wept blood." What matters, then, is not so much what the actors did but how the narrated audience performed their feelings as they turned pale, swooned, and sorrowed. Thus a particular woe is made visible and "universal." Perdita's outward signs of grief give way to the influx of blood within the spectator's heart, and thus we are instructed in how to respond to the even more moving scene of recovery and reconciliation we are to experience in the final scene, when Hermione's statue comes to life. Too accomplished a dramatist to ask an audience for the same response twice in a row, Shakespeare has his Third Gentleman narrate the first reconciliation with implicit instructions on how we are to respond to the second one. We see a similar shaping of audience responses to the heart's business in *Richard II* when the Groom narrates Bullingbrook's conquest of the people's hearts and the suppressed pain that remains in his own heart. Similar narrative techniques come into play in *King Lear* when Edgar describes his father's death and prepares the audience to be even more profoundly touched by the shattering of the king's heart.

The tale that Edgar recounts of his own banishment, his father's blinding, and the new bond that grew between them in exile works simultaneously on the hearts of victim, storyteller, and spectator:

> List a brief tale,
> And when 'tis told, O that my heart would burst!
> The bloody proclamation to escape,
> That follow'd me so near (O, our lives' sweetness!
> That we the pain of death would hourly die
> Rather than die at once!), taught me to shift
> Into a madman's rags, t'assume a semblance
> That very dogs disdain'd; and in this habit
> Met I my father with his bleeding rings,
> Their precious stones new lost; became his guide,
> Led him, begg'd for him, sav'd him from despair;
> Never (O fault!) reveal'd myself unto him,
> Until some half hour past, when I was arm'd.
> Not sure, though hoping, of this good success,
> I ask'd his blessing, and from first to last
> Told him our pilgrimage. But his flaw'd heart
> (Alack, too weak the conflict to support!)
> 'Twixt two extremes of passion, joy and grief,
> Burst smilingly. (*King Lear* 5.3.182–200)

Having related the story twice, first to his father and now to the assembled company, Edgar wishes to die in the same way that Gloucester had and that, subsequently, King Lear will – from the bursting of his overcharged heart. Like the Gentleman in *The Winter's Tale*, Edgar shapes his story with parenthetical interjections, one a philosophical generalization about how, by postponing death we sweetly savor it every hour, a second chastising himself for withholding his true identity from his father for so long, and the last diagnosing his father's final cardiac infirmity. The "flaw'd heart," though not often the subject of anatomical investigation, was known to be vulnerable to an excess of the passions, particularly contrary ones such as "joy and grief." In his final moment, the condition of Gloucester's heart was visible in his face: his heart burst "smilingly." His smile reflects the efficacy of a protracted process of repentance begun when he learned in 3.7 that he had rejected his loving son and embraced the hateful one. That process of suffering and self-despising had brought him to the very brink of bodily self-destruction but ends with the reformation of his heart. Those who hear the process narrated don't need to have it reiterated in the case of Lear. We have been instructed in the interior dynamics of a father's suffering even before Lear enters, howling, carrying the body of his youngest, dearest child.

We can only second Kent's despairing prayer, "Break, heart, I prithee break!" (5.3.313).[18]

Shakespeare's "pretty trick" of embedding narration in dramatic dialogue explicitly establishes a point of view that reminds playgoers of their own positions as spectators. We are subtly invited to share and to evaluate the onstage observer-reporter's responses as versions of our own spectatorship. In the case of the tragedies, the activity that we are thus forced to engage in is both moral and emotional. The rightness of our own conscience, the alignment of our judgments with the suffering we are witnessing – which pain is deserved? which exceeds the sufferer's accumulated follies? – are matters that first require us to be convinced that the depiction of suffering is true to the psychophysiological ways of experiencing pain available in Shakespeare's time, and our own. We are asked to measure our own experiences against those of the onstage observers and describers of the unfolding tragedy. Do our hearts weep blood or burst with contradictory feelings or feel the crushing weight of the hero's sorrow? Are these apt and rhetorically persuasive accounts of what we ourselves feel under the influence of a tragic action?

The answers to these questions vary substantially from play to play. For example, the sense of sheer weight in the heart of Othello by the midpoint of his play resonates with both our own understanding of depression and early modern descriptions of emotion that causes the heart to dilate, become overcharged, and feel too weak to perform its function of supplying the body with essential fluids. His predicament conforms closely to Thomas Wright's description of the heart overwrought with passion:

> The heart being continually invironed with great abundance of spi[rit], becommeth too hote and inflamed, and consequently engendereth much cholericke and burned blood: Besides, it dilateth and resolveth the substance of the heart too much, in such sort, that the vertue and force thereof is greatly weakened.[19]

The super-dilated heart melts or disintegrates ("resolveth"), losing its integrity and power to sustain life. Wright's analysis could be used to describe the terrifying joy that Othello experiences as a stoppage of his heart and names a "discord" (from Latin *cor*, or heart) when he is reunited with

---

[18] The fatal symptoms of cardiac arrest recur frequently in early modern drama, becoming the central image of amorous betrayal and stoic collapse in John Ford's *The Broken Heart*. Shakespeare launches two unlikely characters into a pseudo-medical account of heart failure in *Henry V*. Analyzing Falstaff's death, Nym complains that the king "hath run bad humors on the knight," and Pistol reaches unsuccessfully for the precise medical terms to describe the cause of death: "His heart is fracted and corroborate" (2.1.121, 24). "Fracted," the Latinate term for "broken," is apt enough, but "corroborate," a common term in medical treatises such as Elyot's *Castel of Helth* (London: T. Bertheleti, [1539]), means "strengthened."

[19] Thomas Wright, *The Passions of the Minde in Generall* (London: V. Simme for W. Burre, 1604), 60.

Desdemona (2.1.197–8). It also accords with the "dilation" he suspects of Iago's cryptic utterances and secret thoughts in 3.3:

> such things in a false disloyal knave
> Are tricks of custom; but in a man that's just
> They're close dilations, working from the heart,
> That passion cannot rule. (*Othello* 3.3.121–4)

Modern editors uniformly prefer the Folio reading "dilations" to the Quarto's "denotements" but disagree on what Othello is saying about Iago. The eighteenth-century editor George Steevens, working with the variant spelling "delations," says that Othello is commenting on the guarded narrations or accusations that Iago is making. G. Blakemore Evans similarly provides the gloss "expressions of secret thought." George Lyman Kittridge captures the physiological sense of the lines when he refers to the dangerous swellings of the heart caused by powerful, unruly passions. Reading Iago's hints and innuendos completely wrong, Othello says that his ensign's cautious, halting style of speech is not the sly evasion of a "disloyal knave" but rather a confidential expression of a deeply troubling suspicion that causes his heart to dilate beyond the control of his reason. Two meanings of the term "dilation" thus converge and reinforce one another, the medical (naming a stretching of the heart beyond the normal limits of diastole) and the legal (denoting an accusation of wrong-doing on the part of Desdemona and Cassio). Patricia Parker has discovered in the lines the central dynamic of love and hate that propels Othello toward Iago and away from Desdemona. She then links this emotional dynamic to the repeated, insistent demands for narrative dilation within the play, protracted explanations that delay the tragic outcome.[20] As we have seen in *The Winter's Tale* and *King Lear*, such embedded narrative expansions not only postpone the outcome but also prepare the audience in the correct reading of affect. All these "workings from the heart" promote emotional suspense by invoking a precise, early modern physiological understanding of how the heart is possessed by the passions. As modern readers, we can't afford to ignore descriptions such as these of the body's actions and reactions.

As Othello becomes increasingly possessed by Iago's poisonous hatred, he speaks of the terrible transformation occurring inside him. Gail Kern Paster has argued persuasively that Desdemona offers a telling medical diagnosis of Othello's troubles when she says that something has "puddled his clear

[20] Patricia Parker, "Shakespeare and Rhetoric: 'dilation' and 'delation' in *Othello*," in *Shakespeare and the Question of Theory*, ed. Patricia Parker and Geoffrey Hartman (New York: Methuen, 1985), 54–74.

spirit" (3.4.143). All his natural, vital, and animal spirits, "concocted out of blood and inspired air" have, she says, become muddied.[21] Desdemona's diagnosis is accurate, despite her earlier conjecture that "the sun where he was born / Drew all such [jealous] humors from him" (3.4.30–1). The equatorial heat of Othello's birthplace notwithstanding, his body retains the moisture that fuels the hateful emotion. Even as his humoral body is being stirred into a state of corruption, he tries through innuendo to cast Desdemona's body as the unbalanced, lusting one. Her "liberal heart," he first hints, is a sign of a humoral imbalance ("Hot, hot, and moist" excesses) requiring sequestration or isolation from the rest of her system. His technical term "sequester" has not only medical but also legal and religious overtones, all of which he calls into play as he spars with his wife over the relationship of heart (her internal state) to hand (her outward behavior):

OTH. Give me your hand. This hand is moist, my lady.
DES. It yet hath felt no age nor known no sorrow.
OTH. This argues fruitfulness and liberal heart;
      Hot, hot, and moist. This hand of yours requires
      A sequester from liberty: fasting and prayer,
      Much castigation, exercise devout,
      For here's a young and sweating devil here
      That commonly rebels. 'Tis a good hand,
      A frank one.
DES. You may, indeed, say so;
      For 'twas that hand that gave away my heart.
OTH. A liberal hand. The hearts of old gave hands;
      But our new heraldry is hands, not hearts. (3.4.36–47)

As he holds his wife's hand, Othello labors to suppress the jealous rants of the preceding scene by reciting the temperamental signs and medical symptoms of Desdemona's heart as revealed by her hot, moist hand. This approach to controlling his own emotions quickly gives way to spiritual counsel on the need to castigate, discipline, and "sequester" her body from rebellious temptations by praying and adopting a severe diet ("fasting and prayer, / Much castigation, exercise devout"). In *Anatomie of Vrines* James Hart comments on "the great trouble and encombrance nature hath in the expelling and sequestring such humours."[22] Other relevant meanings of sequestration in this context include the isolation of a nun in a convent and

---

[21] Gail Kern Paster, *Humoring the Body: Emotions and the Shakespearean Stage* (Chicago: University of Chicago Press, 2004), 61.

[22] James Hart, *Anatomie of Vrines* (London: R. Field for R. Mylbourne, 1625), II, 53. One category of "thicke vrines [is] called *turbida*, or troubled and muddie" (53), language reminiscent of Desdemona's description of Othello's spirit.

the power of a judge to separate a litigant from his or her possessions. Othello wishes both to shut his wife away from sexual temptation and to assert his right to her as his own possession.[23] The "young and sweating devil" to whom Othello refers is, evidently, Cassius, who lives "here" in her hand, exercising his diabolical power by corrupting her "liberal heart." Hand and heart seem intimately connected. The hand that gave away her heart in marriage is, like her heart, called "liberal," the connotations of "generosity" giving way to those of sexual promiscuity.

Then, in a sudden about-face indicative of his own instability, Othello denies the link he has been establishing between inner affection and outward action when he invokes a "new heraldry" which, he asserts, "is hands, not hearts." Traditionally, clasped hands on a coat of arms symbolized a bond that had been solemnized in the heart, but Othello charges that the hand-fasting ritual in the marriage vows, particularly in Desdemona's, no longer carries with it the heart's faith.[24] In his essay "Of Complements" William Cornwallis remarks that people used "to giue their hands & their harts together, but we thinke it a finer grace to looke a squint, our hand looking one way and our hart another."[25] Cornwallis's phrase bespeaks a cynical society that finds it more convenient to sever the connection between who one really is and how one appears.

The cultural history of the rupture between the inner person's intentions – the motivating will associated with the human heart – and the instrument-ality of the hand is one of the subjects explored at length in Katherine Rowe's study, *Dead Hands: Fictions of Agency, Renaissance to Modern*. Rowe locates the origins of our modern sense of alienation between the products of our bodily agency and our sense of an inner self in the philosophy of Locke and Hobbes and later in the age of industrialization, when workers were synecdochized as mere "hands." She also recognizes the seeds of the problem of hand-based agency and its tenuous connection with the desires of the heart in the numerous dismembered hands that appear in early modern judicial punishments and stage plays.[26] The division between the heart's

---

[23] Shakespeare uses the term "sequestration" earlier in Iago's famous "put money in thy purse" lecture to Roderigo. He stresses the violent passion that first attracted Desdemona to the Moor, and he predicts, based on an implicit humoral analysis of the couple, an equally sudden separation: "It was a violent commencement in her, and thou shalt see an answerable sequestration" (1.3.344–5).

[24] The marriage-link roundels in certain medieval and early modern genealogies are marked by linked hands, and the joining of the betrothed hands by the priest in the sacrament of marriage was as familiar in Shakespeare's time as in our own.

[25] William Cornwallis, *Essayes* (London: [S. Stafford and R. Read] for E. Mattes, 1600–1), sig. P6^{r-v}.

[26] Katherine Rowe, *Dead Hands: Fictions of Agency, Renaissance to Modern* (Stanford: Stanford University Press, 1999).

desires and the hand's actions reaches a tragic climax when Othello defines himself through speech and action as "an honorable murderer" (5.2.294).

Shakespeare's characters fluctuate between asserting the bond between heart and hand, heart and tongue, and confessing that the bond has been destroyed. The uncertainty that flows from this fluctuation defines the moral dilemmas they agonize over and, just as important, the constant readjustments required of the theater audience. The politics of promise in a play like *Richard II* are shaped by repeated realignments of heart and hand. While consolidating his power, Bullingbrook promises to remember and recompense his friends:

> be sure
> I count myself in nothing else so happy
> As in a soul rememb'ring my good friends,
> And as my fortune ripens with thy love,
> It shall be still thy true love's recompense.
> My heart this covenant makes, my hand thus seals it. (*Richard II* 2.3.45–50)

The future king's coercive covenant gains him the military support he needs by aligning political desire with political action, the heart's wishes with the hand's violence. Such an arrangement becomes untenable for Aumerle once his own father is on the verge of exposing his and the other Oxford conspirators' covenant to overthrow the new king. Aumerle protests to King Henry that his signature on the rebels' document does not carry with it the revised commitment of his heart: "I do repent me, read not my name there, / My heart is not confederate with my hand" (5.3.52–3). Defining his internal relations, those between his heart and his hand, as a "confederacy" belies his guilty conscience about having been discovered in a full-fledged political conspiracy. He must strain hard against the proverbial wisdom that defines honor as acting "with heart and hand."[27]

The ethically charged drama of dissembling keeps the language of the heart and its estrangement from the body's organs of agency, especially the hand and the tongue, consistently before the early modern playgoer. In his abortive prayer for forgiveness, King Claudius is able to force his knees into an attitude of prayer, but his heartstrings prove less pliable, despite his best hopes:

> Bow, stubborn knees, and heart, with strings of steel,
> Be soft as sinews of the new-born babe!
> All may be well. [*He kneels.*] (*Hamlet* 3.3.70–2)

[27] R. W. Dent, *Shakespeare's Proverbial Language: An Index* (Berkeley: University of California Press, 1981), H339.

But all, of course, is not well with his attempt to go through the motions of repentance: "My words fly up, my thoughts remain below: / Words without thoughts never to heaven go" (*Hamlet* 3.3.97–8). As Anthony Dawson has argued, the disjunction of Claudius's words and thoughts transports him into the arena of interior moral debate that is ordinarily thought to be Hamlet's exclusive preserve, at the same time raising contemporary issues of the efficacy of penance in Catholic as well as Lutheran and Calvinist theology.[28] Claudius is paralyzed by his shameful conviction that, like Marlowe's Dr. Faustus, he cannot truly repent, since he continues to enjoy the benefits of his fratricide in the form of his throne and his queen. As Dawson points out, "Shame, like theatre, involves a continuing exchange between outer and inner, the face and the self; and as it is represented here, it is linked to both religious abjection and theatrical watching." Hamlet and the theater audience watch as Claudius mimes the attitudes of the repentant sinner. The audience, however, hears the despairing soliloquy, while Hamlet mistakenly assumes that his uncle's heart has achieved the same penitential posture as his kneeling body. Seeing, without hearing, is a poor basis for believing. The disjunction of inner and outward states that we see enacted here is not just the measure of the villain's self-alienation, as noted in the preceding chapter, but also the occasion of wider doubts about the possibility of repentance for sin. Although a strict reading of Luther's theology of *sola fides* and Calvin's predestination would seem to leave no room for human initiative after the manner of the practice of confession, contrition, and satisfaction, in fact, there was considerable latitude for discretionary action as Protestants worked to achieve remission of sins. The Book of Common Prayer and innumerable sermons, for example, include exhortations to repent before it is too late. That Claudius is unable to achieve this is a clear sign of his lack of faith and the hardness of his heart.

Shakespeare frequently associates the disjunction of heart and tongue with the hardening of the heart so often deplored by Calvin and his followers.[29] Repeated biblical warnings about hardening the sinful heart against God's tender mercy (e.g. Ezek. 11: 19; Matt. 19: 8) find a popular secular analogy in medieval and Renaissance love poems that simultaneously idolize and denounce the flinty hearts of disdainful women. Olivia

---

[28] Anthony Dawson, "Claudius at Prayer," unpublished paper presented in Philadelphia at the Shakespeare Association of America annual conference, 2006.
[29] For example, in a sermon preached at St. Mary's in Beverley, the Puritan preacher John Shawe tells his parishioners that "by nature our hearts are flinty, stony, rocky, hard, need breaking." *A Broken Heart, or the Grand Sacrifice* (London: n.s., 1643), 14–15.

strikes Viola as just such an inwardly unyielding person and condemns her to fall in love with a man who is equally unresponsive. Viola's line, "Love make his heart of flint that you shall love" (*Twelfth Night* 1.5.286), appears to be a self-fulfilling prophecy when Olivia later complains to the unyielding "Cesario" that she has "said too much unto a heart of stone" (3.4.201). Othello carries the trope further when he turns "stone" into a verb to describe the effect of Desdemona's imagined treachery on his heart: "O perjur'd woman, thou dost stone my heart" (5.2.63). His heart has both been pummeled with stones and itself transformed to stone. Having hardened himself against any feelings of pity, he is prepared to call his proposed assault on his wife not murder but sacrifice. Heart and hand cannot be made to accord with one another, since the heart has been isolated from all human feeling. Under such conditions, villainy and tragic self-torment fuse into a single catastrophe.

King Lear contains Shakespeare's most profound insights into the dissociation of inner conviction and outward practice that was both the hope of the Elizabethan Settlement and greatest moral hazard of the age. As he forces the audience to watch the most gruesome bodily torments, he introduces the agony of the overcharged heart unable to communicate its pain through tongue or hand. To Lear on the heath it appears that dissemblers pose the most dangerous threat to personal and communal peace:

> Let the great gods,
> That keep this dreadful pudder o'er our heads,
> Find out their enemies now. Tremble, thou wretch
> That hast within thee undivulged crimes
> Unwhipt of justice! Hide thee, thou bloody hand;
> Thou perjur'd, and thou simular of virtue
> That art incestuous! Caitiff, to pieces shake,
> That under covert and convenient seeming
> Has practic'd on man's life! Close pent-up guilts,
> Rive your concealing continents, and cry
> These dreadful summoners grace. I am a man
> More sinn'd against than sinning. (*King Lear* 3.2.49–60)

The debate over Lear's final claim here will continue so long as men have eyes to read, but his analysis of simulated virtue is rock solid. More profound than the anger caused by dissimulation and betrayal, however, is the self-alienation caused by being unable to speak what is in one's heart. Faced with Lear's coercive demands in the play's opening scene, Cordelia refuses to dissemble: "What shall Cordelia speak? Love, and be silent . . . I am sure my love's / More ponderous than my tongue . . . Unhappy that I am, I cannot heave / My heart into my mouth" (1.1.62, 77–8, 91–2). Here is love that dares not speak its object; only domestic disintegration, shame, and sorrow can follow from her decision to say precisely what is in her heart. She eventually succumbs to the proverbial truth that "What the heart thinks the tongue speaks,"[30] and the outcome is devastating. Lear continues his bullying in the language of the heart ("But goes thy heart with this? ") and proclaims his perpetual estrangement from his youngest daughter in the same terms ("as a stranger to my heart and me / Hold [I] thee from this for ever" (lines 104, 115–16)). His alienation from his family is finally equivalent to self-estrangement. His proclamations no longer come from his heart, and during the central section of the play, like Gloucester, he associates the heart with sin, especially with illicit breeding. While Gloucester struggles to imagine how Edgar had the heart to "breed" his purported conspiracy against his father ("My son Edgar! had he a hand to write this? a heart and brain to breed it in? " (1.2.56–7)), Lear orders, "let them anatomize Regan; see what breeds about her heart" (3.6.76–7). Though the fathers are agonizingly slow to understand what is really going on, they are right that sexual sinning, specifically adultery, joins Edmund, Goneril, and Regan.[31] The moist heat of the heart, as postulated by many medical treatises, can provide the matrix for creating intense emotion, in this case, lust and hatred. This trio will pay for their sin with their lives, and Lear, too, will die, but not before suffering the pain of an uncertain repentance.

The problem of repentance was widely debated in Shakespeare's age and in his plays. Claudius's botched attempt to repent makes an instructive contrast with the uncertainty of Lear's acts of penance during his reconciliation with Cordelia. His experiences on the heath have left Lear unsure about his location, his identity, and the condition of his soul. When Cordelia kneels before him, begging his benediction, he reverses the direction of the request and kneels to her. While Claudius tries to bargain directly with

---

[30] Dent, *Shakespeare's Proverbial Language*, H334.

[31] Olé M. Høystad observes sensibly that "Erotic passion in *King Lear* is often portrayed purely as sexual lust and as the root of all evil." There is a significant leap, however, from this to his more doubtful generalization that "In Shakespeare's work, man's dark side prevails against all idealism." See Høystad's far-ranging anthropological and philosophical study, *A History of the Heart* (*Hjertets kulturhistorie, frå antikken til vår tid*, 2003), trans. John Irons (London: Reaktion Books, 2007), quotation from p. 179. Truer to the play Shakespeare wrote is A. D. Nuttall's question whether *King Lear* is "a negation of all value . . . a final decay of all moral hope," and his answer: "*King Lear* leaves us with a sharpened sense of the difference between good and evil, and, lying behind that, of the difference between goodness and nothingness." *Shakespeare the Thinker* (New Haven: Yale University Press, 2007), 307 and 309. Shakespeare repeatedly locates the moral sense that Nuttall writes about in the heart.

heaven for the restoration of his soul, Lear seeks his salvation on earth, through the child he wronged. The struggle to assume a kneeling posture, so hard for a recuperating old man to manage, becomes the image of his imperfect mind (4.7.62) and determined heart. Shakespeare found a much overdone version of this kneeling sequence in the old Queen's Men's play *King Leir*, where Leir and his daughter bounce up and down two and three times, respectively. By reducing the amount of physical action, Shakespeare intensifies the sense of sincere internal struggle. Stage kneeling is, more often than not, a token of hollow ceremony – as when Bullingbrook abases himself before Richard II, only to be told, "Up, cousin, up, your heart is up, I know, / Thus high at least [*touching his crown*], although your knee be low" (3.3.194–5),[32] or when Lear mocks the very notion of returning, chastened, to live with Goneril: "Dear daughter, I confess that I am old; [*kneeling*] / Age is unnecessary. On my knees I beg / That you'll vouchsafe me raiment, bed, and food" (2.4.154–6). The subsequent genuine act of repentance finds Lear on his knees, facing the kneeling Cordelia. Muriel St. Clare Byrne noted that this arrangement of stage iconography in one Stratford production suggested the joint husband and wife devotions captured for eternity in certain tomb effigies.[33] But what we are watching in the *Lear* reconciliation scene is a return from the brink of the grave and a form of repentance and forgiveness that is entirely of this world. Lear closes the sequence with a supplication that can be addressed only to Cordelia: "Pray you now forget, and forgive; I am old and foolish" (4.7.83). What the Doctor calls "the great rage" is "kill'd in him" (77–8). The war that had raged within his heart against a thoroughly alienated self had been made audible through his lunatic ravings and visible through his physical struggle to achieve the posture of repentance, but now it is over, save for one last, crushing defeat – Cordelia's murder while in custody. That is the blow that breaks his noble but greatly flawed heart.

Like *King Lear*, Shakespeare's Sonnets repeatedly establish the heart as the battlefield where competing aspects of the self engage. In Sonnet 46 ("Mine eye and heart are at a mortal war") the struggle for possession of the beloved is adjudicated by a "quest" or jury of "thoughts, all tenants to the heart" (line 10). As Stephen Booth remarks, this jury is heavily stacked in favor of the heart.[34] The speaker's heart serves as prosecutor, his eye as defendant in the contest between inward affection and visual perception,

---

[32] Compare Thomas Dekker, *Wonder of a Kingdom*: "I know your heart is up, tho your knees downe" (5.2.120f), as quoted in Dent, *Shakespeare's Proverbial Language*, H321.1.

[33] As noted by R. A. Foakes in his Arden 3 commentary on the lines (London: Thomas Nelson and Sons, 1997).

[34] See Stephen Booth, ed., *Shakespeare's Sonnets* (New Haven: Yale University Press, 1977), 209.

the center of the affections being characterized as "A closet never pierc'd with crystal eyes" (line 6). While the term "closet" refers to a chamber without windows, the specific anatomical referent in this case is the pericardium that surrounds the heart (see Vesalius, Figs. 18 and 19 above), protecting it from external invasion.[35] The legal wrangling between the aesthetic eye and the affective heart is resolved by a predictable appeal to distributive justice:

> mine eye's due is thy outward part,
> And my heart's right thy inward love of heart. (lines 13–14)

There is a definite Platonic bias in the poem in favor of the inner, invisible reality of the thinking heart.

The immediately following sonnet, 47 ("Betwixt mine eye and heart a league is took"), celebrates the ongoing pleasures of resolving the conflict of inner and outer modes of experiencing love. Though the heart continues at times to "smother" itself with sighs when deprived of the presence of the beloved, it works in league with the eye to guarantee the perpetual satisfaction of the need for love.[36] Love's portrait, described in the second quatrain, resides in the speaker's heart-thoughts and can be reawakened at any time "to heart's and eye's delight" (line 14). This visual image, then, functions precisely as the icon of the crucifixion did in Luther's account of the hearts of the faithful. The model works less well for Shakespeare, however, under the stress recorded in the Dark Lady sonnets. In Sonnet 141 ("In faith, I do not love thee with mine eyes"), for example, the speaker's "foolish heart" ignores the negative evidence of his eyes, which "in thee a thousand errors note," and, as he says in the sestet, leaves only penitential pain as his benefit:

> But my five wits nor my five senses can
> Dissuade one foolish heart from serving thee,
> Who leaves unsway'd the likeness of a man,
> Thy proud heart's slave and vassal wretch to be:
> Only my plague thus far I count my gain,
> That she that makes me sin awards me pain. (lines 9–14)

---

[35] OED 6a, as noted by Katherine Duncan-Jones in her Arden 3 edition of *Shakespeare's Sonnets* (London: Thomas Nelson, 1997).

[36] The perfect harmony of eye and heart is also captured graphically on the title page of John Saltmarsh's *Holy Discoveries and Flames* (London: R. Y. for P. Nevill, 1640). Within a large heart-shape appear four icons arranged one above the other: a flaming heart, and upcast eye, a holy book, and the dove of the Holy Spirit. The passionate heart and the eye of intellect both tend upward, toward the word and spirit of God.

Nicholas Breton likewise harmonizes the functions of eye and heart, urging his readers to look for love "with the eye of a carefull heart." See *An excellent poeme, vpon the longing of a blessed heart* (London: [R. Bradock] for J. Browne and J. Deane, 1601), sig. A3.

Overcoming ten to one odds, the heart rashly persists in its foolish pursuit of the Dark Lady, leaving the speaker a hollow manikin. Helen Vendler concludes from these lines that the poem's "I" becomes "less than human" because *reason* fails to sway the evidence of his body, but the point at issue is not, I think, reason's governance of the body but the heart's failed role in promoting spiritual health. The speaker's "foolish heart" and the temptress's "proud heart" are both biblical, and the sonnet's final line ("she that makes me sin awards me pain") outlines the experience of spiritual transgression and penance.

Two earlier sonnets in the Dark Lady section, 133 ("Beshrew that heart that makes my heart to groan") and 137 ("Thou blind fool, Love, what dost thou to mine eyes"), drive the wedge still more painfully between the expressive functions of the body and the self-identity under siege in the heart. In Sonnet 133 the Lady is prison guard and torturer of the hearts of both the speaker and his "friend." By the second quatrain it is clear that the resulting fragmentation of the loving self will destroy all efforts to resist the tormentor's victory:

> Me from myself thy cruel eye hath taken,
> And my next self thou harder hast engrossed:
> Of him, myself, and thee I am forsaken,
> A torment thrice threefold thus to be crossed.
>
> (Sonnet 133, lines 5–8)

The mathematical calculation of pain and fragmentation ("torment thrice threefold") will reappear in Sonnet 141, and even the speaker's attempt to protect his friend from the Lady's assaults by placing him inside his own heart are destined to fail:

> Prison my heart in thy steel bosom's ward,
> But then my friend's heart let my poor heart bail;
> Whoe'er keeps me, let my heart be his guard,
> Thou canst not then use rigor in my jail. (lines 9–12)

The plan to "bail" or confine one heart within another for its protection will not shield the friend from torture, since the Lady's body has grossly "engrossed" both hearts. The idea of the heart as a reliable container safely contained in, and only occasionally liberated from, the human breast, which we have seen so powerfully depicted in medical illustrations and religious images, here becomes for Shakespeare the token of inescapable alienation.

The kind of relentless heart attack documented in the eye-versus-heart cluster of sonnets leads Shakespeare to what Stephen Booth calls his "frantic discourse," characterized by disjointed and mixed metaphors. I will look at one final example of this form of distress in Sonnet 137 before attempting some generalizations about the cultural tensions reflected in the Sonnets' personalized narrative of love, jealousy, and self-hatred. In this dark and messy sonnet, the eye is associated with sexual disgust, the heart with sober judgment, and the body with everything from anchoring bays to plots of land to hosts for venereal disease. The heart "think[s]," "knows," and judges, but all in vain:

> If eyes, corrupt by over-partial looks,
> Be anchor'd in the bay where all men ride,
> Why of eyes' falsehood hast thou forged hooks,
> Whereto the judgment of my heart is tied?
> Why should my heart think that a several plot,
> Which my heart knows the wide world's common place?
> Or mine eyes seeing this, say this is not,
> To put fair truth upon so foul a face?
> In things right true my heart and eyes have erred,
> And to this false plague are they now transferred. (lines 5–14)

The reasons for "the wide world's common" opinion of the Dark Lady's indiscriminate sexual availability, her commonness, are clear for the eye to see yet remain unregistered in the heart. The lines of communication being so thoroughly ruptured, the speaker's entire body becomes subject to a "false plague" that most editors gloss as venereal infection.[37] When perception becomes distorted, the heart's judgment, along with the entire corporeal system, becomes infected. The systemic conduits for the passage of syphilis were well established by the late sixteenth century,[38] and Shakespeare makes the venereal dynamic of the lovers' triangle explicit in the conclusion of Sonnet 144:

> I guess one angel in another's hell.
> Yet this shall I ne'er know, but live in doubt,
> Till my bad angel fire my good one out. (lines 12–14)

Despite Francis Meres's famous contemporary assessment of these poems, there is nothing "sugar'd" about this bitter depiction of the body and the soul in crisis.

---

[37] See, for example, Duncan-Jones, *Shakespeare's Sonnets*, 388.

[38] See William Clowes, *A Short and Profitable Treatise Touching the Cure of the Disease Called (Morbus Gallicus) by Vnctions* (London: John Daye, 1579) and Peter Lowe, *Easie, Certain, and Perfect Method, to Cure and Prevent the Spanish Sicknes* (London: James Roberts, 1596). See also Louis F. Qualtiere and William W. E. Slights, "Contagion and Blame in Early Modern England: The Case of the French Pox," *Literature and Medicine* 22 (2003): 1–24.

Although there are notable differences between the ways that Shakespeare treats the alienation of the heart from the other body parts, particularly the hand, tongue, and eye, in the plays and the Sonnets, the awareness of loss in the heart remains constant. One thing is certain: there is nothing idle or mawkish about Shakespeare's language of the heart in the Sonnets. The heart maintains a physical as well as a psychological presence in these poems. It is engrossed and swamped with humoral excess; it senses the needs of the rest of the body and strains to provide those needs. Not only an anatomical but also a religious set of discourses contributes to the centrality of the heart in this body of poetry. While they are not heavily theologized poems, a sizeable handful of the Sonnets draw upon the process of seeking repentance for sins occasioned by erotic frenzy not just once but, with the group of Dark Lady sonnets, twice over. The plays are more explicit than the Sonnets in their re-enactment of the Catholic/Protestant struggle for the penitent heart, but in all his work, Shakespeare balances the violence of earlier heart/conscience attacks with the more private and introspective assessment of the embodied self. We can only guess how influential his Sonnets were as they circulated, first in manuscript among his friends, then in the small print run of 1609. They were certainly quoted and imitated, suggesting that their version of the philosophically and physiologically dissected heart of the lyric subject was as widely influential as the dramatic spectacles of lovers, villains, and belatedly repentant kings in the plays. The link between the heart and the visible, expressive parts of the body – hand, tongue, eye, and other, more private parts – however frayed it becomes, affords the only window we have on inner conviction.

The individual conscience, so insistently identified with the heart in the work of Luther, Calvin, Perkins, and others, takes on an explicitly sexual coloring in Sonnet 151 ("Love is too young to know what conscience is"), a poem that sums up what I have been saying about the centrality of the heart in defining the age of Shakespeare. Everyone, the poet asserts, knows that "conscience is born of love" (line 2), but that knowledge is enormously complicated and its sources difficult to reconcile. It embraces all that we know about our selves and our world, that is, our "consciousness." Next, the conscience is that part of our apparatus for moral reasoning that permits us to apply divine law to particular human circumstances. Finally, in the context of Shakespeare's highly sexualized poem, it becomes knowledge (*science*) of the *con* or female genitalia, what Helen Vendler calls "knowledge of cunt."[39]

---

[39] Helen Vendler, *The Art of Shakespeare's Sonnets* (Cambridge, MA: Harvard University Press, 1997), 639.

Whatever the faculty of moral reason urges, the "perjur'd eye" or "I" of the sonnets (Sonnet 152, line 13) is led about by the penis:

> flesh stays no farther reason,
> But rising at thy name doth point out thee
> As his triumphant prize. Proud of this pride,
> He is contented thy poor drudge to be,
> To stand in thy affairs, fall by thy side. (Sonnet 151, lines 8–12)

Being sexually enslaved by the Dark Lady, rising and falling at her whim, obliterates the first two meanings of "conscience," leaving only the debased third meaning to seal the speaker's confession. The heart's earlier aspirations have been reduced to this shameful state, but there is no available mortification of the flesh to parallel the abjection of Richard II in prison, Lear on his knees before Cordelia, Leonato praying at the tomb of Hero, or Leontes in the posture of humble suppliant before the statue of Hermione.

Shakespeare critics are increasingly coming to the view that until we understand more about the early modern systems of thought that connected the material experience of living to the emotional and intellectual, we will achieve only a very limited response to his works. The systems I have been pursuing through the plays and poems are anatomical and theological ones that found expression in the educational and devotional practices of Shakespeare's culture. The first of these areas relied more and more on what could be seen and recorded during anatomical dissections; the second moved away from the visual representation of spiritual experience in iconic forms and depended instead on the individual's encounter with Scripture and the inner conviction of salvation. Both the theological and anatomical come prominently into play in Shakespeare's conception of the human heart.

The anatomical fugitive sheets of the fifteenth and sixteenth centuries offer an apt model of the culture's fascination with the visible outside and the opaque inside of the human body. Many of these single-page annotated drawings of the body include hinged paper flaps glued over the torso of the figure being described. The goal was to be able to see the shape and position of the organs within the body and also to have the parts labeled and described systematically. Similarly, audiences at Shakespeare's plays are invited to look beneath the gestures of hostility, affection, frustration, and repentance to experience the motions, passions, and humoral condition of hearts that are either expressing or suppressing the characters' psychophysiological states. Henry VIII's wife Katherine isolates as a defining English national trait the alienation between what is held in the heart and what is expressed in the face: "Ye have angels' faces, but heaven knows your hearts" (*Henry VIII* 3.1.145).

That alienation can be the source not only of villainy but of inner torment to Shakespeare's most conscientious characters. The source of this pain is identified as super-dilation of the heart, caused by the accumulation of excess humors in that delicate regulatory organ for the entire body. Leontes tries to minimize the collapse of Hermione in these terms: "Her heart is but o'ercharg'd; she will recover" (*The Winter's Tale* 3.2.150), but when neither she nor their son recovers, he is forced to follow the religious motions of his own heart and repent. He vows, "Once a day I'll visit / The chapel where they lie, and tears shed there / Shall be my recreation" (3.2.238–40). Besides his own tears of abject contrition shed in the chapel, Leontes's re-creation is guided by Paulina, the most rigorous of confessors. Finally, the king's spiritual renovation requires what feels like a Roman Catholic ritual encounter with a miraculously animated, iconic statue of Hermione. This climactic *coup de théâtre* has more in common with the vision of St. Catherine exchanging her heart with Christ (Fig. 8) than with the acts of personal penance most often encountered in Shakespeare, acts that depict hard-won self-knowledge savagely imprisoned between the hope and fear of George Wither's aggressively Protestant emblem "Speqve metvqve pavet" (Fig. 11).

Huston Diehl has generated an ingenious argument concerning the Catholic/Protestant rivalries enacted in the marvelous statue scene that ends *The Winter's Tale*. She contends that Shakespeare mounts an inspired defense of his own theatrical artifice by setting Protestant-approved conceptions of theological wonder against idolatrous Roman Catholic exploitations of wonder. The playwright, she says,

engages competing Protestant and Counter-Reformation theologies of wonder in this play in order to address the legitimacy of his own theatrical representations, a legitimacy that was being vigorously contested by radical Protestants and moralists. In staging a statue that elicits awe, arouses desire, and miraculously appears to come to life, Shakespeare directly addresses the reformers' charge that the theater is idolatrous. But, I contend, he draws on Protestant theories of wonder to defend against those charges. Rather than appropriating Roman Catholic notions of wonder – notions that would make his theater particularly vulnerable to the enemies of the stage – he aligns the wonder his theater arouses with a kind of theological wonder endorsed by the Protestant English Church and thereby makes bold claims about the authority of his own representations. The statue scene raises the specter of idolatry, I am suggesting, in order to liberate theater from the charge it is idolatrous.[40]

[40] Huston Diehl, " 'Strike all that look upon with marvel': Theatrical and Theological Wonder in *The Winter's Tale*," in *Rematerializing Shakespeare: Authority and Representation on the Early Modern English Stage*, ed. Bryan Reynolds and William N. West (Basingstoke: Palgrave, 2005),

But aside from the rhetoric of horror and revulsion shared by the Reformation and Counter-Reformation polemicists in their attacks on stage-playing, there is really little difference between the two faiths' conceptions of the way that certain spectacles can cause spiritual renovation. One wonders, too, just how radical Shakespeare is being when "he deflects his own power to enchant onto a divine creator" (Diehl, "Theatrical and Theological Wonder," 27). It may be stretching a point to insist that Shakespeare is "achieving what we might call a new, Protestant synthesis of art and nature" (28) when Catholic writers from Leonardo to Robert Southwell had been exploring this conjunction for some time. Less controversial and more closely attuned to Shakespeare's art is Diehl's invocation of Robert Weimann's work on contested authority in the period.[41] In the case of *The Winter's Tale* the jostling between Paulina's concluding priestly ministrations and Autolycus's earlier hocus-pocus leaves the issue of wondrous conjuration a site of continuing contestation.

Shakespeare did not create great plays by setting himself up as point man for any side of the ecclesiastical battles of his age. Instead, he pulled these battles onto the stage to provide resonance for the acts of penitence proceeding from the tormented hearts of his most fully conceived characters in whichever genre he was working, from comedy and sonnets to chronicle and tragedy. The acute sense of betrayal that feels like a poisonous snake stinging the heart develops into a still more devastating sense of shame as his characters prove unable to convey what is in their hearts to those they love. Richard II, Othello, Lear, Leontes, and the Sonnets' "I" are all brought to their knees as a visible sign of their inner turmoil. There is not a "right" conscience among them, and the center of their moral doubt is invariably a "fracted," "o'ercharg'd," "sequestered" heart, cut off from all possible forms of communication through the countenance, the trusted handclasp, or any rhetorical expression of sincerity. In its isolation, the heart shrivels and weakens until some genuine, generous act of penance revives it, often shortly before death. The organ that initiates life also signals its cessation: "Now cracks a noble heart" (*Hamlet* 5.2.359).

The tragic potential of the heart in crisis has long been the center of attention for dramatists. Being fully aware of the philosophical, anatomical, religious, and romance traditions in the discourses of the

19–34, quotation from pp. 20–1. Subsequent references will appear parenthetically, using the short title, "Theatrical and Theological Wonder."

[41] See especially Robert Weimann, *Authority and Representation in Early Modern Discourse*, ed. David Hillman (Baltimore: The Johns Hopkins University Press, 1996).

heart, Shakespeare added a kind of subtlety and comprehensiveness to his representations of inner torment that no one in his age quite matched, though I would say that Marlowe and Donne came very close. For me, the true measure of his understanding of the human heart is his willingness to satirize every form of heart discourse, from the astrological to the humoral to the theological, as he does, for example, in the most probing of his comedies, *Twelfth Night*. In his opening turn, the smitten Orsino transforms the hunt for the hart into his own version of love at first sight based on the Ovidian legend of Acteon:

> That instant was I turn'd into a hart,
> And my desires, like fell and cruel hounds,
> E'er since pursue me. (*Twelfth Night* 1.1.20–2)

The over-the-top rhetoric of the lover's devoured heart deflates the entire mythological and romance tradition that we saw in Chapters 1 and 4. Nor is Orsino the only heart-struck lover submitted to derisive laughter. Olivia resurrects the image of the dear/deer, heart/hart as she sweeps the bewildered Sebastian away to her house, confessing that Sir Toby "started one poor heart of mine" from its covert (4.1.59). Such enthusiastic gush simply reveals the confusion of inner desire with outer reality. Sebastian is not Viola, let alone "Cesario." Launching into the world of myth compounds the confusions, as we see again when Orsino invokes Cupid's "golden shaft" (1.1.34) to unify and organize the humoral and political hierarchies of Olivia's "liver, brain, and heart" (line 36). The functions of these organs in systematizing the affections fail utterly to unscramble Orsino's jumbled fantasy. Nor does Sir Andrew Aguecheek's stab at grasping the astrological influences on the body parts succeed in clarifying matters for him, especially since Sir Toby Belch willfully miscorrects Andrew's error:

SIR ANDREW   Taurus? That's sides and heart.
SIR TOBY   No, sir, it is legs and thighs. (1.3.139–40)

Notions of spherical predominance over the heart are apparently as foolish as mythological indulgence. The preacher's systematic method is also mocked as a way to interpret the biblical or the amorous heart as Viola/Cesario tries to deliver word of her master's affections:

OLIVIA   Where lies your text?
VIOLA   In Orsino's bosom.
OLIVIA   In his bosom? In what chapter of his bosom?
VIOLA   To answer by the method, in the first of his heart. (1.5.223–7)

Orsino later outrages the disguised Viola with his assertion that only the male heart can experience real, abiding love:

> There is no woman's sides
> Can bide the beating of so strong a passion
> As love doth give my heart; no woman's heart
> So big, to hold so much; they lack retention. (2.4.93–6)

None of these languages of the heart approaches the characters' inner truths, and even their outward identities are disguised. When Orsino denounces Viola for hiding "a raven's heart within a dove" (5.1.131), he still has no idea who he is talking to. While the characters in *Twelfth Night* are not heartless, neither have their hearts been fitted with windows offering a clear view of their thoughts and desires. What they wear on their sleeves are broad parodies of inwardness. Perhaps only Olivia, trapped for so long in the to-ing and fro-ing of unrequited love, is capable of the profundity and dignity of the philosophical heart.

Finally, Shakespeare finds the motive force of drama not in the kind of detailed scrutiny of the heart's core that would come to fill the novels of the eighteenth and nineteenth centuries but rather in the disconnection between the inward desires that we glimpse in his characters' unguarded moments and the self-betraying grasp of their hands and eloquent folly of their words. The disconnection is sometimes ironic, as in *Twelfth Night* and the later sonnets, sometimes farcical, as in the earliest comedies, but most often it signals the sad and inevitable dissolution of the dreamed-of integral self. The Shakespearean heart, then, is not one thing but an accumulation of the forms and pressures of the times, classical and medieval as well as early modern.

Conclusion: The heart of hearts

Fergus Henderson has said, "The heart is the most expressive muscle in any animal . . . It's amazing, a muscle that works so endlessly and tirelessly to keep us alive. And yet it emerges tender and distinctive."[1] Henderson is a London chef who has built an international reputation by specializing in the preparation of heart and other internal organs at his many-starred restaurant. His tenderness is not quite the love poet's, but it is not entirely different. The amatory, sacred, and anatomical heart has long shared the stage with the gustatory heart prepared in many ways. It is one thing for King Richard to devour a lion's heart raw in the great hall and quite another for the Lady of Faguell to be served the heart of her lover carefully prepared by her husband's cooks. These hearts of the warrior-hero and the lover are strictly gendered, one tough, aggressive, and courageous, the other tender, moist, and vulnerable. The humoral basis of Hippocratic and Galenic traditions links the motions of the cool, moist lungs inseparably with those of the tough, hot heart in a narrative readily adaptable to the gender struggles that are resolved into harmonious balance in tales of romance. These stories of the heart, recast in the sixteenth and seventeenth centuries under the influence of anatomical exploration, Protestant theology, and graphic representation, remained gendered. To recapture the changing conceptions of how male and female desires struggle for control in these narratives of the heart has been a major part of the present study.

Attempts to create windows on the gendered heart were occasionally met with approval but more often with scornful skepticism in Shakespeare's age. The openness of an Ophelia or a Desdemona stands in stark contrast to the secret anguish of their lovers, the prince and the professional soldier who try to elude victimization by concealing their inner vulnerabilities from the prying eyes of their enemies. Communicating the secrets of one's heart to God and one's fellows, desirable though it may seem, emerges as a tremendously

---

[1] Adam Gopnik, "Two Cooks: Taking Food to Extremes," *The New Yorker* (September 5, 2005), 95.

risky business in early modern drama. Assessing those risks is the work of both the fictional characters and cultural commentators of the period. Looking toward the middle of the seventeenth century, we see a rapid increase in the number of sermons on the secrets of the sinner's heart and of tracts on the dissident conscience figured as the heart, suggesting that political vulnerability, not just narrative conflict, was driving a reconfiguration of the heart.

A century earlier in England, an awkward and incomplete transition had taken place between the traditional Catholic representations of the Passion, the Wounds of Christ, and the Devotion of the Sacred Heart and more restrained, internalized Protestant conceptions of the Christian heart. Explicit scenes of sacrifice and suffering, of violence and bloodshed, were eventually expunged from churches following the Elizabethan Settlement, but, as Eamon Duffy, Joseph Leo Koerner, and others have shown, the "stripped" altars of the Reformation retained a good deal of the imagery and power of their predecessors. The bleeding heart remained a salient image in the poetry of the Counter-Reformation at the same time that a subtly inflected language of penitential suffering was emerging in Protestant discourse to express the experience of interiority. Smoldering hearts continued to be worshiped and excoriated; satiric anatomies cut deep into the hidden corruption of villains and heroes alike; and calm meditations brought peace to the hearts of many members of the Church of England.

However much male authors feminized the passionate heart on the early modern stage, they also located the inner debates that determine the fate of nations within the aggressively male hearts of princes. The viciousness of a Richard III or a Barabas turns on the physiological and psychological motions or *alteration* that Timothy Hampton postulates as the nub of early conceptions of the self.[2] Even as Hamlet praises Horatio for his stoic control of the passions, he invokes the passion of a quintessential heart that binds man to man:

> Give me that man
> That is not passion's slave, and I will wear him
> In my heart's core, ay, in my heart of heart,
> As I do thee. (*Hamlet* 3.2.71–4)

At the level of philological wit, the second of his memorably balanced phrases, "my heart of heart," redoubles his thought by translating what the Latinists in his audience had just heard as "my heart's *cor*." In philosophic

---

[2] See Timothy Hampton, "Strange Alteration: Physiology and Psychology from Galen to Rabelais," in *Reading the Early Modern Passions: Essays in the Cultural History of Emotion*, ed. Gail Kern Paster, Katherine Rowe, and Mary Floyd-Wilson (Philadelphia: University of Pennsylvania Press, 2004), 272–93.

terms, the introspective intensity and self-reliance of Lipsian neo-stoicism combines paradoxically in these lines with Hamlet's perception that the heart is the prime source of attachment to other people. Martha Nussbaum gets to the root of this paradox in her study of "the intelligence of [the] emotions." Rather than hostility to the emotional core of human life, Nussbaum finds in the philosophy of stoicism grounds for moral relations between people.[3] Her protracted argument relies on some significant adjustments to ancient and Renaissance stoic thought, but they are all ones that are consonant with the uses to which Shakespeare puts this philosophical stance in *Hamlet*. While Hamlet refuses to become a slave to womanish passions, he declares his reliance on a confidant whom he can trust to share his most secret desires. The touchstone of interiority in the period, Hamlet combines feminine tenderness with masculine political and personal vengeance in his heart's heart. Shakespeare's Wittenberg-trained prince conceives of his predicament as an extended moral and political meditation in the tradition of the great Protestant thinkers of his time. He is responsible for his own salvation (and that of his kingdom), but he is also precariously dependent on friends, family, and ultimately his stern God.

The heart increasingly becomes a political instrument in the seventeenth century. In the process of defining the political virtues and vulnerabilities of the nation, the anatomical-political poems by John Davies of Hereford and Phineas Fletcher assign a crucial role to the regal heart. Similarly, the government of the body by the motions of the heart adumbrates a sustained, coherent, Hobbesian theory of state in William Harvey's *De motu cordis*.

English drama of the seventeenth century consistently blends within the heart political determination, erotic attraction, and moral turmoil. In Shakespeare's plays the word "heart" and its derivatives and compounds occur over 1,400 times, a third again as often as "hand" and more than twice as often as "head," the next most prominent and active body parts in the corpus. While we might anticipate higher numbers of heart references in the early romantic comedies, the evidence of word frequencies reveals a uniform distribution of these references across the dramatic genres, with chronicle histories, satiric comedies, and tragedies showing roughly equal numbers. More important than mere frequency, the strategic concentration and placement of heart references that we identified in Chapter 6 suggests their centrality to the dramatist's conception of past memories, present engagements of the passions, and future consequences of tragic choices.

---

[3] Martha C. Nussbaum, *Upheavals of Thought: The Intelligence of Emotions* (Cambridge: Cambridge University Press, 2001).

Speaking from the heart could have nationwide repercussions. In *King Lear*, for example, Shakespeare organizes a cluster of heart references around the emotional history of Lear and his daughters in the opening division-of-the-kingdom scene, another around Lear's furious misjudgments on the heath (2.4), and a third grouping in the final scene when hearts burst and home truths project a grim future. Each of these moments directly affects the political future of Britain.

Besides contributing to the structural orchestration of political narrative, the hearts strategically placed in Shakespeare's plays are crucial to the humanizing of his characters. In *Troilus and Cressida* the self-indulgent senses of the titular heroes are directed by their hearts. As the betrayal scene unfolds, first Cressida, then Troilus, admits to falling under the heart's sway:

> CRES. Troilus, farewell! one eye yet looks on thee,
> But with my heart the other eye doth see.
> Ah, poor our sex! this fault in us I find,
> The error of our eye directs our mind.
>
> (*Troilus and Cressida* 5.2.107–10)

Her double-crossing vision is the result of one eye being directed by the lust in her heart for Diomedes while the other remains fixed on Troilus. Next, Troilus, who has seen the betrayal "co-acted," confesses an analogous inversion between his sense perception and his inner beliefs:

> yet there is a credence in my heart,
> An esperance so obstinately strong,
> That doth th'attest of eyes and ears,
> As if those organs had deceptious functions,
> Created only to calumniate. (5.2.120–4)

His heart is poised between faith and terror in precisely the way that George Wither's emblematic Christian heart is (Fig. 11). Despite extensive discussions of will and willfulness in the play, the characters come to view the motions of their heart as involuntary. They convince themselves that they could no more alter the direction of their inclinations than stop their heart beating and start it up again. Something similar happens in John Ford's *'Tis Pity She's a Whore*, where compulsion leads inexorably to incest and then to sororicide. The extraction of Annabella's heart only appears to strip it of its metaphorical power. Instead, the heart remains here and throughout the period the center of identity, (mis)understanding, and love.[4]

---

[4] Lisa Hopkins, in her characteristically insightful way, points out that, having worried the term "heart" long and hard through much of his career, Ford is content in his later works to "let its most obvious and traditional meanings stand . . . unchallenged." Chief among those meanings is to be

The growing interest in representing interior states of being on the English stage found in the extensive array of anatomical and religious discourses of the heart an infinitely adaptable symbol for interior corruption as well as for love. Iago, Macbeth, Bosola, and the rest of the fraternity of stage villains vociferously deny having hearts capable of tenderness or remorse, yet eventually all are vulnerable to perceived attacks on their sense of self. Resentments are nurtured in the heart and, just occasionally, glimmers of renovation. More often, secret motives that have only been glimpsed remain buried there. While anatomists purported to be revealing the body's secrets, the dramatists of Shakespeare's age continued to tantalize their audiences with interior spaces barely hinted at and motives only partly revealed.

There would, then, appear to be no grand, panoramic window on the heart, only, as it were, narrow slits through which we gain partial knowledge of the concept of interiority in the age of Shakespeare. No single master narrative of the heart emerges. Instead, a series of interrelated narratives provides useful insights into what it might have meant to be aware of inner conflict and inner peace. Milad Doueihi concludes that we can identify not one but two hearts in the period:

> Th[e] shattered and inscribed heart opens up a space for the visibility of the divine and of its writing in images and words, in combinations of images and words located within the heart. The eaten heart, on the contrary, hides and covers up its mysterious interiorization. Between the two hearts, between pure visibility and the image on the one hand, and the secret and its complementary withdrawal on the other, are drawn the lines separating the transparency through the image and the absolute mystery of interiorization of the missing divine body. Between the two hearts and the models they make possible, a whole intellectual history is waiting to be read.[5]

What Doueihi offers is not a direct reading of the visible and invisible hearts but rather a reading of the "intellectual history" crouching in the interstices between the two. I have tried to suggest that we can map the coordinates of a broader cultural history by identifying more hearts than these two. Both the languaged and the absconded heart loom large in the early modern discourse of the heart, but as recent scholars working on the problem are well aware, these hearts have been constructed from a range of textual and graphic evidence that allows for other interpretations. Just when we think that the story of the heart has been comprehensively told and explained, other versions emerge to complicate it. Even such a

---

guarantor of identity, love, and faith. See Lisa Hopkins, *John Ford's Political Theatre* (Manchester: Manchester University Press, 1994), 154.
[5] Milad Doueihi, *A Perverse History of the Human Heart* (Cambridge, MA: Harvard University Press, 1997), 139.

decided transformation as the Protestant Reformation in England leaves us with more questions than have yet been answered about the place of the heart in the body of Christian thought, poetry, and art. Doctrinal and affective distinctions that we took as givens fifty years ago have begun to shift and collapse. The piercing of the ecstatic St. Teresa's heart is as intense a revelation for English readers of Crashaw's "The Flaming Heart" as it is for the international audience of Bernini's *Ecstasy of St. Teresa* in Rome. Both communicate in an aesthetic language beyond sectarian debate, in emotions more deeply felt and convictions more profoundly held than any polemic text could capture.

So too does the anatomical heart of the Renaissance offer insights that combine a classical, humoral, felt experience of the body with a minutely observed and measured Harveian analysis of the motions of the engine of circulation. The culture of Shakespeare's age found the heart symbol indispensable for its sense of itself in love, health, and faith but also in hatred, sickness, and doubt. Without it, the culture becomes incomprehensible and with it, a challenge to be met again and again.

The pre-Cartesian "age of Shakespeare" inherited a natural philosophy in which the physical motions of the heart were one with the affections of the mind. In the course of the sixteenth and seventeenth centuries, however, human agency came to be associated with the hand at work in the material world and estranged from the intentions of the humanists' conception of the heart. Narratives of sacred and sexual passion came increasingly to measure the distance between the secrets of the heart and the public posturing of the visible human body. The villains of early modern drama are indicative of this development, as they profess one set of values and act on another, vigorously denying that they have affections or a conscience but at the same time revealing their inner vulnerabilities. The public performance of penance in the plays of Shakespeare and his contemporaries stands in stark contrast to the interior states of characters disabled by a sense of sin. This Protestant reconfiguration of the drama of the penitent sinner leads to the contradictory convictions that God sees the secrets of the human heart and that political success depends on concealing, indeed, denying the existence of any core of inner convictions. The Reverend Thomas Watson, exhorting his parishioners to be conscious of divine surveillance, resorts to Lucian's metaphor of a window in our heart of hearts and turns God into a theatrical spectator and critic:

God, my brethren, hath a window that looks into our heart. *Momus* complained of *Vulcan*, that he had not set a grate at every man's breast. God hath such a grate, he is the great Superintendent; we come into the world as upon a Theatre, every man acts his severall Part or Scene, God is both the Spectator and the Judge.[6]

Watson sounds a good deal like the melancholy Jaques, but his God is more than a helpless spectator in the *theatrum mundi*; He retains control of the hearts of the faithful in the precarious time of mid-seventeenth-century civic turmoil. By invoking the term "Superintendent," one used by radical reformers since the late sixteenth century as a coded alternative to "bishop," Watson insists on the rights of Englishmen to protect their inner convictions from ecclesiastical surveillance, leaving God alone to judge their troubled consciences. Three decades before Watson combined the idea of God anatomizing men's hearts with the trope of an interior theatrical performance, Helkiah Crooke, physician to James I, had identified the dramatic role of the heart in "the Theater of the body" as that of the sun-king.[7] Just as the anatomist and physician created an exacting language of psychophysiology that could be appropriated for the embodiment of dramatic characters, the drama provided concepts of power through spectatorship that could explain the hierarchy of the organs in the body. This kind of interchange continued undiminished throughout the age of Shakespeare, providing us a far more valuable window on the place of the heart in early modern culture than the one denied to Momus.

---

[6] Thomas Watson, *Gods Anatomy upon mans heart or, a sermon preached . . . at Margarets Westminster, Decemb. 27* (London: R. Smith, 1649), 6.

[7] Helkiah Crooke, *Mikrokosmographia: A Description of the Body of Man* (London W. Jaggard, 1615), 410.

Bibliography

Anthony, Francis. *An Apologie, or defence of . . . a medicine called arum potable . . . for the strengthning* [sic] *of the heart.* London: J. Leggatt, 1616.

Aquinas, St. Thomas. *Summa Theologiae*, 59 vols. London: Blackfriars, in association with Eyre and Spottiswoode, 1964.

Arden of Faversham, ed. Martin White, New Mermaids. New York: W. W. Norton, 1982.

Aristotle. *Nicomachean Ethics*, trans. H. Rackham, Loeb Classical Library. London: William Heinemann, 1968.

   Parts of Animals, trans. A. L. Peck, Loeb Classical Library. London: William Heinemann, 1937.

Bacon, Francis. "Of Simulation and Dissimulation," in *The Essayes or Counsels, Civill and Morall* (1625), ed. Michael Kiernan, the Oxford Francis Bacon. Oxford: Clarendon Press, 1985.

   Sylva sylvarum, or a naturall history in ten centuries (1626). London: J. F. for W. Lee, 1651.

Barish, Jonas A. *The Antitheatrical Prejudice.* Berkeley: University of California Press, 1981.

Barnet, Sylvan. "Coleridge on Shakespeare's Villains," *PMLA* 7 (1956): 10–20.

Bath, Michael. *Speaking Pictures: English Emblem Books and Renaissance Culture.* London: Longman, 1994.

Beirnaert, Louis, S. J. "Note sur les attaches psychologiques du symbolisme du cœur chez Sainte Marguerite-Marie," in *Le Cœur*, Les études Carmélitaines. Bruges: Desclée de Brouwer, 1950, 228–33.

Benet, Diana Treviño. "Crashaw, Teresa, and the Word," in *New Perspectives on the Life and Death of Richard Crashaw*, ed. John R. Roberts. Columbia: University of Missouri Press, 1990, 140–56.

Bietenholz, Doris. *How Come This ♡ Means Love? A Study of the Origin of the ♡ Symbol of Love.* Saskatoon, Canada: D. Bietenholz, 1995.

Block, Chana. *Spelling the Word: George Herbert and the Bible.* Berkeley: University of California Press, 1985.

Blundeville, Thomas. *The Arte of Logick.* London: W. Stansby, 1617.

Boccaccio, Giovanni. *Decameron*, 3 vols., trans. John Payne, revised and annotated by Charles S. Singleton. Berkeley: University of California Press, 1982.

Book of Common Prayer, 1559: The Elizabethan Prayer Book, ed. John E. Booty. Charlottesville: University Press of Virginia for the Folger Shakespeare Library, 1976.

Book of the Life of the Ancient Mexicans: containing an account of their rites and superstitions: an anonymous Hispano-Mexican manuscript preserved at the Biblioteca Nazionale Centrale, Florence, Italy. Facsimile with introduction, translation, and commentary by Zelia Nuttall and Elizabeth Hill Boone, in two parts. Berkeley: University of California Press, 1983.

Booth, Stephen. *Shakespeare's Sonnets*. New Haven: Yale University Press, 1977.

Boyadjian, N. *Le Cœur, son histoire, son symbolisme, son iconographie et ses maladies*. Antwerp: Esco Books, 1980.

Breton, Nicholas. *An excellent poeme, vpon the longing of a blessed heart*. London: [R. Bradock] for J. Browne and J. Deane, 1601.

Brockleby, R. *Reflections on Ancient and Modern Musick, with the Application to the Cure of Diseases*. London, 1749.

Bunyan, John. *The Acceptable Sacrifice*. London: for G. Larkin, 1689.

　　The Pilgrim's Progress, ed. James Blanton Wharey, revised by Roger Sharrock. Oxford: Clarendon Press, 1960.

Burckhardt, Jacob. *The Civilization of the Renaissance in Italy*, trans. S. G. C. Middlemore. London: Phaidon, 1945.

Bynum, Caroline Walker. *Fragmentation and Redemption: Essays on Gender and the Human Body in Medieval Religion*. New York: Zone Books, 1991.

　　"Violent Imagery in Late Medieval Piety," *GHI Bulletin* 30 (2001): 3–36.

Calvin, John. *Commentaries (Commentaries on the Epistles of Paul the Apostle to the Philippians, Colossians, and Thessalonians)*, trans. Rev. John Pringle. Edinburgh: Calvin Translation Society, 1851.

　　Commentaries (Commentary on the Book of Psalms), 5 vols., trans. Rev. James Anderson. Edinburgh: Calvin Translation Society, 1845–49.

　　Commentaries (Commentary on the Gospel According to John), 2 vols., trans. Rev. William Pringle. Edinburgh: Calvin Translation Society, 1847.

　　Institutes of the Christian Religion, 2 vols., ed. John T. McNeill, trans. Ford Lewis Battles. Philadelphia: Westminster Press, 1960.

Camille, Michael. "Reading the Printed Image," in *Printing the Written Word: The Social History of Books, circa 1450–1520*, ed. Sandra Hindman. Ithaca: Cornell University Press, 1991, 259–91.

Carlino, Andrea. *Books of the Body: Anatomical Ritual and Renaissance Learning*, trans. John Tedeschi and Anne C. Tedeschi. Chicago: University of Chicago Press, 1994.

　　Paper Bodies: A Catalogue of Anatomical Fugitive Sheets, 1538–1687, trans. Noga Arikhas. London: Wellcome Institute for the History of Medicine, 1999.

Christiansen, Keith, Laurence B. Kanter, and Carl Brandon Strehlke, eds. *Painting in Renaissance Siena, 1420–1500*. New York: Metropolitan Museum of Art, distributed by H. N. Abrams, 1988.

Christianson, Paul. *Reformers and Babylon: English Apocalyptic Visions from the Reformation to the Eve of the Civil War*. Toronto: University of Toronto Press, 1978.

Cicero. *Tusculan Disputations*, trans. J. E. King, Loeb Classical Library. London: Heinemann, 1927.

Clark, Ira. *Christ Revealed: The History of the Neotypological Lyric in the English Renaissance*. Gainesville: University of Florida Press, 1982.

———. "'Lord, In Thee the Beauty Lies in the Discovery': 'Love Unknown' and Reading Herbert," *ELH* 39 (1972): 560–84.

Clowes, William. *A Short and Profitable Treatise Touching the Cure of the Disease Called (Morbus Gallicus) by Vnctions*. London: J. Daye, 1579.

Coeffeteau, Nicolas. *A Table of the Humane Passions*, trans. Edward Grimestone. London: N. Oakes, 1621.

Cohen, I. Bernard. "Harrington and Harvey: A Theory of the State Based on the New Physiology," *Journal of the History of Ideas* 55 (1994): 187–210.

Coleridge, Samuel Taylor. *Coleridge's Shakesperean Criticism*, ed. T. M. Raysor. Cambridge, MA: Harvard University Press, 1959.

Coop-Phane, Corrine. "L'âme au cœur," *M/S: médicine science* 14 (1998): 1089–96.

Cornwallis, William. *Essayes*. London: [S. Stafford and R. Read] for E. Mattes, 1600–1.

Cramer, Daniel. *Emblemata sacra*. Frankfurt am Maine, 1624.

Crashaw, Richard. *The Poems English, Latin and Greek of Richard Crashaw*, ed. L. C. Martin. Oxford: Clarendon Press, 1957.

Crooke, Helkiah. *Mikrokosmographia: A Description of the Body of Man, Collected and Translated out of All the Best authors of Antiquity*. London: W. Jaggard, 1615.

Cunningham, Andrew. *The Anatomical Renaissance: The Resurrection of the Anatomical Projects of the Ancients*. Aldershot: Scolar Press, 1997.

Dante Alighieri. *Vita Nuova*, trans. Dino S. Cervigni and Edward Vasta. Notre Dame: University of Notre Dame Press, 1995.

Davies, Sir John. *Hymnes of Astraea in acrosticke verse*. London: [R. Field] for J. S [tandish], 1599.

Davies, John of Hereford. *Microcosmos: The Discovery of the Little World, with the government thereof*. Oxford: J. Barnes, 1603.

Dawson, Anthony. "Claudius at Prayer," unpublished paper presented at the Shakespeare Association of America annual conference, Philadelphia, 2006.

Debroise, Olivier. "Heart Attacks: On a Culture of Missed Encounters and Misunderstandings," in *El Corazón Sangrante/The Bleeding Heart*. Catalogue of an exhibit mounted by the Institute of Contemporary Art, Boston. Seattle: University of Washington Press, 1991, 12–61.

Deguileville, Guillaume de. *Le pèlerinage de vie humaine* (en castellano) [El pelegrino de la vida], trans. Vincente de Mazuelo. Toulouse: H. Mayer, 1490.

Dent, R. W. *Shakespeare's Proverbial Language: An Index*. Berkeley: University of California Press, 1981.

Diehl, Huston. *An Index of Icons in English Emblem Books, 1500–1700*. Norman: University of Oklahoma Press, 1986.

———. *Staging Reform, Reforming the Stage: Protestantism and Popular Theater in Early Modern England*. Ithaca: Cornell University Press, 1997.

"'Strike all that look upon with marvel': Theatrical and Theological Wonder in *The Winter's Tale*," in *Rematerializing Shakespeare: Authority and Representation on the Early Modern English Stage*, ed. Bryan Reynolds and William N. West. Basingstoke: Palgrave, 2005, 19–34.

Donne, John. *The Poems of John Donne*, 2 vols., ed. Herbert J. C. Grierson. Oxford: Oxford University Press, 1912.

Sermons, 10 vols., ed. George R. Potter and Evelyn M. Simpson. Berkeley: University of California Press, 1953–62.

Doran, Madeleine. "Iago's 'if': An Essay on the Syntax of *Othello*," in *The Drama of the Renaissance: Essays for Leicester Bradner*, ed. Elmer M. Blistein. Providence, RI: Brown University Press, 1970, 53–78.

Doueihi, Milad. *A Perverse History of the Human Heart*. Cambridge, MA: Harvard University Press, 1997.

Duffy, Eamon. *The Stripping of the Altars: Traditional Religion in England, c. 1400–c. 1580*. New Haven: Yale University Press, 1992.

Duncan-Jones, Katherine, ed. *Shakespeare's Sonnets*, Arden Third Series. London: Thomas Nelson and Sons, 1997.

Eliot, T. S. *Selected Essays*. New York: Harcourt, Brace, 1950.

Elyot, Thomas. *The Castel of Helth*. London: T. Bertheleti, [1539].

Engle, Lars. "'I am that I am': Shakespeare's Sonnets and the Economy of Shame," in *Shakespeare's Sonnets: Critical Essays*, ed. James Schiffer. New York: Garland, 1999, 185–98.

Erickson, Robert A. *The Language of the Heart, 1600–1750*. Philadelphia: University of Pennsylvania Press, 1997.

Evans, G. Blakemore, *et al.*, eds. *The Riverside Shakespeare*. Boston: Houghton Mifflin, 1997.

Ferry, Anne. *The "Inward" Language: Sonnets of Wyatt, Sidney, Shakespeare, Donne*. Chicago: University of Chicago Press, 1983.

Fletcher, John. *The Mad Lover*, ed. Robert Kean Turner, *The Dramatic Works in the Beaumont and Fletcher Canon*, Fredson Bowers, gen. ed., vol. 5. Cambridge: Cambridge University Press, 1982.

Fletcher, Phineas. *The Purple Island. The Poetical Works*, 2 vols., ed. Frederick S. Boas. Cambridge: Cambridge University Press, 1909.

Ford, John. *'Tis Pity She's a Whore*, ed. N. W. Bawcutt, Regents Renaissance Drama Series. Lincoln: University of Nebraska Press, 1966.

Foakes, R. A., ed. *King Lear*, Arden Third Series. London: Thomas Nelson and Sons, 1997.

Forker, Charles, ed. *King Richard II*, Arden Third Series. London: Thomson Learning, 2002.

Foucault, Michel. *Discipline and Punish: The Birth of the Prison*, trans. Alan Sheridan. New York: Pantheon Books, 1977.

The Order of Things: An Archaeology of the Human Sciences. New York: Pantheon Books, 1970.

Freedberg, David. *The Power of Images: Studies in the History and Theory of Response*. Chicago: University of Chicago Press, 1989.

Galen. *On the Usefulness of the Parts of the Body [De usu partium corporis humani]*, 2 vols., trans. Margaret Tallmadge May. Ithaca: Cornell University Press, 1968.

Geminus, Thomas. *Compendiosa totius anatomie delineatio*. London: J. Herford, 1545.

Geneva Bible: A Facsimile of the 1560 Edition, intro. Lloyd E. Berry. Madison: University of Wisconsin Press, 1969.

Gilman, Ernest B. *Iconoclasm and Poetry in the English Reformation*. Chicago: University of Chicago Press, 1986.

Goldberger, Ary L. and David R. Rigney. "Nonlinear Dynamics at the Bedside," in *Theory of the Heart: Biomechanics, Biophysics, and Nonlinear Dynamics of Cardiac Function*, ed. Leon Glass, *et al.* New York: Springer-Verlag, 1991, 583–605.

Gopnik, Adam. "Two Cooks: Taking Food to Extremes," *The New Yorker*, September 5, 2005.

Graham, Peter W. "Harvey's *De motu cordis*: The Rhetoric of Science and the Science of Rhetoric," *Journal of the History of Medicine* 33 (1978): 469–76.

Greenblatt, Stephen. *Marvelous Possessions: The Wonder of the New World*. Chicago: University of Chicago Press, 1991.

Renaissance Self-Fashioning: From More to Shakespeare. Chicago: University of Chicago Press, 1980.

Gross, Kenneth. *Spenserian Poetics: Idolatry, Iconoclasm, and Magic*. Ithaca: Cornell University Press, 1985.

Gurewich, Vladimir. "Observations on the Iconography of the Wound in Christ's Side, with Special Reference to Its Position," *Journal of the Warburg and Courtauld Institutes* 20 (1957): 358–62.

Hampton, Timothy. "Strange Alteration: Physiology and Psychology from Galen to Rabelais," in *Reading the Early Modern Passions: Essays in the Cultural History of Emotion*, ed. Gail Kern Paster, Katherine Rowe, and Mary Floyd-Wilson. Philadelphia: University of Pennsylvania Press, 2004, 272–93.

de Hamusco, Juan Valverde. *Anatomia del corpo humano*. Rome, 1560.

Hanson, Elizabeth. *Discovering the Subject in Renaissance England*. Cambridge: Cambridge University Press, 1998.

Harcourt, Glen. "Andreas Vesalius and the Anatomy of Antique Sculpture," *Representations* 17 (1987): 28–61.

Harrington, James. *The Common-wealth of Oceana*. London: J. Streater for L. Chapman, 1656.

Hart, James. *Anatomie of Vrines*. London: R. Field for R. Mylbourne, 1625.

Harvey, Christopher. *Schola cordis, or the heart of it selfe, gone away from God . . . in 47 Emblems*. London: for H. Blunden, 1647.

Harvey, William. *An Anatomical Disquisition of the Motion of the Heart and Blood in Animals [De motu cordis]*, trans. Robert Wills. London: J. M. Dent & Sons, 1907.

Anatomical exercitations concerning the generation of living creatures. London: J. Young for O. Pulleyn, 1653.

De motu cordis, Movement of the Heart and Blood in Animals, trans. Kenneth J. Franklin. Oxford: Blackwell Scientific Publications, 1957.

Exercitatio anatomica de motu cordis sanguinis in animalibus. Francofurti: G. Fitzeri, 1628.

Herbert, George. *The Works of George Herbert*, ed. F. E. Hutchinson. Oxford: Clarendon Press, 1941.

Herrick, Robert. *The Complete Poetry of Robert Herrick*, ed. J. Max Patrick. New York: New York University Press, 1963.

Herrlinger, Robert. *History of Medical Illustration from Antiquity to* A.D. *1600*. London: Pitman Medical and Scientific Publishing, 1970.

Hillman, David. *Shakespeare's Entrails: Belief, Scepticism and the Interior of the Body*. Basingstoke: Palgrave, 2007.

Hillman, David and Carla Mazzio, eds. *The Body in Parts: Fantasies of Corporeality in Early Modern Europe*. New York: Routledge, 1997.

Hobbes, Thomas. *The English Works of Thomas Hobbes*, 11 vols., ed. Sir William Molesworth. London, 1839–45; reprinted Aalen, 1962.

Hodges, Devon L. *Renaissance Fictions of Anatomy*. Amherst: University of Massachusetts Press, 1985.

Hopkins, Lisa. *John Ford's Political Theatre*. Manchester: Manchester University Press), 1994.

Høystad, Olé M. *A History of the Heart*, trans. John Irons. London: Reaktion Books, 2007.

Hunter, G. K., ed. *All's Well That Ends Well*, Arden Edition. Cambridge, MA: Harvard University Press, 1959.

Instruction, pratiques, et prières pour la dévotion au Sacré-Cœur de Jésus: L'Office, vespres et messe de cette dévotion. Paris, 1752

Jager, Eric. *The Book of the Heart*. Chicago: University of Chicago Press, 2000.

James, Susan. *Passion and Action: The Emotions in Seventeenth-Century Philosophy*. Oxford: Clarendon Press, 1997.

Jardine, Lisa. *Ingenious Pursuits: Building the Scientific Revolution*. New York: Doubleday, 1999.

Jonas, Raymond Anthony. *France and the Cult of the Sacred Heart: An Epic Tale for Modern Times*. Berkeley: University of California Press, 2000.

Jordanova, Ludmilla. "Happy Marriage and Dangerous Liaisons: Artists and Anatomy," in *The Quick and the Dead: Artists and Anatomy*, ed. Deanna Petherbridge and Ludmilla Jordanova. Berkeley: University of California Press, 1997, 100–13.

Kahn, Victoria. *Wayward Contracts: The Crisis of Political Obligation in England, 1640–1674*. Princeton: Princeton University Press, 2004.

Keele, K. D. *Leonardo da Vinci on Movement of the Heart and Blood*. London: Harvey and Blythe, 1952.

Kemp, Martin. "'The Mark of Truth': Looking and Learning in Some Anatomical Illustrations from the Renaissance and Eighteenth Century," in *Medicine and the Five Senses*, ed. W. F. Bynum and R. Porter. Cambridge: Cambridge University Press, 1993, 85–121.

Keynes, Geoffrey. *Life of William Harvey*. Oxford: Clarendon Press, 1978.

Kish, George. "The Cosmographic Heart: Cordiform Maps of the 16th Century," *Imago Mundi* 19 (1965): 13–21.

Kittridge, George Lyman, ed. *Othello*. Waltham, MA: Blaisdell, 1941.

Koerner, Joseph. *The Reformation of the Image*. London: Reaktion Books, 2004.

The Knight of Curtesy and the Fair Lady of Faguell, ed. Elizabeth McCausland. Northampton, MA: Smith College, 1922.

Lambert, Samuel W., Willy Wiegand, and William M. Ivins Jr., *Three Vesalian Essays to Accompany the "Icones Anatomicae" of 1934*, foreword by Archibald Malloch. New York: Macmillan, 1952.

Le Goff, Jacques. "Head or Heart? The Political Use of Body Metaphors in the Middle Ages," trans. Patricia Ranum, in *Fragments for a History of the Human Body*, ed. Michel Feher, Ramona Naddaff, and Nadia Tazi. New York: Zone Books, 1989, 3: 13–26.

Lindemann, Mary. *Medicine and Society in Early Modern Europe*. Cambridge: Cambridge University Press, 1999.

Lowe, Peter. *Easie, Certain, and Perfect Method, to Cure and Prevent the Spanish Sicknes*. London: J. Roberts, 1596.

Lucian. *Works*, trans. A. M. Harmon, 8 vols., Loeb Classical Library. London: William Heinemann, 1913–67.

Luther, Martin. *Luther's Works*, 55 vols., American edn. ed. Jaroslav Jan Pelikan, Hilton C. Oswald, and Helmut T. Lehmann. Philadelphia: Fortress Press, 1955–.

Luxon, Thomas H. *Literal Figures: Puritan Allegory and the Reformation Crisis in Representation*. Chicago: University of Chicago Press, 1995.

Luzvic, Stephanus. *The Devout Hart or royal throne of the pacifical Salomon*. Rouen: J. Cousturier, 1634.

Manning, John R. "Whitney's *Choice of Emblemes*: A Reassessment," *Renaissance Studies* 4 (1990): 155–200.

Marchitello, Howard. "Vesalius' *Fabrica* and Shakespeare's *Othello*: Anatomy, Gender and the Narrative Production of Meaning," *Criticism* 35 (1993): 529–58.

Marlowe, Christopher. *Tamburlaine the Great, Parts I and II*, ed. John D. Jump, Regents Renaissance Drama Series. Lincoln: University of Nebraska Press, 1967.

Marshall, Cynthia. *The Shattering of the Self: Violence, Subjectivity, and Early Modern Texts*. Baltimore: The Johns Hopkins University Press, 2002.

Martin, Philip. *Shakespeare's Sonnets: Self, Love and Art*. Cambridge: Cambridge University Press, 1972.

May, Edward. *A most certaine and true relation of a strange monster or serpent found in the left ventricle of the heart of Iohn Pennant . . .* London: G. Miller, 1639.

d[e] M[ello], G[abriel]. *Les divines opérations de Jésus dans le cœur d'une Ame fidèle*. Paris, 1673.

Miller, Jonathan. "The Pump: Harvey and the Circulation of the Blood," in *Blood: Art, Power, Politics and Pathology*, ed. James M. Bradburne. Munich: Prestel, 2002, 100–7.

Milton, John. *John Milton: Complete Poems and Major Prose*, ed. Merritt Y. Hughes. New York: Odyssey Press, 1957.

Mitchell, W. J. T. *Iconology: Image, Text, Ideology.* Chicago: University of Chicago Press, 1986.

Moravia, Alberto. *L'uomo come fine e altri saggi.* Milan: Bompiani, 1964.

Neill, Michael. "'What Strange Riddle's This?': Deciphering *'Tis Pity She's a Whore,*" in *John Ford: Critical Re-Visions*, ed. Michael Neill. Cambridge: Cambridge University Press, 1988, 153–79.

Nunn, Hillary M. *Staging Anatomies: Dissection and Spectacle in Early Stuart Tragedy.* Aldershot: Ashgate, 2005.

Nussbaum, Martha C. *Upheavals of Thought: The Intelligence of Emotions.* Cambridge: Cambridge University Press, 2001.

Nuttall, A. D. *Shakespeare the Thinker.* New Haven: Yale University Press, 2007.

O'Malley, C. D. *Andreas Vesalius of Brussels, 1514–1564.* Berkeley: University of California Press, 1965.

Opie, Lionel H. *The Heart and Its Functions.* Cape Town: University of Cape Town, 1981.

Page, Samuel. *The Broken Heart: or, Davids Penance.* London: T. Harper, 1637.

Park, Katharine. "The Criminal and the Saintly Body: Autopsy and Dissection in Renaissance Italy," *Renaissance Quarterly* 47 (1994): 1–33.

Parker, Patricia. "Shakespeare and Rhetoric: 'dilation' and 'delation' in *Othello,*" in *Shakespeare and the Question of Theory*, ed. Patricia Parker and Geoffrey Hartman. New York: Methuen, 1985, 54–74.

Paster, Gail Kern. *The Body Embarrassed: Drama and the Disciplines of Shame in Early Modern English.* Ithaca: Cornell University Press, 1993, 23–63.

    Humoring the Body: Emotions and the Shakespearean Stage. Chicago: University of Chicago Press, 2004.

Paster, Gail Kern, Katherine Rowe, and Mary Floyd-Wilson, eds. *Reading the Early Modern Passions: Essays in the Cultural History of Emotion.* Philadelphia: University of Pennsylvania Press, 2004.

Pender, Stephen. "Signs of Interiority, or Epistemology in the Bodyshop," *The Dalhousie Review* 85 (2005): 221–37.

Peterson, Robert T. *The Art of Ecstasy: Teresa, Bernini, and Crashaw.* New York: Atheneum, 1970.

Petherbridge, Deanna. "Leonardo da Vinci and the Grammar of Anatomical Drawing," in *The Quick and the Dead: Artists and Anatomy*, ed. Deanna Petherbridge and Ludmilla Jordanova. Berkeley: University of California Press, 1997, 43–8.

Peto, James, ed. *The Heart.* New Haven: Yale University Press; London: Wellcome Collection, 2007.

Phillips, John. *The Reformation of Images: Destruction of Art in England, 1535–1660.* Berkeley: University of California Press, 1973.

Plato. *Laches*, trans. W. R. M. Lamb, Loeb Classical Library. London: William Heinemann, 1924.

    Timaeus, trans. Rev. R. G. Bury, Loeb Classical Library. London: William Heinemann, 1929.

Playfere. Thomas. *Hearts Delight. A Sermon preached at Pauls Crosse in London in Easter terme. 1593.* Cambridge: J. Legat, 1603.

Problemes of Aristotle. Edinburgh: R. Waldgrave, 1595.

Prynne, William. *Histrio-mastix. The Players Scourge.* London: E. A [llde, A. Mathewes, T. Cotes] and W. I[ones] for M. Sparke, 1633.

Puttenham, George. *The Arte of English Poesie.* London: R. Field, 1589.

Qualtiere, Louis F. and William W. E. Slights. "Contagion and Blame in Early Modern England: The Case of the French Pox," *Literature and Medicine* 22 (2003): 1–24.

Richard the Lion-Hearted and Other Medieval English Romances, trans. Bradford B. Broughton. New York: Dutton, 1966.

Roberts, K. B. and J. D. W. Tomlinson. *The Fabric of the Body: European Traditions of Anatomical Illustration.* Oxford: Clarendon Press, 1992.

Robicsek, Francis and Donald M. Hales. "Maya Heart Sacrifice: Cultural Perspective and Surgical Technique," in *Ritual Human Sacrifice in Mesoamerica,* ed. Elizabeth H. Boone. Washington, DC: Dumbarton Oaks, 1984, 49–90.

Rogers, John. *The Matter of Revolution: Science, Poetry, and Politics in the Age of Milton.* Ithaca: Cornell University Press, 1996.

Ross, Alexander. *Arcana microcosmi, or, the hid secrets of man's body discovered.* London: T. Newcomb, 1652.

Rowe, Katherine. *Dead Hands: Fictions of Agency, Renaissance to Modern.* Stanford: Stanford University Press, 1999.

Saltmarsh, John. *Holy Discoveries and Flames.* London: R. Y[oung] for P. Nevill, 1640.

Sargent, Emily Jo. "The Sacred Heart: Christian Symbolism," in *The Heart,* ed. Peto, 102–14.

Sawday, Jonathan. *The Body Emblazoned: Dissection and the Human Body in Renaissance Culture.* London: Routledge, 1995.

"In Search of the Philosopher's Stone: Montaigne, Interiority and Machines," *The Dalhousie Review* 85 (2005): 195–220.

"The Transparent Man and the King's Heart," in *The Arts of 17th-Century Science: Representations of the Natural World in European and North American Culture,* ed. Claire Jowitt and Diane Watt. Aldershot: Ashgate, 2002, 12–21.

Schoenfeldt, Michael C. *Bodies and Selves in Early Modern England: Physiology and Inwardness in Spenser, Shakespeare, Herbert, and Milton.* Cambridge: Cambridge University Press, 1999.

Shakespeare, William. *The Riverside Shakespeare,* ed. G. Blakemore Evans, *et al.* Boston: Houghton Mifflin, 1997.

Sharp, Robert L. "Donne's 'Good-morrow' and Cordiform Maps," *Modern Language Notes* 69 (1954): 493–5.

Shawe, John. *A Broken Heart, or the Grand Sacrifice. As it was laid ovt in a sermon preached at St. Maries in Beverley ... 1642.* London, 1643.

Sir Gowther. Six Middle English Romances, ed. Maldwyn Mills. London: Dent, 1973, 148–68.

Siraisi, Nancy G. *Medieval and Early Renaissance Medicine: An Introduction to Knowledge and Practice.* Chicago: University of Chicago Press, 1990.

"Vesalius and Human Diversity in *De humani coporis fabrica*," *Journal of the Warburg and Courtauld Institutes* 57 (1994): 60–88.

"Vesalius and the Reading of Galen's Teleology," *Renaissance Quarterly* 50 (1997): 1–37.

Slights, Camille Wells. *The Casuistical Tradition in Shakespeare, Donne, Herbert, and Milton.* Princeton: Princeton University Press, 1981.

"A Hero of Conscience: *Samson Agonistes* and Casuistry," *PMLA* 90 (1975): 395–413.

Slights, William W. E. "Ain't It a Shame: History and Psychology in *Richard II* Criticism," in *Re-visions of Shakespeare: Essays in Honor of Robert Ornstein*, ed. Evelyn Gajowski. Newark: University of Delaware, 2004, 243–59.

"Textualized Bodies and Bodies of Text in *Sejanus* and *Coriolanus*," *Medieval and Renaissance Drama in England* 5 (1991): 181–93.

Soellner, Rolf. "The Four Primary Passions: A Renaissance Theory Reflected in the Works of Shakespeare," *Studies in Philology* 55 (1958): 549–67.

Southwell, Robert. *The Complete Poems of Robert Southwell, S.J.*, ed. Rev. Alexander B. Grosart [1872]. reprinted Westport, CT: Greenwood Press, 1970.

Spenser, Edmund. *Edmund Spenser's Poetry*, ed. Hugh Maclean, 2nd edn. New York: Norton, 1982.

Stein, Arnold. *George Herbert's Lyrics.* Baltimore: The Johns Hopkins Press, 1968.

Stevens, Scott Manning. "Sacred Heart and Secular Brain," in *The Body in Parts: Fantasies of Corporeality in Early Modern Europe*, ed. David Hillman and Carla Mazzio. New York: Routledge, 1997, 262–82.

Strier, Richard. *Love Known: Theology and Experience in George Herbert's Poetry.* Chicago: University of Chicago Press, 1983.

Strong, Roy. *Gloriana: The Portraits of Queen Elizabeth I.* New York: Thames and Hudson, 1987.

Taylor, Jeremy. *The Whole Works of the Right Rev. Jeremy Taylor*, 15 vols., ed. Reginald Heber. London, 1828.

Thomas, Keith. *Religion and the Decline of Magic.* New York: Scribners, 1971.

Tilley, Morris Palmer. *A Dictionary of the Proverbs in England in the Sixteenth and Seventeenth Centuries.* Ann Arbor: University of Michigan Press, 1950.

Tillyard, E. M. W. *The Elizabethan World Picture.* Harmondsworth: Penguin Books, 1943.

Tricomi, Albert H. *Reading Tudor-Stuart Texts through Cultural Historicism.* Gainesville: University of Florida Press, 1996.

van de Velde, Jan. *Openhertighe Herten.* Brussels, *c.* 1618–21.

van Haeften, Benedict. *Schola Cordis* (1629), trans. Christopher Harvey. London: for H. Blunden, 1647.

van Vaeck, Mark. "The *Openhertight Herten* in Europe: Remarkable Specimens of Heart Emblematics," *Emblematica* 8 (1994): 261–91.

Vendler, Helen. *The Art of Shakespeare's Sonnets*. Cambridge, MA: Harvard University Press, 1997.

Vesalius, Andreas. *De humani corporis fabrica libri septem*. Basel: J. Oporinus, 1543, rev. 1555.

The Epitome of Andreas Vesalius, trans. L. R. Lind. New York: Macmillan, 1949.

On the Fabric of the Human Body, Book I, trans. William Frank Richardson and John Burd Carman. San Francisco: Norman Publishing, 1998.

Vicary, Thomas. *A Profitable Treatise of the Anatomie of Mans Body*. London: H. Bamforde, 1577.

da Vinci, Leonardo. *Corpus of the Anatomical Studies in the Collection of Her Majesty the Queen at Windsor Castle*, 3 vols., ed. Kenneth D. Keele and Carlo Pedretti. New York: Harcourt Brace Janovich, 1978–80.

Vinken, Pierre. *The Shape of the Heart*. Amsterdam: Elsevier, 1999.

Waith, Eugene M. "Concern for Villains," *Renaissance Drama* n.s. 24 (1993): 155–70.

Watson, Thomas. *Gods Anatomy upon mans heart or, a sermon preached ... at Margarets Wesminster, Decemb. 27*. London: R. Smith, 1649.

Heaven Taken by Storm; or, The Holy Violence a Christian is to Put Forth in the Pursuit after Glory. London: for R. W. by T. Parkhurst, 1669.

Webster, John. *The Duchess of Malfi*, ed. Brian Gibbons, New Mermaids, 4th edn. New York: Norton, 2001.

The White Devil, ed. Christina Luckyj, New Mermaids, 2nd edn. New York: Norton, 1996.

Weimann, Robert. *Authority and Representation in Early Modern Discourse*, ed. David Hillman. Baltimore: The Johns Hopkins University Press, 1996.

Wells, Francis. "The Renaissance Heart: The Drawings of Leonardo da Vinci," in *The Heart*, ed. James Peto, 70–94.

Welstead, Robert. *The Cure of a Hard-Heart. First preached in diuers sermons*. London: W. Stansby for S. Man, 1630.

Whitney, Geffrey. *A Choice of Emblems and Other Devices*. Leiden: F. Raphelengius for C. Plantin, 1586.

Wiggins, Martin. *Journeymen in Murder: The Assassin in English Renaissance Drama*. Oxford: Clarendon Press, 1991.

W[ilmot], R[obert]. *The Tragedy of Tancred and Gismund*. London: T. Scarlet, 1592.

Wither, George. *A Collection of Emblemes*. London: A. M[atthews], 1635.

Wright, Thomas. *The Passions of the Minde in Generall*. London: V. Simmes [and A. Islip] for W. Burre [and T. Thorpe], 1604.

Yates, Frances A. *Astraea: The Imperial Theme in the Sixteenth Century*. London: Routledge & Kegan Paul, 1975.

"Queen Elizabeth as Astraea," *Journal of the Warburg and Courtauld Institutes* 10 (1947): 27–82.

Yoder, Audrey. *Animal Analogy in Shakespeare's Character Portrayal*. New York: King's Crown Press, 1947.

Young, Louisa. "The Human Heart: An Overview," in *The Heart*, ed. James Peto, 1–30.

Index